Cheryl Robson FRSA
Editor

Cheryl created the award-winning publishing company Aurora Metro Books in 1980, which is well-known for its diverse and inclusive range of titles with works in translation from over 20 languages. The press was a finalist for Small Press of the Year in 2025, British Book Awards. aurorametro.com

As an editor, Cheryl has edited over 100 books. Her work has won the Pandora Prize, the Raymond Williams/Arts Council Publishing Prize, a Special Jury Prize for Peace, Best Innovative & Best Seasonal Foodbook from Gourmand World Cookbooks, and was a finalist for the People's Book Prize. The press was also a finalist for the IPG National Diversity Awards in 2019 and 2020 and Cheryl was a finalist for the ITV National Diversity Awards in 2019 and 2022.

An award-winning playwright, she has also had writing published in *The Guardian*, the *Chicago Tribune, Culture Trip, Riviera News* and more.

As a producer/director, her feature documentary film *Rock 'n' Roll Island,* won several awards at film festivals and was broadcast on BBC4 in 2020, garnering a *Sunday Times* Critics' Choice and *Radio Times* Pick of the Week.

Cheryl is perhaps best-known for her successful 5-year campaign with sister charity (aurorametro.org.uk) to erect a full-size bronze statue of Virginia Woolf which was unveiled in November 2022 on Richmond riverside and has proven a popular attraction.

She co-owns the independent bookshop Books on the Rise in Richmond, which offers weekly literary, music and arts events and hosts Feminist Book Fortnight. booksontherise.com

For more see cherylrobson.net

First published in the UK in 2025 by Supernova Books, an imprint of Aurora Metro Publications Ltd. 80 Hill Rise, Richmond, TW10 6UB, UK. www.aurorametro.com @aurorametro FB/AuroraMetroBooks

Instagram: @aurora_metro X: @aurorametro

At the Heart of Conflict: Talking Resolution © copyright 2025 Cheryl Robson

Editor: Cheryl Robson

Front cover image © copyright 2025 Deposit images

Introduction © copyright 2025 Helen Kezie-Nwoha

Foreword © copyright 2025 Oliver P Richmond

Afterword © copyright 2025 Jonathan Cohen

Cover design Aurora Metro Books © copyright 2025 Aurora Metro Publications Ltd.

Printed on sustainably resourced paper.

ISBNs:
978-1-913641-42-9 (print version)
978-1-913641- 43-6 (ebook version)

At the Heart of Conflict:
Talking Resolution

Foreword by
Oliver P. Richmond

Introduction by
Helen Kezie-Nwoha

Afterword by
Jonathan Cohen

Compiled and edited by
Cheryl Robson

SUPERNOVA
BOOKS

SUPERNOVA BOOKS

At the Heart of Conflict: Talking Resolution

20
Exclusive
First-Person
Interviews

SUPERNOVA
BOOKS

SUPERNOVA BOOKS

CONTENTS

FOREWORD

By Oliver P. Richmond

This collection of interviews of local and international peacemakers offers an insightful and valuable resource for practitioners, scholars, and students. Very few such records exist as the 'archive of peacemaking' normally only records the voices of political elites, mediators, politicians, diplomats, and officials and their often-scant contributions (usually found in self-congratulatory, polemical, and hagiographic autobiographies and biographies). The archives of academics and their scholarly contributions are intellectually far more substantial and are perhaps more closely entwined with the thinking and outputs of civil society organizations and wider social networks. Yet, such work has proven mostly inaudible and has been widely rejected by official actors and leadership who tend to insist on authoritarian, neoliberal, populist, and related violence-oriented political systems.

As with the current US President, Trump, a victor's peace or the balance of power system of peacemaking has long been an elite and hegemonic preference. Authoritarian and isolationist actors have often rejected the costs and complexity of maintaining a liberal international order. In even more advanced form, they reject a peace that is predicated on responding to subaltern claims about social justice. Historically, such regressive views are eventually inoculated by war, but at great cost to global society, because this type of peacemaking is often reactive and subject to power-relations which favour the political utility of violence.

This collection provides unique perspectives from key exponents of the various forms of peacemaking that transgress old boundaries of thought and practice, in different contexts, acknowledging their acute pressures, and the tactics and strategies that are required to deal with them, which bridge both distant scholarship and the polemics of politics. It reads like a historical review – and at times a nostalgic one – of the pros and cons of peacemaking during the post-Cold war liberal moment. During this era, the platform of human rights and democracy allowed unforeseen social experimentation with, and broader access to, peacemaking than ever before, as well as some leverage over violence-prone actors and leaders. This process led to the emergence of a very substantial international peace architecture, and if still fragile, its results have been extraordinary when compared to the recent and distant past. Yet our conceptualisation of peace is still inadequate in terms of accruing wider, global legitimacy and connecting peace with global forms of justice (as opposed to the victor's peace model).

Of course, all of the advances in the era of 'liberal peace'– as perhaps attempted in Timor-Leste, Bosnia Herzegovina, and Kosovo – depended on the support of external actors and an alignment with their interests and values. Scholars noticed quite early on that its outcomes were more hybrid than liberal, as in Timor, and that authoritarian actors were determined to maintain the utility of violence in their political toolkit and so pushed hard to block rights and democracy in a kind of 'counter-peace' process, which unfolded in countries spanning Cambodia to Afghanistan.

Even this weak alignment has now broken down since US President Obama failed to respond to the use of chemical weapons in the early stages of the Syrian conflict in 2013, then the subsequent failures of UN mediation in Syria, the US withdrawal from Afghanistan in 2021 (initiated by President Trump), and the drawdown of many UN peacekeeping missions in sub-Saharan Africa over the last decade. Matters have been made even worse by the withdrawal of donor support from civil societies worldwide (as with Trump's 2025 closure of USAID), and ultimately after Russian President Putin's 1930s style invasion of Ukraine in 2022.

In addition, in the Global South there has been localised and scholarly rejection of northern peacebuilding praxis, associating it with former colonial practices, as well as with northern capitalism. There has also been growing elite and popular nationalism, along with increasing isolationism on the part of former donors. The reactionary dynamics of nationalism and populism have re-emerged, despite the cautionary lessons of history, making the insights of this volume all the more important as a guide for the more substantial praxis of peacemaking that must now be renewed and redeveloped.

FOREWORD

The book represents a kind of soliloquy for the liberal era, which now seems to be over. Its representation of peacemaking by leading transversal, trans-scalar[1], and transnational voices indicates their extraordinary fortitude and sacrifice, needed to lead the debate on reconciliation, non-violence, and pluralism in any war and violence prone setting. Their collective critique of the liberal peace era, the current more fragmented, multipolar situation, and their discussion of how to persevere with peacemaking raises the question of how one makes peace after liberalism, in a way that preserves dignity, rights, and the possibility of non-violent political orders. What sort of system would it maintain, and what tools would it have? In particular, how would local and subaltern actors find their place in a renewed system of peacemaking?

The scholarship on such matters has some answers here, and they have often been acknowledged in global institutions even if only as unimplemented doctrine (as in the recent Sustaining Peace agenda of the UN (2018)). However, the scholarship often draws its conclusions from the raw data as presented in this collection of interventions and essays, so we should pay particular attention to the rich, experiential knowledge of peacemakers such as these, who recognise the incredible privations that both the utility of war and experiments in peacemaking rest upon, as well as the innumerable gains that the evolution of peacemaking praxis may lead to.

The lessons that emerge from these chapters indicate that peacemaking 'after liberalism' needs to build upon the key elements of solidarity, empathy, networks, sustainability, and recognition of rights in evidence during the liberal era. This approach needs to be combined with a very substantial, polyversal global dialogue (top down, bottom up, fluid and networked). Dialogue of this kind resulted in the loosening of the dominance of the 'victor's peace' as seen through the state, geopolitics and regional power structures. This has shifted peace towards a closer attachment, in today's scholarship and some policy doctrine at least, to global justice questions: environmental, gender, racial, economic, and historical, among others. Global political, economic, and social reform is required by extension.

---

1   A "trans-scalar peace system" is based on a "consistency of purpose" and a "parity of esteem" for actors across global, regional, international, national, and local scales. Millar G (2021) "Ambition and ambivalence: Reconsidering positive peace as a trans-scalar peace system". *Journal of Peace Research* 58(4): 640–654.

The social dynamics of peacemaking remain under-developed as this book illustrates, but it also provides insights into how they are evolving and expanding in a world of global complexity and mutual responsibility. The valuable archive of the wide range of recent contributions to expanded forms of peacemaking that this book represents offers an essential platform for further work and development, to stabilise and augment the international peace architecture.

Professor Oliver Richmond is a renowned scholar in International Relations, Peace, and Conflict Studies. He is the founder of the MA in Peace and Conflict Studies at the University of Manchester, where he also teaches core modules in the Department of Politics. Recognized for his significant contributions to the field, he received the 2019 Eminent Scholar Award from the International Studies Association. With extensive fieldwork experience in conflict zones, he has worked closely with international organizations, including the UN, and civil society groups. Richmond's publications include *The Grand Design: Peace in the 21st Century* (Oxford University Press, 2022) and *Peace in International Relations* (Routledge, 2020, 2nd ed.).

He has led several global research projects, including the AHRC-funded The Art of Peace and the Blockages to Peace projects. He also serves as a Visiting Professor at several prestigious universities, and co-edits key academic journals.

INTRODUCTION

by Helen Kezie-Nwoha

The Institute for Economics and Peace (IEP) 2024 report indicates that there are currently 56 active conflicts globally, the most since the end of the Second World War. This is an alarming trend with fewer conflicts being resolved, either militarily or through peace agreements. A limited number of conflicts have ended in a decisive victory during the last 50 years, falling from 49 per cent in the 1970s to 9 per cent in the 2010s, while successful peace agreements also declined from 23 per cent to 4 per cent over the same period (IEP, 2024:2).

This shift signals several key challenges for conflict resolution efforts. Firstly, the reduced number of decisive military victories suggests that contemporary conflicts are more likely to become prolonged, stalemated, or "frozen," with no clear winner or resolution. Many modern conflicts involve non-state actors, insurgencies, and decentralized militant groups, making traditional military victories harder to achieve. The fragmentation of warring parties and the involvement of multiple actors (both local and international) complicate the conflict dynamics, making comprehensive military solutions less feasible. Secondly, the decline in peace agreements highlights the growing complexity of achieving negotiated settlements. The decreasing willingness of parties to engage in peace talks may reflect entrenched positions, distrust between conflicting parties, or the influence of external actors with competing geopolitical interests. Modern conflicts are often intertwined with identity-based grievances, extremism, or issues like access to natural resources, all of which hamper efforts at conflict resolution.

The interviews in this book, which were conducted with 20 people who have worked in various institutions delivering peace building and conflict resolution, highlight the complexities of peacebuilding in conflict zones. Understanding conflict resolution is fundamental to building sustainable peace, particularly in regions plagued by violence and instability. There are various approaches to resolving conflicts, each suitable for different scenarios, depending on the parties involved, the nature of the conflict, and the desired outcome. The most common of these include negotiation, mediation, arbitration, collaboration, accommodation, compromise, and avoidance (Olga et al, 2018).

Negotiation is a process in which the conflicting parties directly engage in dialogue to reach a mutually acceptable agreement. It is a voluntary and non-binding process, making it one of the most widely used methods in conflict resolution. The success of negotiations depends on the willingness of parties to compromise, communicate openly, and prioritize peace over conflict.

Mediation involves a neutral third-party facilitating dialogue between the conflicting parties. The mediator does not impose solutions but helps the parties communicate effectively, explore options, and reach a resolution. Mediation is commonly used in international diplomacy and community-level conflicts.

Arbitration involves a neutral third party who has the authority to make binding decisions. Arbitration is typically used in legal disputes and labour conflicts, where the disputing parties agree to accept the arbitrator's ruling.

Collaboration is a conflict resolution approach where parties work together to find a win-win solution that benefits everyone involved. This method emphasizes cooperation and creativity, seeking long-term, mutually beneficial outcomes.

Accommodation is a reconciliation whereby one party agrees to yield to the wishes or demands of the other. While it can be effective in maintaining peace in the short term, accommodation often leaves underlying issues unresolved, which may resurface later.

Compromise involves both parties making concessions to arrive at a solution that is acceptable to all. Although no party achieves everything they want, compromise ensures that neither party feels entirely defeated, making it an effective strategy in negotiations.

Avoidance is the decision to ignore or sidestep a conflict, often in the hope that it will resolve itself or diminish over time. While this approach can prevent immediate escalation, it often leads to long-term issues as the root causes of the conflict remain unaddressed.

Despite the various methods of conflict resolution, ending violent conflicts remains a monumental challenge due to a range of factors. As we can see today with the escalation of conflict in the Middle East, conflicts are often driven by deep-seated grievances, such as ethnic or religious differences, political oppression, and historical injustices. These grievances make it difficult to find common ground, as parties are not only fighting over tangible resources but also over identity, dignity, and recognition. In many conflict-prone areas, weak governance exacerbates violence. Corruption, lack of rule of law, and inability to provide basic services can fuel discontent and drive citizens to support armed groups. External actors, including foreign governments and multinational corporations, often have vested interests in conflicts. These actors may provide financial or military support to one side, prolonging the conflict and making resolution more difficult. Conflicts are often sustained by economic factors, such as control over natural resources like oil, minerals, or land. Warlords and corrupt officials benefit from the instability, making peace undesirable for them.

Gender and Conflict Resolution

It's almost 25 years after the passing of the landmark United Nations Security Council Resolution 1325 on women, peace, and security. The Resolution redefined the role of women in peacebuilding and conflict resolution (Ileke and Imene-Chanduru, 2020). Despite some progress, there is widespread acknowledgment that much work remains to be done to fully implement this resolution. Efforts must better address the various ways in which women and men are treated differently in peacebuilding and conflict resolution processes (Ladan et al ,2021). Women play an essential role in peacebuilding, yet they are frequently excluded from formal peace processes. Their contributions, particularly at the grassroots level, are invaluable in rebuilding communities and fostering reconciliation after conflict. However, their involvement is hindered by several challenges. In many societies, women are not viewed as decision-makers or leaders in peace processes, which limits their participation. These patriarchal norms not only marginalize women but also deprive peace processes of their unique perspectives on security and social cohesion (Rehn and Sirleaf, 2002, UN Women, 2015). Formal peace processes often fail to include women. When women are absent from negotiations, issues such as gender-based violence, sexual violence, and women's economic and political empowerment are often sidelined, leaving these critical areas unaddressed. Women involved in peacebuilding, particularly in conflict zones, face threats of violence and harassment, discouraging them from taking active roles. Additionally, women who do participate are often targets of intimidation by armed groups or political factions (O'Reilly et al, 2015, UN Women 2015).

Global Issues and their Impact on Conflict Resolution

Global issues, such as climate change, technological advances, migration, and economic inequality, are increasingly influencing conflict dynamics. One of the most significant of these is climate change. Climate change is exacerbating resource scarcity, such as water and arable land, particularly in regions like the Sahel and the Horn of Africa (Barnett and Adger, 2007). This scarcity drives competition between communities, leading to conflicts over survival resources. Climate-induced migration further strains already fragile states, increasing the potential for violence. Conflicts and climate change are leading to mass migrations, particularly from conflict-prone areas in the Middle East and Sub-Saharan Africa. These movements put pressure on neighbouring countries and can lead to new conflicts as resources become overstretched and tensions arise between migrants and host communities (IOM, 2017).

Issues such as climate change and migration complicate conflict resolution in several ways. Climate change-driven resource scarcity escalates competition over vital resources like water and land. These environmental pressures can create tensions that are difficult to mediate because they revolve around survival. This makes negotiated settlements challenging, as basic resource needs often supersede diplomatic solutions. Migration, particularly climate-induced migration, further destabilizes fragile states and exacerbates tensions between migrants and host comm-unities. Countries already grappling with internal instability find it harder to resolve conflicts when an influx of migrants puts additional strain on resources, infrastructure, and social services. This complexity requires conflict resolution processes to integrate migration management and equitable resource distribution to prevent new conflicts from emerging.

Rising global inequality, where wealth is concentrated among a small elite group while large populations remain in poverty, is driving discontent and political unrest. This inequality fuels violent uprisings and insurgencies, particularly among marginalized groups (IPCC, 2022; Oxfam International 2017). Conflict resolution efforts are hindered by entrenched socio-economic disparities, as marginalized groups may be reluctant to participate in peace processes if their grievances stemming from economic injustice are not addressed.

The Role of International Institutions

International institutions like the United Nations (UN) and NATO play vital roles in peacekeeping, conflict resolution, and atrocity prevention as we will read from the stories of peacebuilders in this book. The UN is at the forefront of conflict resolution efforts globally, with its peacekeeping missions, mediations, and humanitarian aid operations. However, the effectiveness of the UN is often constrained by the political interests of its member states, leading to delays in intervention or biased peace processes. NATO has traditionally played a role in military interventions to stabilize regions affected by conflict. However, its involvement is often controversial, as military interventions can sometimes escalate tensions rather than resolving the underlying issues. Despite their importance, international institutions often struggle with resource constraints, lack of political will, and geopolitical rivalries that limit their ability to enforce peace agreements or prevent conflicts from escalating.

The perspectives on internationalization of peacebuilding versus internal resolution and national ownership from the various authors highlight a recurring theme; while international actors play important roles in facilitating peace processes, lasting peace must be driven and owned by national actors. **Victor Ângelo** argues that external interventions should not replace local leadership, emphasizing that solutions must be shaped by those directly affected. Similarly, **Gershon Baskin** critiques over-reliance on global powers like the US in the Israeli-Palestinian conflict, advocating instead for grassroots and civil society-led peace efforts. **Emily Winterbotham** and **Caroline Brooks** echo this, warning that international peacebuilding often sidelines local actors and fails to reflect on-the-ground realities. **Heela Yoon** critiques the cultural disconnect and short-term approach of international interventions in Afghanistan, calling for meaningful inclusion of local youth and women. **Paulo Gonçalves** and **Simon Mann** question the effectiveness of top-down UN missions that lack contextual grounding. **Sandra Melone** supports a balanced, hybrid model where local media and civil society initiatives are supported but not dominated by international partners. Together, these voices underscore that legitimacy, relevance, and sustainability in peacebuilding can only be achieved when local ownership is prioritized.

Future Drivers of Conflict

Advances in technology, including cyber warfare, are becoming new drivers of conflict. As technology progresses, cyber warfare has emerged as a significant factor in destabilizing nations. Both state and non-state actors are now capable of launching cyber-attacks that can paralyze critical infrastructure, disrupt communication networks, and sow societal discord by spreading disinformation. For instance, cyber-attacks on power grids or financial systems can lead to widespread chaos, economic hardship, and even political instability, as governments struggle to respond (Clarke and Knake 2010; Singer and Friedman 2014). The rise of fake news and online propaganda has further blurred the lines between truth and manipulation, making conflict resolution more difficult. Cyber-attacks can trigger physical conflicts or exacerbate existing tensions, leaving states vulnerable to new, unseen forms of aggression. States and non-state actors can now launch cyber-attacks that disrupt essential services, spread disinformation, and destabilize governments, leading to new forms of conflict (Van Niekerk, 2018).

In regions where there is a high concentration of unemployed youth, there is an increased risk of violence and radicalization. When young people are left without access to economic opportunities, they are more susceptible to radicalization, recruitment by violent extremist groups, or participation in criminal networks (ILO, 2020). Unemployed youth often feel marginalized and frustrated by the lack of prospects, which can fuel grievances that lead to social unrest, protests, or insurgencies. Countries with high levels of youth unemployment, especially in conflict-prone regions, are at greater risk of experiencing future conflicts unless these challenges are addressed.

Another emerging theme from the interviews is climate crisis. **Victor Ângelo** highlights how desertification in Africa has intensified conflicts between nomadic herders and settled farmers, contributing to rising rural-urban migration and straining urban infrastructure and social stability. **Simon Mann** builds on this, noting how environmental degradation in the Sahel region has made communities more vulnerable to recruitment by jihadist groups, who exploit grievances tied to shrinking livelihoods. **Sandra Melone** draws attention to transhumance-related conflicts, where traditional pastoral routes now overlap with contested territories due to shifting climate patterns, fueling local tensions. Meanwhile, **Paulo Gonçalves** underscores how climate-induced migration, especially from Portuguese-speaking Africa to Europe, has led to instability in both origin and destination countries, affecting social cohesion. Finally, **Anjan Sundaram** addresses environmental conflict from a justice perspective, documenting indigenous resistance to extractivist practices in Latin America, where communities oppose land exploitation linked to climate and ecological destruction, often at great personal risk. Collectively, these perspectives frame climate change as a powerful, transnational driver of both direct and structural violence.

Moving from war mentality to peace

One prominent approach of conflict resolution is peace education, which is critical for transforming societies from war-torn states to peaceful ones. By teaching conflict resolution skills, such as empathy and the importance of cooperation, peace education helps lay the foundation for a culture of peace. Moreover, moving from a war mentality to a peace mentality requires addressing the narratives that perpetuate violence. This involves promoting reconciliation, focusing on shared humanity, and creating opportunities for dialogue between formerly warring groups. Shifting societal attitudes from revenge and retribution to healing and rebuilding is key to achieving lasting peace. Conflict resolution, peacebuilding, and preventing future violence are complex and multifaceted tasks. By understanding the different methods of conflict resolution, addressing the challenges to peace, and recognizing the evolving nature of global conflicts, we can create more effective strategies for lasting peace. Women's participation, international cooperation, and a focus on education are crucial for transforming violent conflicts into opportunities for reconciliation and economic development.

CONFLICT RESOLUTION APPROACHES

The various experiences shared in the chapters of this book highlight the complexities of conflicts, particularly in hybrid-warfare contexts. Traditional peacebuilding models are becoming less effective in dealing with modern conflicts that are influenced by globalization, advanced technologies, and misinformation. The interviews collected in this book reflect the first-hand experiences of a wide range of those involved in various types of conflict resolution as indicated below.

Negotiation and Mediation

Negotiation is often emphasized as a key approach to conflict resolution, where diplomacy plays a crucial role in resolving disputes between opposing parties. For instance, **Simon Mann** discusses the limitations of military interventions and stresses the importance of diplomatic negotiations in reaching long-term peace settlements in the context of Bosnia and Herzegovina. Mediation, as practised by international actors such as the UN, is central to conflict resolution, particularly in places like Afghanistan, where United Nations Assistance Mission in Afghanistan (UNAMA) facilitated dialogues between Afghan political leaders and insurgents. **Victor Ângelo** used mediation and diplomacy to resolve conflict between the Indigenous population and white farmers in Zimbabwe, while **Gershon Baskin** shares how he applied informal negotiations channels in the Israel – Palestine peace process.

Military Interventions

Simon Mann and others acknowledge that military interventions are sometimes necessary to halt violent conflicts. However, they also stress that military action should be aligned with broader political strategies to ensure long-term peace. In countries like Angola and Sierra Leone, military interventions were used to suppress conflicts but had limited success without accompanying political negotiations.

Community Engagement and Trust-Building

Local engagement is seen as vital in conflict resolution, with a strong emphasis on trust-building between local communities, civil society, and peacekeepers. Community-based bottom-up approaches, particularly involving grassroots actors, are crucial for sustainable peacebuilding (see **Ângelo, Gonçalves, Melone, Yoon** and **Baskin**). These efforts focus on resolving tensions at the local level before they escalate into larger conflicts.

Humanitarian Aid and Peacekeeping

Humanitarian efforts, combined with peacekeeping missions, are essential for addressing both the immediate and long-term needs of conflict-affected populations. International actors, including non-governmental organizations (NGOs) and agencies like the United Nations High Commission for Refugees (UNHCR) and International Committee of the Red Cross (ICRC), provide essential humanitarian aid in conflict zones. They offer food, shelter, medical care, and psychosocial support to displaced populations and communities affected by violence.

Media, Civil Society and Public Dialogue

Sandra Melone's experience with Search for Common Ground emphasizes the innovative use of media (such as radio and soap operas) to transform harmful narratives and promote conflict transformation. Media engagement is seen as a vital tool in reshaping public perceptions and promoting reconciliation. **Caroline Brooks'** work in Syria under-scored the critical role of civil society in peacebuilding. Engaging local actors and empowering grassroots movements are key strategies to promote peace in communities affected by conflict. This is also linked to multi-track diplomacy, where local initiatives are connected to national and international peace processes.

    Nurcan Baysal reiterated the role of media and civil society in conflict resolution and peacebuilding, citing examples from Northern Ireland and Colombia and the benefit of their involvement in ensuring that social issues are addressed. Similarly, **Saskia Binet** highlighted the role of civil society in developing mechanisms for accountability by peacebuilding actors.

Psychological Support and Wellbeing

Mental health and psychological wellbeing are increasingly recognized as critical components of peacebuilding, as seen in **Heela Yoon's** work. Providing safe spaces for women to express their emotions and heal from trauma is part of the broader peacebuilding strategy, reflecting the psychological toll that conflict takes on individuals.

    The conflict resolution methods, challenges, and strategies from the interviews demonstrates that a multi-faceted approach blending diplomacy, local engagement, psychological support, and media outreach is essential for sustainable peacebuilding and each depends on the nature of conflict and the context.

Principles of Inclusivity in Conflict Resolution

Inclusivity is a critical principle in conflict resolution, particularly in gender inclusion and youth engagement within peace processes. In societies like the Democratic Republic of Congo (DRC), engaging women in peacebuilding efforts is essential, as gender dynamics often limit their participation in male-dominated environments.

Several authors (**Emily Winterbotham**, **Caroline Brooks**, **Nurcan Baysal,** and **Saskia Binet**) emphasized women's unique contributions to peacebuilding by focusing on family cohesion, community rebuilding and long-term peace sustainability. They advocate for inclusive peace -building that centres the needs of marginalized groups, including women and children.

Heela Yoon's work emphasizes the importance of youth, especially young women, in peace processes. Through her organization, Afghan Youth Ambassadors for Peace (AYAPO), she empowers young leaders to play active roles in peacebuilding. Including youth in these efforts allows for fresh, innovative approaches to conflicts, as they bring perspectives deeply affected by the violence they experience.

Local ownership of peacebuilding processes is another key theme. **Yoon** highlights that those grassroots efforts, particularly in conflict zones like Afghanistan, must be culturally sensitive and driven by the community. External models often fail when implemented without understanding local dynamics. Tailoring peace initiatives to specific needs ensures sus-tainability and resonates with the local population, fostering long-term solutions.

Challenges of Conflict Resolution

The challenges of conflict resolution are multifaceted, with misinform-ation and disinformation being a critical issue in the interviews (see **Winterbotham, Norman, Holmes and Gonçalves**). Social media and Artificial Intelligence (AI) are increasingly used to spread false narratives that undermine the neutrality of peacekeeping missions, heightening distrust among local populations and putting peacekeepers at risk.

AI generated content distorts perceptions of conflict, creates confusion over truth and contributes to political polarization. These challenges require peace-builders to adopt new strategies to provide clear and truthful information. **Tony Schiena** warns of the catastrophic consequences of AI if AI-controlled weapons fall into the wrong hands, whether rogue states, private military companies or terrorist groups. He also flags cyber-AI as a new battlefield, where entire governments and infrastructures could be compromised through cyber attacks with AI powered malware and deepfakes. **Paulo Gonçalves** notes that AI could also be deployed to deepen authoritarian control, speed up escalation and entrench militarized politics. Despite its challenges, AI could also be used to combat misinformation and enhance dialogue. **Saskia Binet** argues that if well regulated, AI could be used in trend analysis and detecting online drivers of conflict.

Gershon Baskin underscores the difficulty of initiating peace when parties are not emotionally or politically ready, often delaying negotiations until after extensive suffering. **Victor Ângelo** identifies demographic shifts and exclusionary governance as major conflict drivers, compounded by a persistent militaristic mindset. **Simon Mann** critiques the overreliance on military solutions that suppress but fail to resolve deeper grievances. **Sandra Melone** notes the challenge of transforming public narratives dominated by divisive media, while **Anjan Sundaram** draws attention to the criminalization of indigenous resistance in the face of extractivist violence. Another significant challenge is the gender-based credibility issues women face in leadership roles within peacekeeping missions. Additionally, peacekeeping missions often suffer from resource limitations and poor communication, making it hard to respond to crises and fostering mistrust among local populations.

Furthermore, complex and fluid conflict environments, like those in Syria, make long-term planning challenging, while civil society actors often experience fatigue and frustration due to limited resources and slow progress. Trust issues, skepticism towards peace initiatives, and cultural sensitivity further hinder effective peacebuilding efforts, particularly in patriarchal societies where engaging women and youth is met with resistance. This is especially true in contexts such as Afghanistan where women are being increasingly disempowered and discriminated against.

Strategies for addressing challenges

Strategies to address peacebuilding challenges from the interviews emphasize local ownership, communication, and resilience. Empowering local communities by involving leaders and civil society organizations in decision-making is key. Clear communication, including outreach programs and proactive counter-misinformation campaigns, helps build trust and ensures that communities understand peacekeeping mandates. For example, using local media and trusted figures to disseminate accurate information is essential.

Targeted gender outreach, particularly engaging women in peace processes, ensures that their voices are heard in shaping the future. Addressing gender-based disparities also involves creating specific programs to encourage participation. Similarly, building trust through partnerships with civil society actors empowers local stakeholders to take ownership of peacebuilding efforts.

In conflict environments like Syria, adaptability is crucial. Constantly re-evaluating plans based on evolving dynamics ensures that peacebuilding efforts can continue in unstable situations. Supporting youth resilience through education, employment, and positive role models helps deter recruitment into violent groups. Mental health support, such as art therapy programs for women, promotes healing and empowerment, fostering long-term peace. Additionally, addressing hybrid warfare and misinformation requires integrating advanced tools like AI for monitoring conflicts and engaging multiple stakeholders to create unified, sustainable peace strategies.

GENDER AND CONFLICT RESOLUTION

From the interviews, the role of women in peacebuilding is a recurring theme, emphasizing their essential contributions to conflict resolution and the challenges they face.

The Role of Women in Peacebuilding

- *Unique Perspectives and Priorities:* Women often bring unique perspectives to peace processes, focusing on issues related to family, community cohesion, and long-term sustainability of peace agreements. Their involvement ensures that the specific needs of women, children, and marginalized communities are addressed, such as preventing sexual violence and advocating for inclusive human-centred approaches to peacebuilding (see **Winterbotham** and **Brooks**).

- *Grassroots Engagement:* Women are heavily involved in peacebuilding at the grassroots level, serving as mediators and community leaders. They engage directly with local communities to prevent violence and promote reconciliation. Women's efforts in humanitarian aid also complement their peacebuilding roles, particularly in war-torn areas where they work to rebuild communities (see **Yoon** and **Hadjipavlou**).

- *Advocacy for Gender-Specific Issues:* Women play a crucial role in pushing for the inclusion of gender-specific issues in peace agreements. For example, they work to prevent gender-based violence, promote gender equality, and ensure women have access to resources, healthcare, and education. These issues are often sidelined in male-dominated peace processes, making women's involvement crucial (see **Melone**).

Challenges Faced by Women in Peacebuilding

Patriarchal norms and traditional gender roles often prevent women from participating in formal peace processes. In many conflict-affected regions, women are not viewed as leaders or decision-makers, limiting their ability to influence high-level negotiations (see **Winterbotham,** and **Brooks**). These cultural barriers are particularly pronounced in societies like Afghanistan, where women's participation is viewed with suspicion, and their contributions are undervalued (see **Yoon**).

Despite their active roles at the grassroots level, women are frequently excluded from high-level peace negotiations. This exclusion often results in peace agreements that fail to address the needs and priorities of women and children, which undermines the overall effectiveness of peace processes (see **Gonçalves, Mann** and **Brooks**). Women peacebuilders including women human rights defenders frequently face threats of violence, harassment, and retaliation, especially in conflict zones (see **Corey, Binet, Norman** and **Baysal**). This poses a significant challenge, as security concerns limit their mobility and ability to engage in peacebuilding efforts (see Winterbotham). Women in leadership positions also face credibility issues in male-dominated environments, making it harder for them to assert authority and build trust.

Women's peacebuilding efforts are often underfunded, with women-led organizations struggling to secure resources. International funding tends to prioritize larger, male-dominated organizations, leaving women's groups marginalized and limiting their ability to sustain their work (see **Yoon**). In some conflict zones, misinformation and disinformation can undermine the credibility of peace processes and put women peacebuilders at risk. This is especially problematic in regions where local populations view peacekeepers and international actors with skepticism (see **Winterbotham** and **Brooks**). Despite the vital role women play in peacebuilding, they face numerous structural barriers that limit their participation and effectiveness as indicated from the interviews included in this book. Addressing these challenges requires targeted efforts to include women in formal peace processes, to provide adequate security and financial support, and dismantle patriarchal norms that hinder their involvement (see **Hadjipavlou**). Additionally, countering misinformation and promoting gender-sensitive peacebuilding approaches will be essential in ensuring that women's contributions are fully recognized and integrated into lasting peace works. Moreover, it is essential to promote gender-sensitive policies, including enacting laws and quotas to mandate women's participation in peace negotiations and decision-making roles. Capacity building is also crucial, providing women with training and resources to empower them in leadership positions. Enhancing security for women peacebuilders is necessary to ensure their safe involvement. International organizations and governments must collaborate to create protection mechanisms, such as rapid response systems and secure transportation, to shield women from violence. These measures collectively foster a more inclusive and effective approach to peacebuilding and conflict resolution.

THE ROLE OF INTERNATIONAL ACTORS

The role of international actors in conflict resolution varies widely, with both positive contributions and significant challenges highlighted in interviews across multiple contexts. Key international organizations such as the UN, NATO, and the European Union (EU) have been pivotal in providing military support, peacekeeping, humanitarian aid, and capacity-building in conflict zones. Their efforts, however, are often criticized for inconsistencies, lack of coordination, and a tendency to adopt a top-down approach, which can disconnect international interventions from the realities on the ground.

Caroline Brooks points out that while international institutions provide essential support, including financial aid and technical assistance, they often impose solutions that do not align with local needs. **Emily Winterbotham** echoes this critique in the Afghanistan context, noting that international peace efforts, particularly military interventions by NATO and the US, initially stabilized the country but failed to address the root causes of conflict, such as ethnic tensions and governance issues. The rapid withdrawal of forces led to the collapse of fragile systems, underscoring the limitations of externally driven solutions. **Heela Yoon** emphasizes the limitations of international institutions when they fail to adapt to the specific cultural and political dynamics of countries like Afghanistan. While the UN has provided funding and advocated for human rights, their interventions have often been symbolic and short-term, without adequately supporting the grassroots organizations critical to sustaining peace and social justice. Similarly, **Paulo Gonçalves** and **Simon Mann** critique the bureaucratic constraints and inefficiencies of international organizations like the UN. **Gonçalves** underscores the disconnect between high-level peacekeeping missions and the realities of conflicts on the ground, while **Mann** stresses that international actors often fail to engage in meaningful military action when necessary. In Zimbabwe, Ângelo highlights the challenge of navigating both formal and informal power structures, emphasizing the need for local ownership of peace processes with international actors playing a facilitative role.

The interviews highlight that while international actors have been essential in providing immediate relief, facilitating political settlements, and offering technical support, their efforts are often hindered by a lack of local ownership, political constraints, and a disconnect from the grassroots level.

Future Drivers Of Conflict

The future drivers of conflict, as highlighted in the interviews, revolve around various global and regional challenges such as climate change, resource scarcity, technological advancements, and social inequality.

Many interviewees, including **Simon Mann**, emphasize that climate change is a critical future driver of conflict. Drought, desertification, and diminishing resources such as water and arable land will lead to competition and displacement, as seen in regions like the Sahel. This resource competition increases the likelihood of violent conflict over survival necessities.

Technological advancements like AI and cyber warfare are also seen as future conflict drivers (see **Latif Fayaz**). While technology can be used to promote peace, it is also increasingly being weaponized to manipulate information and escalate tensions, such as through disinformation campaigns during elections or in conflict zones.

Patrick McGrann and **John Holmes** discuss how inequality, particularly in land distribution and access to resources, continues to fuel tensions. In countries like Colombia, economic disparities are a root cause of conflict, especially when vulnerable communities are exploited by industries such as illegal mining or drug trafficking. **Jehan Perera** and others note that unresolved historical grievances and ethnic tensions, such as those in Sri Lanka and Afghanistan, could continue to drive conflicts. For example, the resurgence of the Taliban and the oppression of ethnic minorities like the Hazaras in Afghanistan highlight how social and political divisions remain potent drivers of conflict.

According to **Victor Ângelo,** demographic shifts due to urban migration and environmental degradation, particularly in Africa, will create tensions between different social and ethnic groups. The movement of populations from rural to urban areas, exacerbated by climate change, will result in competition for resources and could lead to urban conflicts. Moving from a war mentality to a peace mentality requires addressing these root causes, fostering global cooperation, and shifting from military interventions to diplomatic, humanitarian, and developmental approaches. Peacebuilding strategies will need to focus on inclusivity, sustainability, and adaptability to tackle these emerging challenges.

Conclusion

Conflict resolution remains a complex and multifaceted challenge, shaped by various types of conflict, gender dynamics, future conflict drivers, and the role of the international community. The interviews reveal that while conflict resolution techniques like negotiation, mediation, military intervention, and grassroots engagement have been effective in certain contexts, many conflicts continue to persist due to deep-rooted socio-political, economic, and environmental factors. Additionally, issues such as rape and sexual assault, orphaned children, sex trafficking and the use of child soldiers arising from numerous conflicts highlight the need for women's greater inclusion in peace processes, as their participation often brings a more holistic and inclusive perspective to resolving conflicts and the social devastation in their wake. However, patriarchal norms, security risks, and lack of resources continue to hinder their full engagement.

Future conflict drivers such as climate change, resource scarcity, economic inequality, technological advances, and migration pose additional challenges to peacebuilding. The shift from a war mentality, which relies on militaristic approaches, to a peace mentality that focuses on diplomacy, development, and addressing root causes, is critical. Addressing these future drivers requires proactive, inclusive, and sustainable peacebuilding efforts that are adaptive to local contexts and global trends.

The role of the international community in conflict resolution is essential but often inconsistent. While international actors provide vital support through peacekeeping, humanitarian aid, and capacity-building efforts, their interventions are frequently top-down, overlooking local dynamics. To ensure effective conflict resolution, the international community must prioritize collaboration with local actors, particularly civil society, women, and marginalized groups. This local-global synergy is crucial for sustainable peace, as imposed solutions without grassroots involvement are likely to falter.

RECOMMENDATIONS

1. **Inclusive Peace Processes:** To ensure sustainable conflict resolution, peace processes must actively include women, youth, and marginalized groups at all levels of negotiation and decision-making. Quotas and gender-sensitive policies can be employed to ensure equal representation, while local grassroots actors should be empowered to contribute meaningfully.

2. **Address Future Conflict Drivers:** Climate change, economic inequality, and technological advances must be addressed as key drivers of conflict. Investment in sustainable development, climate adaptation, and creating economic opportunities for vulnerable communities can reduce the risks associated with these challenges.

3. **Local Ownership and Empowerment:** The international community should move away from imposing top-down solutions and instead support local ownership of peacebuilding efforts. This requires investing in local leadership, capacity building, and grassroots organizations that understand the specific needs of their communities.

4. **Enhanced Collaboration:** International actors must coordinate more effectively with one another and with local governments and civil society to create comprehensive, long-term strategies for conflict prevention and resolution. A unified approach that blends diplomatic, military, humanitarian, and developmental efforts is essential for lasting peace.

REFERENCES

Barnett, Jon, and W. Neil Adger (2007) *Climate Change, Human Security and Violent Conflict.* Political Geography, 26(6), 639–655.

Clarke, Richard A., and Robert K. Knake (2010). *Cyber War: The Next Threat to National Security and What to Do About It.* HarperCollins.

Ileka, Nekwaya and Imene-Chanduru, Julia (2020). 'How Namibia Helped Birth UN Resolution 1325 on Women, Peace and Security', Africa Renewal, 27 October, 2020.

International Labour Organization (ILO) (2020). "Global Employment Trends for Youth 2020: Technology and the Future of Jobs"

International Organization for Migration (IOM) (2019). World Migration Report 2020. IOM Publications Platform") Available from https://publications.iom.int › pdf › wmr_2020 [Accessed 12 September 2024]

Institute for Economics & Peace. Global Peace Index 2024: Measuring Peace in a Complex World, Sydney, June 2024. ("Cluttons Portugal - Instagram") Available from: http://visionofhumanity.org/resources [accessed 29 August 2024)

Intergovernmental Panel on Climate Change (2022). Climate Change 2022: Impacts, Adaptation and Vulnerability. Available at https://www.ipcc.ch/report/ar6/wg2/ [Accessed 12 September 2024]

Olga Stepanova, Merritt Polk and Hannah Saldert (2018). "Understanding mechanisms of conflict resolution beyond collaboration: an interdisciplinary typology of knowledge types and their integration in practice." Sustainability Science (2020) 15:263–279 https://doi.org/10.1007/s11625-019-00690-z [Accessed September 10, 2024]

Oxfam International (2017). "An Economy for the 99%: It's Time to Build a Human Economy that Benefits Everyone, Not Just the Privileged Few." ("An economy for the 99%: it's time to build a human economy that ...")

Singer, P.W., and Allan Friedman (2014). *Cybersecurity and Cyberwar: What Everyone Needs to Know*. Oxford University Press.

UN Women (2015). Preventing Conflict, Transforming Justice, Securing the Peace: A Global Study on the Implementation of United Nations Security Council Resolution 1325. ("FACT SHEET THE GLOBAL STUDY ON 1325: KEY MESSAGES, FINDINGS, AND ...") http://wps.unwomen.org/en [Accessed September 9, 2024]

Rehn, E. and Sirleaf, E. J. (2002). Women, War and Peace: The Independent Experts' Assessment on the Impact of Armed Conflict on Women and Women's Role in Peace-Building. United Nations Development Fund for Women, New York, USA.

Marie O'Reilly, Andrea Ó Súilleabháin, and Thania Paffenholz, (2015) Reimagining Peacemaking: Women's Roles in Peace Processes, New York: International Peace Institute, June 2015 ("Policy Brief Role of Women in Peacebuilding Processes")

Van Niekerk, Brett (2018). *The Strategic Implications of Cyber Security in Africa. African Security Review*, 27(3), 214–233.

Kaldor, Mary (2013). *New and Old Wars: Organized Violence in a Global Era*. Polity Press.

AT THE HEART OF CONFLICT - TALKING RESOLUTION

Helen Kezie-Nwoha is a feminist scholar, peace-builder, and human rights advocate with over two decades of experience advancing gender equality in conflict and post-conflict settings. She is the Founder and Lead Researcher at Researchers Without Borders and former Executive Director of the Women's International Peace Centre. Her work spans Africa and beyond, providing strategic policy advice to regional institutions such as the African Union, particularly on the implementation of the Women, Peace and Security agenda. Helen currently serves as the Chair of the Gender is My Agenda Campaign (GIMAC) at the African Union and is a member of FEMWISE, the African Network of Women Mediators. She holds a Ph.D. in Women and Gender Studies from Makerere University and has published extensively on feminist peacebuilding, political participation, and transitional justice. Through her leadership and scholarship, she has influenced national and regional policies that centre women's voices in peace processes and governance.

INTERVIEWS

VICTOR ÂNGELO

Could you share some highlights of your 32-year career with the work at the UN?

Certainly, I had the privilege of working with the United Nations for an extended period, though it is essential to note that prior to this, I served with the Portuguese Government in the National Statistics Institute. This was during the first Election Commission following the 25 April 1974, which oversaw the preparations for the first free elections after the fall of the dictatorship. I was quite young at the time, around 24 years of age. One of my responsibilities at the Institute was to represent Portugal in meetings in Paris with the Organisation for Economic Co-operation and Development (OECD).

It was during those meetings that I encountered individuals from various OECD countries, as well as representatives from international organizations, including from the UN in New York. Through these contacts, in 1978, I was invited by the UN to assist in establishing a planning and statistics system in São Tomé and Príncipe. The assignment was initially intended to last for one year, with the aim of conducting a census, rebuilding the national statistics system – which had been dismantled following the departure of the Portuguese – and implementing a system of economic planning.

Ultimately, I remained in São Tomé and Príncipe for two and a half years. After that, the UN offered me a more permanent position in Mozambique. From 1980, I became deeply involved in family planning, demography, and the protection of women and children, not only within Mozambique but across Southern Africa. This was a large-scale initiative that also encompassed Angola, São Tomé and Príncipe, and Equatorial Guinea, all of which were Portuguese or Spanish-speaking countries.

My work then transitioned towards development, and in 1985, I was appointed as the United Nations Development Programme (UNDP) representative to the Central African Republic. At that time, the Central African Republic was a largely unknown and underdeveloped nation.

When New York offered me the opportunity, I had to consult a map to identify its location. The UN presented me with two options: to work on development in the Central African Republic or to remain focused on demography and population issues, with a posting in Rio de Janeiro. I chose the Central African Republic, believing it would offer both a more rewarding challenge and greater career advancement, given that it was a country few were willing to work in and where the need for development was urgent.

I spent four years there, assisting the government in establishing basic governance structures. My role was broad, addressing a variety of national needs rather than focusing on a specific sector.

Following this, I was assigned as the UN representative to The Gambia, a country that was attracting attention for its status as one of the few democratic nations in Africa at the time. In 1989, The Gambia sought to become a leader in the fight against poverty, and I was tasked with leading the development and implementation of an integrated poverty reduction plan. I spent nearly five years in The Gambia, overseeing the creation of the plan and mobilising resources from the international community.

Due to the success of my work in The Gambia, the UN subsequently appointed me to Tanzania, a country of great significance in Africa at the time. I went to Tanzania with two purposes: to support the transition from a Marxist-Leninist economy to a market-driven one and to manage the influx of refugees fleeing the Rwandan massacre. I arrived in Tanzania during the height of the Tutsi genocide and remained there for almost four years. During my tenure, I organised the first free elections in Tanzania and played a pivotal role in resolving the conflict between Tanzania and Zanzibar, which was then under a dictatorial regime.

Following my time in Tanzania, I returned to New York, where I served for three years as Director of Operations for the development of Africa.

When did you work as Special Representative of the U.N. Secretary-General (Peacekeeping Operations)?

I left New York for East Timor right after the referendum of 1999, which declared the country independent from Indonesia. There, I prepared the political presence for peace operations to come in. I also mediated the armed conflict in the Philippines between the Muslim population of Mindanao and the central government.

What did your day-to-day work involve in that role?

Within this role, I pursued two principal objectives: de-escalating tensions between conflicting parties and organizing an electoral process that was both credible and widely acceptable. Achieving the former required preventing armed confrontations and engaging in negotiations to secure the release of hostages. The latter involved carefully balancing the demands of the general population with those of opposing group leaders.

Shifting to another politically charged context, I was assigned to Zimbabwe during the period when Robert Mugabe initiated the controversial occupation of white-owned farmlands. My primary goal was to negotiate an agricultural reform process that ensured access to land for the indigenous population while preserving the capacity of white farmers to sustain commercial agriculture, a fundamental practice for Zimbabwe's economic stability.

This created enormous and widespread conflicts. It encompassed external invasions, armed clashes between factions, and escalating tensions between Zimbabwe and the international community, particularly the United Kingdom.

My role was to mediate negotiations and reach for an agreement that would guide the redistribution of land ownership. This was one of the most challenging tasks, as Mugabe's government was both ruthless and deeply hostile toward the white minority. Violent attacks on white-owned properties and individuals were frequent, and the response from the white community was often armed too.

After this, I joined the Peace Operation in Sierra Leone. The primary focus of this mission was the reintegration of former soldiers who had perpetrated heinous acts of violence during the civil war, into the national armed forces and police. Part of this reintegration process required fostering acceptance of democratic governance among the ex-combatants and in turn, persuading the government of Sierra Leone to accept their inclusion.

I spent three and a half years working on the peace process in Sierra Leone, engaged in efforts to rebuild a country that was divided and fractured by civil war and exacerbated by profound ethnic divisions between northern and southern tribes. As I organized the nation's first free and credible elections, I faced attempts from both sides to manipulate and falsify the results. This included interference from highly influential government figures with great international reputations.

The government ended up losing the elections. This marked the first instance in Africa where a government in power was defeated in a democratic election. One of my critical responsibilities was ensuring the government accepted the results. To that end, I had to discreetly protect the president of the Supreme Court of Justice, giving him the time and space to announce an impartial declaration of the results, free from government intervention.

Following my time in Sierra Leone, I went to the Sahel region to address a complex web of conflicts. These included disputes between the governments of Chad and Sudan, and a rebellion zone in the Central African Republic. My mission was to negotiate peace agreements aimed at fostering a good 'neighbourly' relationship between Chad and Sudan, creating a foundation for peaceful coexistence.

In addition to addressing the conflicts, I worked on two other critical issues. The first was managing massive refugee movements. Thousands of Sudanese refugees had sought shelter in Chad, while many Chadians went to the Central African Republic. My role involved protecting these populations and ensuring the safety of humanitarian workers amidst ongoing hostilities. The second concern was the rampant poaching of wildlife in Chad and the Central African Republic. Poached animals were sold to finance the purchase of weapons, perpetuating the cycle of violence.

To address these challenges, we had 6,000 soldiers, a police force of 2,000, and numerous NGOs to safeguard vulnerable populations and counteract the destructive consequences of poaching.

Of all the conflicts you worked on, was there one that was particularly challenging? Why?

Each conflict I worked on presented its own unique challenges, as they all differed in nature and had distinct characteristics. I will give you a few examples.

The conflict between the rebels in Chad and the military stands out for its sheer intensity and the brutal conditions in which it unfolded. Both sides were primarily composed of people from the northern regions of the country, accustomed to the harsh desert environment. For those of us intervening, it wasn't something we were used to. Our soldiers were not equipped to survive, let alone fight, for weeks in the desert. Only the individuals who had been born and raised there were able to fight and win in those conditions.

Fighting in the desert and the most arid areas was a nearly impossible challenge for us not only because of the conditions, but also because most of the UN soldiers had limitations imposed by their governments that prevented them from going to areas of the desert that had worse living conditions and no access to hospitals. Injuries, which were inevitable, required helicopter evacuations – sometimes proving impossible due to bad weather, sandstorms, visibility issues.

Another even bigger challenge arose in Sierra Leone, where we faced the task of persuading the government to accept its electoral defeat. They were absolutely sure they were going to win, and so the loss came as a shock.

To make matters even more complex, several senior government officials, including the President, were people I knew personally. They thought I would be on their side, but I couldn't choose sides. They had assumed I would help them to win the elections. That created huge tensions between former colleagues and me who never thought someone they had known for so many years would just be impartial. But upholding neutrality was so important.

I also encountered significant challenges working with Robert Mugabe. He was an extremely intelligent, cultured individual, very strategic in his way of thinking and so we needed to be very careful with what we discussed with him because he could always turn conversations to his advantage. Engaging with him required extreme caution; for instance, if we pointed out that a certain decision violated the rule of law, he might simply respond that it wasn't a problem because you could change the law tomorrow.

I had a similar experience with figures like Jean-Bédel Bokassa, the President of the Central African Republic. He was astute in the way he saw things, how he spoke and had a knack for turning arguments on their head.

On the other hand, I also had the privilege of working with very interesting leaders who, despite their power, displayed remarkable humility. Julius Nyerere, often regarded as the father of the republic

Tanzania and a key figure in bringing about the country's independence, was one such leader. During the Rwandan and Burundian conflicts, which overlapped with my time in Tanzania, I observed his unwavering humility despite his immense power and influence.

In which conflicts were you most successful?

Sierra Leone stands out as one of the most significant successes. Despite the challenges, the mission achieved its objectives largely because the UN – particularly my team – remained strict in its impartiality and unwavering in its principles.

Another notable success was East Timor. I was involved in the mission's early stages, immediately following the referendum when tensions erupted. The population rose against the Indonesians, leading to widespread destruction as homes and infrastructure were set ablaze. I spent about six months there, focused on preparing the groundwork for the mission led by Sérgio Vieira de Mello. Once he arrived, I returned to New York. Ultimately, the East Timor mission was another example of effective international intervention.

However, Zimbabwe was a different story entirely. That mission, unfortunately, can only be described as a true failure.

What happened in Zimbabwe?

The greatest disappointment was Zimbabwe, in the sense that it was not possible to achieve the agrarian reform we had envisioned. There was no agreement between the African and white populations, and after four years of UN presence, the country's economy was in complete ruins.

When I arrived in 2000, Zimbabwe was a functioning nation. By the time I left in 2004, however, it had become one of the poorest and most chaotic countries, with the most severe social problems. The justice system, which had once worked well, was completely overtaken by Robert Mugabe's influence and had ceased to function well.

This was, without a doubt, my greatest failure. The international community, namely the UN, my mission, and myself always maintained a strong and firm dialogue with Robert Mugabe, but he was a little bit like Vladimir Putin. Much like Putin, he dismissed external advice and acted solely on his own convictions, irrespective of the consequences. His actions, unfortunately, led to the country's ruin.

It was the most difficult mission I undertook and, ultimately, a total failure. However, it led to a significant promotion of my position within the UN following my departure from Zimbabwe. This recognition from the UN and the international community indicated their understanding that we had done everything within our power to prevent the catastrophe. Despite our efforts, the outcome was beyond our control.

Do you have any advice for people trying to navigate current conflicts?

The most important advice is explaining to the people in the country that it is their problem, and they are the ones who must solve it. We are not there to solve the problem: we are there to try and help all parties reach a deal. But it is ultimately their problem.

I'm saying this because, for example, even yesterday European Foreign Affairs Ministers and some Arabic ones spent a day trying to come up with a peace strategy for Israel and Palestine, but without Israel and Palestine. That's exactly the opposite of what should happen. A peace plan must be made by Israel and Palestine, and others should only facilitate and support. That was one of the biggest lessons: to explain to the governments or members of the opposition that it's their problem, and they must find a solution. Our aim was to help them to look for that solution, to ensure that the process they had created made sense, and to try to bring some international support to move the process along.

But it is important to understand that is not the responsibility of foreign countries to solve other country's issues, especially because they (the population) are the ones who know the society, who know who has influence and who doesn't. Where the true leaders are. A lot of the times we think a person has a lot of influence because he is the president or the prime minister, but he doesn't, because sometimes there can be a traditional leader with a much bigger influence. In Zimbabwe, I had a situation in which my driver had more influence than some ministers because my driver belonged to the dominant tribe.

For example, once there was a delegation which came from New York and wanted to speak to the president but didn't have access to him. They had spoken with the Minister for Foreign Affairs, the Minister for Labour, who was a close friend to the President, the Defence Minister, but still couldn't get to him. So, I asked if they had spoken to my driver.

They thought it was a joke. Why would we speak to the driver? Then

I told them: for access. They didn't believe me, but then they did speak to the driver. A day later, they had a meeting with the president. He was a young driver, but he belonged to one of the most influential tribes.

That was one of the things I learned. A lot of the time, formal and informal power don't coincide. We are used to dealing with formal power – Ministers, Governors – but in reality they're only a sort of screen, because the real power is behind, in the traditional leaders, the powerful families, the dominant tribes or ethnicities. We always have to understand, in every situation, where power lies. The power in that country lies on what? In the UK, the elections, the Parliament. In other countries, that's not necessarily the case.

Another lesson is that whatever the issue, it's a national issue and must be resolved with national solutions, by the population – and it has to be in line with what people consider to be a solution. If it's something which comes from the outside, it won't last.

How do you view the current conflict between Russia and Ukraine and the Israel-Hamas conflict?

Each of those conflicts has its own characteristics. The conflict between Russia and Ukraine is completely different from the one between Israel and Palestine. The conflict between Russia and Ukraine is fundamentally an aggression from the outside. The most important thing is to understand what must happen for the aggressor to stop the aggression.

In a situation such as that one, there are several possible solutions: one of them is getting the aggressor to stop, convince him through international diplomacy, through the international organizations, etc.

In the case of Israel, it's necessary to solve the situation of two populations who live in the same territory, or live in a territory which, in theory, should be shared. The idea that the solution has to come from the outside won't work. The solution has to come from the inside. Otherwise, it won't solve anything. Yesterday, European Foreign Affairs Ministers and some from Arab countries came together and gave it a year for the development of a peace strategy. Why a year? Are we going to wait for things to get worse over 12 months? And, as I'd said, Palestine and Israel are not included in the process, so, it's impossible. It's not going to work.

Do you believe the desertification of Africa and the impact of climate change can lead to increasing conflicts and migration from certain areas of the world?

I believe so, and it's already happening at a growing speed, since the late 90s. The nomadic populations who depend on livestock, the shepherds, started moving south and invading areas which usually were only used for agriculture, with no animals – no cows, no camels or anything. That created conflicts between shepherds and farmers. That's increasingly frequent. On the other hand, what we see both in Western Africa and in Central Africa is increasing desertification.

For example, Gambia today is much more like a desert than it was 20 or 30 years ago. That also leads to the migration of populations, to conflicts between shepherds and farmers, but also migration to the urban areas. What we have seen in the last twenty years is a huge growth in the larger African cities which don't have the conditions to accommodate all of these people coming from the more rural areas.

That obviously creates conflicts, leads to instability and to safety problems in those cities. It has already led to the migration of populations in the Sahel region for the coastal countries, like Togo or Benin. Those movements of populations coming from the countryside to the coastal areas creates tension between the indigenous populations of those areas and the foreign.

The growing desertification and climate change is already creating enormous conflicts and will continue to do so in Africa and, especially, Western Africa, Sahel and Central Africa.

Do you believe future leaders can use AI weapons for territorial expansion or access to resources such as oil or natural gas?

It's hard to predict what will be done with artificial intelligence. I'd start by saying that nowadays, there are two other huge issues somewhat related to that. One of them is that younger people in Africa don't have enough education to use new technologies because the education system is still extremely fragile. Often, governments don't have the means to establish schools. What happens then is that the radical religious movements, currently ones related to Islam, from countries such as Saudi Arabia, even Pakistan, open schools that aren't really schools but are called that. They're religious education centres, which means they teach religion in a radical way.

VICTOR ÂNGELO

In the last 20 or 25 years we have seen the weakening of formal education and an expansion of education related to religious movements. That somewhat explains why there has been an increase in radicalism and terrorism: these are countries that can't get out of poverty, the education system and everything else from the state's administration stops working and so the radical groups, with money from Gulf countries, create an alternative system profoundly impacted by religious extremism. That leads to confrontation between the populations that, on the one hand had a "western" education, and others who were educated on radical religion.

That's what has been happening, namely in Sahel. The population growth in these areas is notorious, and most of the young population can't find a job – so they resort to violence, both political and social. With the movement of population from the rural areas to the urban centres, there's a movement of that violence too, and more and more the larger African cities are chaotic, with no conditions and infrastructure, aside from enormous problems in terms of safety.

Victor Ângelo is a seasoned diplomat with over 32 years of senior-level experience at the United Nations. He has held key roles, including Special Representative of the Secretary-General for Peacekeeping Operations at the Deputy Secretary-General level, Director of Operations for Africa, Resident Coordinator, Humanitarian Coordinator, and UNDP Resident Representative. Additionally, Ângelo served as a Special Envoy on various missions. Outside the UN, he was a founding member of the Swiss Foundation "PeaceNexus" Board of Directors from 2009 to 2022, where he supported peacebuilding in regions such as West Africa, the Sahel, and Central Asia. He also worked as an Associate Member and Senior Advisor at the Geneva Centre for Security Policy (GCSP). Between 2010 and 2017, he provided strategic advice as Senior Consultant to the Executive Secretary of the Community of Portuguese Language Countries (CPLP) and as a Senior Civilian Advisor for NATO. A commentator on international affairs, Ângelo contributed to various media, including Rádio Macau.

GERSHON BASKIN

You've had a long career in peacebuilding, in particular in the conflict between Palestine and Israel. How has the conflict changed over the decades?

I have been doing this for 45-46 years. There used to be a lot more hope than there is today. That's the nature of a conflict that has gone through a failed peace process. Before there was a peace process or during a time when there was a peace process, there was hope. When it failed and exploded in acute violence and lots of people lost their lives, it became so much more difficult to renew hope. People lose their belief that the other side wants peace.

What we have had for the last 24 years – since the second Intifada exploded in September of 2000 – is a very strong belief, on both sides of the conflict, that each side says "we want peace" but they don't actually. Unfortunately, over the past 24 years, both sides have done an enormous amount to reinforce the belief that the other side does not want peace.

How has that changed the approach to peacebuilding and conflict resolution?

In the field, we have experienced a cycle of seeking external assistance, facing disappointment with the international community, and ultimately turning to civil society to foster grassroots peacemaking from the bottom up. This is extraordinarily difficult when no official peacemaking efforts are underway, the conflict remains violent, and there is a growing sentiment – particularly among Palestinians – that engagement should be avoided. This policy, known as anti-normalization, has led to Palestinians interested in dialogue with Israelis facing intimidation and threats.

Then, we've had ups and downs of other international actors, usually the United States. If you look back to 2008, during the so-called "Annapolis process," John Kerry was trying to do something. But the basic problem is that we have leaders on both sides who are unwilling and incapable of leading their people towards peace. On the Israeli side we have had a very clear strategic decision by the person who has led Israel for most of the years since 2009, to make sure that there is no Palestinian partner for peace.

The Palestinian leadership, which has been delegitimized by Israel has done everything possible to delegitimize itself at the same time. What we've had is very long periods of time when everyone around the world knows more or less what the solution to the conflict is or could be, and there's been little more than lip service towards that.

You've written that both the Israeli and the Palestinian leadership must go. How would that change things?

One of the unexpected outcomes of the Hamas attack on Israel on October 7, 2023, and the subsequent Gaza war has been the renewed international focus on a two-state solution. For years, this idea had been largely dismissed, but now, the global community is once again recognizing that there is no military solution – only a political one. There is a sense that, perhaps, this time, the idea will be taken seriously.

Achieving real progress will require strong regional involvement. Recent events have highlighted the importance of alliances in the Middle East. While each country acts in its own interest, there is a growing recognition that stability in the region is tied to resolving the Palestinian issue. Many countries are now making this clearer than ever before.

At the same time, political shifts in the United States and elsewhere are influencing international responses. The unconditional backing Israel has long received is being questioned in new ways. More voices in Congress and even within the White House are expressing concerns that were rarely heard in the past. While the US has not yet taken decisive action to end the war in Gaza, there is a noticeable shift in rhetoric and policy.

These changing dynamics could influence Israeli public opinion, even if they do not immediately sway political leaders. The idea that the Israeli-Palestinian conflict can simply be managed or sidelined is losing credibility. The expectation that Israel could continue to expand regional agreements without addressing Palestinian statehood is also being challenged. In this shifting landscape, there may be an opportunity for meaningful change – if the right political will emerges.

Can outside help really work, or does the solution for this problem have to come from the inside?

No, as opposed to all the previous years when people like Hillary Clinton used to say the Israelis and the Palestinians have to want it more than us. That's no longer the case because this conflict has not kept within the boundaries of the river and the sea. It goes into the region, and it threatens regional security, it threatens international shipping which impacts the whole global economy, and it could lead to a much wider war which, at the end of the day could involve Russia and the United States. I mean, this is really dangerous stuff.

So, it's no longer the case that the Israelis and the Palestinians can be left by themselves. They can't. There is a responsibility in the international community and quite frankly I'm fed up with countries like most of the Organisation for Economic Cooperation and Development (OECD) countries who, for 30 years, have talked about a two-state solution, but only recognize one of the states.

There should be a call for anyone who supports the two-State solution that all 193 member states of the United Nations need to recognize both of the states, and Palestine needs to become state number 194 in the United Nations membership. These are the changes that we need now. That doesn't end the occupation, but it changes the parameters of future negotiations, which should not be bilateral between Israel and Palestine. They should be regionally focused on creating an architecture of stability, security, and economic development and on confronting climate change and all the other things that the world is concerned with.

The playing field is so unbalanced between Israel and Palestine that it can't just be a bilateral only negotiation. It has to involve the other regional partners. And it should not be led by the United States, who don't know how to do this, are always ending up being partial toward Israel, and never do the job that they need to do as the objective, impartial mediator. They're not objective and impartial in this conflict, and therefore the table needs to include other parties.

For example?

Well, mainly focused on the region. First of all, the countries that Israel has peace with, Egypt and Jordan and the United Arab Emirates, Bahrain and Morocco. And it must include the Saudis. The Saudis have to be at the table because they're such an important player, and they are in fact the biggest incentive for Israel to make concessions. The concessions have to be made in a way that guarantees Israel's security.

The deal that needs to be made here, in very crude terms, is Palestinians get independence and dignity, and Israel gets security. Each side has to understand that Israel doesn't get security if Palestinians don't have independence, liberation and dignity and Palestinians don't get independence, liberty and dignity without Israel getting security.

The two-State solution is the only way to end this conflict?

There is no possible other solution at this time, particularly after October 7th. There were dreamers who thought that we could have a one-state solution, but the idea of these two peoples living in one state is beyond imagination at this point. Anyone who does support the one-state solution has to understand that first the Palestinians have to have independence and freedom and take responsibility over their own lives and sovereignty. In the future, Israel and Palestine can negotiate other agreements whether that be Federation or Confederation involving Jordan and others.

There are all kinds of possibilities, but first the occupation has to end, and Israel has to be secured enough that it's willing to make additional concessions in the future on different aspects of its sovereignty. The two-state solution cannot be a two-state solution built on walls and fences because that's not a viable solution that will lead to peace. It will only lead to more conflict. We have to imagine realities where there is actually going to be cooperation between the two states and permeable borders and people and goods moving across those borders.

Of course, there has to be some kind of sovereign Palestinian connection between the West Bank and Gaza and Jerusalem as an open shared city of the capital of two countries. Today that's beyond human imagination or what's realistic in terms of achieving peace.

In 2006 you created a back channel between the officials in Jerusalem and in Gaza, with Ghazi Hamad. What led you to do that?

What led me to do that was my wife's first-cousin being kidnapped and killed by Hamas and then a chance meeting with a Professor of Economics from the Islamic University of Gaza who is a member of Hamas. We met at a conference in Cairo, and after spending about six hours talking to each other, I proposed to him that we try to create a dialogue between Hamas academics and Israeli academics.

To make a long story short, that never happened because the Hamas leadership vetoed it, but it did bring me to Gaza, to the Islamic University to meet with him and his colleagues. The two of us went to the Hamas prime minister's office and met with one of the top advisors who said that he would join the talks. That didn't happen. I ended up inviting the professor to a conference in Istanbul that I organized for Israelis and Palestinians. It's also based on the reality that there were free, fair, and democratic elections in Palestine in 2006 and Hamas won them. Hamas was not my choice, but the Palestinian people chose them, which meant that we had to deal with them and find a way to talk to them.

At the end of June 2006, Palestinian commandos from three different organizations including Hamas attacked an Israeli army base, killed two soldiers and abducted another. Immediately, Israel began a military operation in Gaza. A week later, the professor called me and said, "Gershon, we have to do something. Let's try to open up a channel between the two sides." He went to the Hamas prime minister's office, and they called me. That was July 1st, 2006. It was the first of over 1,000 conversations that I had with Ghazi Ahmad and other members of Hamas over the next 17–18 years. My network of contacts in Hamas has since spread to the leadership in exile in Doha, and within Gaza.

What were the challenges of setting up that channel?

One challenge is that it's against the law. I have been breaking the law for 17 years. Everyone in the world knows it, it has been in the press, and yet it continues because there's a need for it.

I would say the main challenge is that we have dealt with life and death issues, and they don't get addressed until both sides are ready to – and that takes an awful lot of time. With Gilad Shalit, the Israeli soldier, it took five years before the sides were seriously willing to make a deal. I spent eight years trying to negotiate the release of two bodies of Israeli soldiers and two living civilians in Gaza. That never reached a point when the sides were ready to make a deal.

Now we have been in a war for six months, with 35,000 people killed at least in Gaza, 70% of Gaza demolished, 1,200 civilians killed in Israel and over 600 soldiers killed in Israel. The war goes on, not at the same pace it was going a couple of months ago, but it still goes on. There are still 133 Israeli hostages in Gaza. The parties are not yet ready to make a deal.[1]

---

1 Since this interview was conducted in March 2024, approximately 51,000 Palestinians have been killed and more than 100,000 injured. 1,200 Israelis have been killed and over 5000 injured. It is believed that Hamas holds 24 people as hostages in Gaza. Israel has detained over 10,000 Palestinians, with over 3000 held as prisoners.

That back channel you created helped release over 1,000 prisoners. How did you navigate those negotiations?

First of all, I never made the decision on the terms of the deal or who was to be released. At the end of the day, that was Prime Minister Netanyahu. Of the 26 ministers of his government who voted for the deal, only three ministers voted against, and the entire national security establishment of Israel advised the government to vote for it. So, we're talking about the head of the Mossad, the head of the Shin Bet, the chief of police, the chief of staff of the Israeli army – they all recommended to the government of Israel to vote for it.

I never had anything to do with selecting the names of the people who were released. I facilitated negotiations and opened up a channel which led to a breakthrough document of principles for a deal which was accepted by the prime minister and then led to negotiations that moved to Cairo under the auspices of the intelligence service of Egypt.

How did you go about that?

It's very frustrating because I'm not a decision maker. I can't make offers that I can't back up, without knowing that they're going to be implemented. I had a lot of freedom for many years while I was doing these talks with people in Hamas to throw out ideas. Even when my channel became official, I had enough trust from the Mossad officer involved to be free to put out my own ideas and also circumvent the direct channel that I had.

I mean, I went to Cairo and talked to the Egyptian intelligence officer, which I did on my own: I didn't ask for permission, and I didn't say what I was doing in advance, and I helped move it forward. But that was a very unique situation where there was really one person in charge, when we're talking about one Israeli soldier, it's very different from the reality of today. Today we're dealing with 133 Israeli hostages. The overwhelming majority of them are civilians who were taken out of their homes. They were not combatants. They were not soldiers who were captured on a military base.

There are more than 200 people involved in the negotiations on the Israeli side. They are led by the head of the Mossad, the head of the Shin Bet and a retired military general – the three leaders of the Israeli negotiations – but they are very constrained in what they are permitted to do by direct order from the prime minister who, quite frankly, is not that interested in reaching a deal, or I should say not interested in reaching the kind of deal that Hamas would agree to.

You once mentioned how both sides are keeping the dead bodies of their enemies as bargaining chips. Can you tell me about that?

Before October 7th, Hamas was holding the bodies of two Israeli soldiers. And Israel has hundreds of bodies of Palestinians. They're usually buried in a cemetery with graves marked by numbers, not names. Since this war has begun, we have no idea how many of the hostages are alive and how many of them are dead. There's a working assumption within Israel that more than half of the hostages are dead. And Hamas is either holding their bodies or knows where their bodies are – or their bodies are under the rubble of buildings that were blown up by Israel and they may never be found.

Israel has, of course, bodies from the West Bank, as well as bodies that were apparently taken out of Gaza as well, though there's no publication or admittance of it. I have had conversations with Hamas people in the past and I asked them, "Is it important for you to get back bodies?" And their answer to me was no.

They said, "We understand it's important for the families to bury their loved ones, but from our principles or, more correctly, our beliefs, their souls are already in heaven. Wherever they're buried, they're buried in Palestine. Because whether you call it Israel or you call it whatever, for us, between the river and the sea is all Palestine. So, they're buried in holy ground. It doesn't matter what you call it for them."

Despite the Israeli belief that they could exchange a body for bodies, that was never a deal that could be made, and Hamas never even wanted it. In all the years that I've been negotiating with Hamas, the issue of bodies was never brought up by them.

It doesn't really have an impact in the negotiations?

Well, it does in the minds of Israelis because it is so important, within Israeli society, within Jewish culture and Jewish religion to have a place to bury the dead. They want them buried in a Jewish cemetery. This is something that, you know, I have no capacity of understanding. We don't live together, and we can't even die together. There are Jewish cemeteries, there are Muslim cemeteries, there are Christian cemeteries, and it seems absurd to me. But that's the reality in which we live.

Have you had contact with the population or just the higher representatives?

I have lots of friends in Gaza. I have thousands of Palestinian friends that I've worked with and been friends with over the 46 years that I've been doing this work. In the first days of the war, I wrote directly to more than 100 people in Gaza who are friends and colleagues to wish them well and express my hope that they will survive. I wanted them to know that I was thinking about them as they were being bombed by Israeli planes. Many of them answered me.

What are the population's thoughts on the conflict – those you've had contact with?

In Gaza? There's been a change, obviously, over the last six months. And the change that has happened, that is happening now much quicker than before, is a growing resentment and hatred of the population toward Hamas. There's a great Palestinian YouTuber from Gaza who lives in London. His name is Abu Julia. Maybe you can find someone who knows Arabic to look him up. He picked the name Abu Julia because he likes Julia Roberts, apparently. That's what they say. But he did mostly food, culinary kind of videos. But in the first week or the second week of the war, he did a rant, which was not scripted. It was just him speaking really emotionally.

He described the reality of life in Gaza. But the bottom line of his message was, as people in Gaza were celebrating after October 7th, because they had succeeded in invading Israel and capturing civilian communities and killing so many people and taking so many hostages, Abu Julia's bottom line message was, "Don't give me a week of happiness and a lifetime of misery." That's what the Palestinians in Gaza are realizing today. There's a growing hatred toward Hamas. I don't think it's anything that pollsters can get. I'm not sure that it's possible to even conduct a reliable public opinion poll during wartime. But you hear more and more of these voices.

There are still many, many who are afraid to speak against Hamas because of the kind of regime that Hamas held, and because opposition to Hamas in the past, when they were in power, ended up with people getting killed. I think there's still a great fear because no one knows what's going to happen tomorrow. Hamas might reemerge and they might still be in power tomorrow. So, people are cautious, but I think it's clear that that's the sentiment. As opposed to the sentiment in the West Bank, where Hamas's support is still very, very strong, much stronger than it was before October 7th.

Does that kind of difference of opinion also impact on how this conflict might be resolved?

It could. The greatest crime of the current government of Israel is its failure to understand that there is no military solution to the conflict; there's only a political solution. They refuse, starting with Netanyahu, to recognize that there must be a day-after plan, that Israel must have someone to turn the keys of Gaza over to.

Because the longer that Israel stays in Gaza, the more there is guaranteed armed insurgency against Israel and the more the power of extremists grows, even perhaps more extreme than Hamas. The only way to change the situation and put us on a different path is for there to be a legitimate, accepted Palestinian leadership taking over from the current Palestinian leadership in the West Bank and Gaza.

What needs to happen for that to be a reality?

A combination of three forces working together, the most important is within Palestine itself. They need to decide that it is time for the leaders of both Abbas and Hamas to move aside. There are people who could be acceptable to Palestinians in the West Bank and Gaza who would offer a different direction. Part of it also has to be done by Israel because Israel has to engage those people.

One of the most important people is sitting in an Israeli prison for 22 years already, Marwan Barghouti, and the Israelis need to be talking to him, not torturing him as they're doing now. There are other Palestinian leaders who were exiled by Mahmoud Abbas because they did not toe the line of his group of cronies.

The international community needs to weigh in, especially in the region. People like King Abdullah in Jordan and Mohammed bin Salman and Mohammed bin Zayed in the Emirates need to tell Mahmoud Abbas that he needs to step aside. I have a very good Palestinian friend who is an activist from Fatah his whole life. He's 52 years old. He talks about meeting Mahmoud Abbas when he was in his 20s, and hearing Mahmoud Abbas tell this group of young Fatah leaders that "you people are the leaders of tomorrow". And he says, "tomorrow never came."

We have an almost 90-year-old leader who's been sitting in the same seat for 18 years, in four-year terms, and it's time for change. The Palestinians need to say, "After this war in Gaza, there is no military solution for us. The arms struggle is a strategy of death and destruction for Palestine. We cannot use the arms struggle anymore." They need to change their own internal discourse. They need to say to the Jewish people, "We understand that there's a real connection between the Jewish people and this land. But the Jews need to understand that they never were here alone. There were always others in this land, and we are those others." That's the essential construct.

I had a conversation with a Palestinian, who's part of Fatah, but he calls himself part of the opposition to Abbas within Fatah. He was saying that we need to have a coup d'état in Palestine. It's the only way we're going to get rid of Abbas and his cronies – by taking control. And maybe they need to do that. But that's not the way forward.

Why?

Well, because they're not considered legitimate by the Palestinian people and because as long as the government of Netanyahu is in power, he will never enable a real legitimate Palestinian authority to have power.

You are also the director of the "Holy Land Bonds". Can you tell me about that?

The "Holy Land Bonds" is kind of frozen right now. It was created by an organization called International Communities Organization, which is a British non-governmental organization that defines itself as working in conflict zones with failed peace processes. I am the director of Middle East operations for the International Communities Organization.

We were in the midst of various negotiations on ways of putting our investment in place, and then the war broke out, and we decided to hold off and see what we're going to do after the war. We're looking into creating a private sector investment bond for the reconstruction of Gaza now. But we'll see. The commitment to put investment funds into the conflict in order to help to facilitate a different kind of conflict resolution is certainly on our agenda and we will do it at some point when it's more feasible.

One of the things that the NGO did was find housing for Palestinians in Israel. I imagine that to be very challenging?

There were two areas of housing that we were looking into. One was Palestinian housing in East Jerusalem, where there's a real shortage of housing. What we wanted to do is provide investment money for Palestinian developers who get licenses from the Jerusalem municipality. Our initial strategy was to fund developers directly, but then we learned that there were three Palestinian banks that had established companies in Jerusalem for facilitating loans that could be offered to Palestinians in Jerusalem. Even though their banks were registered in Palestine, they created investment companies in Israel.

We began a negotiation with three Palestinian banks where we would provide loan guarantees and they would be the actual lenders. This way we could enable the banks to loan money directly by giving them 100% guarantees on their funds, which means that they could lower their interest rates and give better offers to Palestinian developers. We can make a lot more money available.

The second thing that we were doing, and we conducted a market survey, was to determine if we could build and develop integrated Jewish-Arab housing in Israel's mixed cities, where there are Jewish and Palestinian populations living in the same cities, sometimes, in the same neighbourhoods, sometimes in the same buildings, but never by choice.

We wanted to look into several of these cities and buy properties from developers to then market as equally as we could to Jewish and Palestinian citizens of Israel. We would create a social development program that would work with them over a number of years to build community and not just throw people in the water and say, sink or swim. The idea is still on paper. We conducted a market survey and determined that there is a feasibility for it. That was before the war. Things may be different now. We were negotiating with a couple of developers on buying a couple of properties, but we froze it.

You're also a founder of the Israel-Palestine Center for Research and Information. What does the Center do?

It doesn't do anything anymore because unfortunately, the people who inherited it from me shut it down two years ago. I founded it in 1988, in the fourth month of the First Intifada. It was going to be a joint institution of Israelis and Palestinians working together in the same office at total parity and equality, with our working model being that the two-state solution is the solution, and that's not under debate. The question was how to make it real, how to engage in reverse engineering.

In the 24 years that I co-directed Israel Palestine Centre for Research and Information (IPCRI), we held more than 2000 working groups of Israeli and Palestinian professionals in every field imaginable, from security and border management to economic development in business, agriculture, tourism, antiquities, agriculture, trade, everything.

During the course of those 24 years, I also became an advisor on the peace process to two Israeli Prime Ministers, Yitzhak Rabin and Ehud Barak. We brought together thousands of people. We also had a very large peace education program with a budget of nearly a million dollars a year, in which we had about 15,000 Israeli and Palestinian high school students participating, and hundreds of Israeli and Palestinian teachers being trained every year in teaching a peace education curriculum in Israeli and Palestinian schools.

So, it's quite a big centre. I left it in the beginning of 2012. I thought that after 24 years we needed a new generation of leaders with new ideas to come along. My goal was actually to have two women take it over. I was successful in getting a Palestinian woman and an Israeli man who ran the centre for the next years. But as I said, two years ago, they shut it down. A very big shame.

They also never renewed the website, so the domain got stolen by someone else, who shut the website down. I hired someone out of my own pocket to get the website back up because it's an enormous archive of material that should be on record forever.

What were the challenges of being an advisor on conflict resolution and what kind of care did you have to have?

You know what, it's not something I applied for, and things generally happened by chance. After I started IPCRI in 1988, I immediately got put on the Israeli blacklist, on the security list. I was harassed, stopped, searched, and checked every time I left and came back into the country for four years. After four years, I managed to get an Israeli security officer to meet with me. After a very difficult two-hour meeting with this person, he finally agreed that they would remove me from the list.

Why were you put on the list?

What I was told and what I understood is that they put me on the list not because they suspected that I would do something against Israel, but they understood, from my personal background and history, that I deeply understood Palestinian culture. The security guy mentioned my Palestinian partner by name – I had never mentioned his name – and he said that if someone heard I was travelling abroad and asked him to give me a package, I, because I understand the culture so well and act accordingly, wouldn't be able to say no. I responded, "Listen, I don't take packages from anyone." He said, "I can't take that as an answer because if they ask you, you can't say no."

But I said, "Listen, I promise you that if ever anyone gives me a package, as soon as I get to the airport, I will find the first security person I see and say, 'Someone gave this to me. Can you check it?'" And then he looked at me and said, "With a heavy heart, I'll recommend they release you from the list." Two weeks later, I travelled abroad, and it was the first time in four years that I had the stamp on my passport. It was like the Liberty Bell. It was amazing to go to the airport and not be stopped.

I travelled to Jordan before Israel had peace with Jordan. I had applied with the Israeli security to cross the Allenby Bridge from Israel to Jordan because we were organizing a business conference between Israel and Palestine, and we thought the Jordanians should participate as well. After three weeks, they gave me my permit to cross the bridge. They told me I had to leave my Israeli passport at the Israeli side of the bridge, which I did. I had a very successful trip in Jordan.

On the last day of the trip, we were invited to the palace and had a three-hour meeting with one of the closest advisors to King Hussein. He was the head of the royal court. When I got back to Israel, I gave a short interview to Haaretz newspaper, one of Israel's leading newspapers, and talked about the meetings that we had in Jordan.

A couple of days later, I got a phone call from the army telling me I'm invited to a security interview (it's the nice way they put it). They told me where to go and when to get there. But when I was there, my name wasn't at the gate. I waited until someone showed up, a guy who was probably a reserve officer. He came to the gate without any ranks on his uniform and no insignia of what unit he was from and took me into the military compound in the centre of Jerusalem from the British-mandate period. It was this old wood building with no windows and a wooden chair and two wooden tables.

Like every intelligence officer, he takes out a little pad from his pocket, starts writing, and says to me, "You went to Jordan."

I said, "Yeah, I got permission. I applied to the Ministry of the Interior, and they told me that it was sent to the security, to the Shin Bet, before they gave me a clearance. And I got a clearance. It was even stamped in my passport".

He said then "But you didn't inform your unit in the army".

I started laughing. I said, "Do you know what I do in the army? I'm a lecturer at the College for the Education of Officers. I lecture Israeli officers about Palestinians."

He said, "It doesn't matter what you do in the army. You traveled to an enemy country. You were supposed to inform your unit that you went to an Arab country."

I said I didn't know. This was so hysterical.

After asking me a few more questions, the soldier put the pad back in his pocket, and he said, "Is it OK if we continue talking?"

I said to him, "I'm willing to talk to anyone who's willing to talk to me".

He started asking me all these really good questions about the work that I was doing. At the end of the talk, we sat for about an hour.

He said to me, "Do you mind if I give your name to people who might be interested in talking to you?"

I said to him, "As I said to you, I'm willing to talk to anyone who's willing to talk to me."

A week later, I got a phone call from a guy who introduces himself with a name and tells me to come to a building in Tel Aviv, which is the office of the prime minister's research department.

They set the date and the time. I, in the meantime, checked out and discovered that the prime minister's office had no research department. But I went to the building at the designated time, and there was a plaque on the door that said, Prime Minister's Office Research Department. I buzzed on the door, they opened it up, and I see it's a hallway with interrogation rooms. I go into one of these interrogation rooms, and this intelligence officer, very nice guy, explains to me that Prime Minister Rabin established a team of five intelligence officers to advise him on the peace process.

It was top secret because the intelligence service isn't supposed to work on a peace process. That's not their job. But Rabin didn't trust the politicians in his own government, and he needed experts. He was a military person his whole life. He needed experts from the military who could advise him.

There I went and spent more than 200 hours with this team as an advisor to them. Until Rabin was killed, and then Peres took over and it continued. When Netanyahu, when Sharon, came into power, he cancelled the team.

So, it was all by chance.

What was it like working in that team?

I would meet with them about, on average, once every 10 days, and we would set a time and a date. I would get a phone call in the morning telling me what hotel to go to and what room to go to. It was really top secret. When we would order coffee from room service, I would have to hide in the bathroom. It was kind of James Bond-ish. It was really interesting. Mostly they wanted to know what Palestinians were thinking. What kind of words I heard about the peace process, what were the issues of concern for them.

Because I was leading so many working groups of Israelis and Palestinians at the time, I also gave them lots of policy ideas and proposals. I mean, they spent a couple of hours every single week, just the five of them with Rabin. Even the chief of staff of Rabin's office didn't participate in these meetings. There were the five of these intelligence officers and Rabin, once a week. I had direct impact.

How has social media impacted what happens in the conflict in the Middle East?

Look, there are the positive sides of it: that communication is so much easier, and you can reach so many more people so easily. My Twitter/X exploded after October 7th. I have three times the number of followers today than I had before October 7th. In six months, it's about 28,000 people, which is quite amazing. And of course, reaching out to people that you can't talk to. Whenever I've lectured to young people, they ask me, "What can we do?"

I always say one thing that you can do is knock on the door of someone from the other side of the conflict who you know just by their name or where they're from on Facebook and say, "Hey, I'd really like to know you and know what you think. Tell me your story." I would tell people that I've never met anyone or almost anyone who, when I said "I want to listen to you. Tell me your story," have said no. I advise people don't argue and don't make counterarguments, listen, actively listen. So, it can be a very positive tool.

But it's also a very negative tool because it's a tool where you can anonymously sit behind a keyboard and say horrible things. And as we've learned over the past years, it's also a very good tool for fake news.

What's the impact of a lot of misinformation?

It's very dangerous; it's not benign. People use it because it's dangerous. So, you have to be careful, and I hope that people become more and more aware and intelligent in using social media. My hunch is that it's probably going to get a lot worse with AI being used to create images of real people saying horrible things in their own voices.

Gershon Baskin is the Middle East Director of International Communities Organization. With a background in activism dating back to his youth in the US, he has dedicated much of his life to promoting coexistence and conflict resolution. Baskin played a significant role in shaping peace efforts, including the initiation of secret back-channel negotiations between Israelis and Palestinians and the creation of various joint initiatives. Notably, he was involved in mediating the release of Gilad Shalit and advocating for peace agreements, such as the 2024 Israeli-Palestinian peace proposal with Ehud Olmert and Nasser Al-Kidwa. He writes a column in the *Times of Israel* and *Al Quds* newspapers as well as being a commentator on media around the world. He has also worked to advance socio-economic projects, renewable energy in Palestine and Egypt, and educational initiatives, including a summer course on coexistence at Hebrew University. Baskin's extensive efforts have earned him recognition, including the Luxembourg Peace Prize in 2023.

NURCAN BAYSAL

Can you tell me what you are working on at the moment?

I do a lot of things at once. That's the way my life has always been. I write regularly. This week, my first English book will be published. It is called *WE EXIST – Being Kurdish in Turkey*. Next month, a 4-book set of my 10-year testimonies of war and destruction will be published. It is a collection of 600 of my writings over the 10 years from 2013, when peace talks between the PKK and the Turkish state began, to 2023. In addition to these, I am writing a book on conscience.

I also write as a columnist for the *Oksijen* Newspaper about the Kurdish question, human rights, and poverty. In addition to these, I work on human rights and poverty projects in the earthquake region and Kurdish provinces. In addition to providing consultancy to some non-governmental organizations, I have voluntary work on landmine victims and other human rights activism.

And I am a mother of two adolescent boys.

From your experience and from the work you do, what are the challenges to conflict resolution today?

Each conflict has both similarities and differences, and they all have many dimensions. Most of them are rooted in a system based on discrimination and inequality. They have historical dimensions, international dimensions, and of course, there are economic and armament dimensions. We are in a period when authoritarian and populist powers are gaining strength in the world, and these powers are not in favour of solving the conflict by expanding democratic spaces, as in the past. They try to 'solve' conflicts in a more repressive way, by destroying the 'enemy' or keeping them under heavy pressure. Sometimes they think that they will 'neutralize the enemy' by focusing on the arms and defence industry. They are partially successful. However, there is an important point they forget: At the root of every conflict, there are certain feelings. For example, the language of that minority may have been taken away, and as is the case for Kurdish children, the pressure on their language has been at such a point that what it means to be Kurdish has been shaped through this 'language wound'. The feeling of worthlessness, the fear of being killed at any moment, of being humiliated, of being constantly discriminated against makes for intolerable suffering... This is in addition to many concrete reasons for conflicts such as land claims, the theft of minerals and raw materials, the state of the economy, and the imposition of borders. A fundamental reason for conflict is how the country in which you grow up and live makes you feel. The feeling of being a second-class citizen, the feeling that the country is not yours, the feeling that at any moment you can be deprived of your freedom just because you speak your mother tongue... So feeling constant insecurity and fear as well as a sense of not belonging in your own land.

An important part of the process in conflict resolution is to bring social understandings of the conflicting parties closer. However, I do not think that authoritarian powers are willing to engage with this process.

You have worked as a journalist in Turkey. Can you tell us what is happening now in the country in terms of Human Rights?

Turkey is experiencing human rights violations on a scale unprecedented in its history. The 1990s were also a bad period in terms of human rights. Especially in the Kurdish provinces, gross human rights violations were constantly taking place. Today, human rights violations have increased all over Turkey and are much more widespread. Law has been completely instrumentalised. The concept of the rule of law no longer exists in Turkey. The courts are completely politicised. If you send a single tweet criticizing the President, that night your house can be raided by heavily armed special teams, and you can be immediately arrested. Court processes do not work to protect citizens from abuse.

We are all under heavy pressure. Journalism which reflects the real state of affairs is now very difficult in Turkey. Today, because most Turkish media is under the control of the Turkish government, social media has become the only means of understanding what is happening in Turkey, and, simultaneously, it is a danger zone. The pressures on us to be extremely cautious in our use of social media increase every day. These increasing restrictions cause not just ordinary citizens to censor themselves, but also journalists and writers. It is now exceedingly difficult to write about what's happening in Kurdish cities, a task requiring exceptional courage. Because every word that I write affects not just my life, but also the life of my children. Every word that I write returns to them in the form of raids, fear, and trauma. Today in Turkey, it requires a lot of courage to use those most beautiful words, 'peace, life, freedom, justice, equality.' Many journalists and writers, including me, practise self-censorship. Most of us have a list of 'objectionable words,' and when we write, we take care not to use these words or we choose not to write at all on certain topics.

You come from Diyarbakir in Turkey and have spoken of witnessing as a child the funeral of Kurdish rights activist Vedat Aydin being attacked. How has this experience informed your work as an activist?

Let me first tell you about my childhood and the famous 90s: I spent my childhood in the Şehitlik neighbourhood of Diyarbakır, the unofficial capital city of the Kurds. Back in the 80s, Şehitlik was, like it is today, a neighbourhood of impoverished families with a lot of children. Another characteristic of Şehitlik was that violence and death were rife. When, in the late 80s, the OHAL/State of Emergency Governorate chose the neighbourhood as the location for its headquarters, Şehitlik also became the centre of special forces, unsolved murders and the infamous white Toros cars.

The 90s were a period when the war between the Turkish state and the Kurdistan Workers' Party (PKK) was at its most intense – and also the years when death was around every corner in Kurdish cities. The rule of law had been suspended. People in the city centres were devastated by the murders committed by unknown assailants, numerous detentions, home raids and torture, while in rural areas, villages were being evacuated and burned down on the pretext of "restricting the PKK's zone of influence". A huge disaster of forced migration ensued and Kurdish villagers who were evicted from their villages and torn from their land, desperately scrambled to the cities. Within a mere few years, millions of Kurdish villagers were forcibly removed from their land. The fundamental citizenship rights of Kurds had been suspended both in the cities and the villages.

The state of emergency regional governors, who resided in Diyarbakır and were given extensive powers that led them to be referred to as "super governors", ruled over the Kurdish provinces with army commanders, police forces and paramilitary forces in tow. In the face of all this repression and intimidation, Kurdish youth fled to the mountains to join the PKK. Kurdistan was suffering direct and continuous cultural and structural violence.

War and violence were part of our everyday life in Şehitlik. The state was staging all manner of dirty tricks. On 5th July 1991, Vedat Aydın, the Provincial Chairperson of HEP and our dear neighbour, was taken from his home in the entrance to the neighbourhood, for "his statement to be taken". A few days later, his tortured body was found under a bridge close to the Maden district of Elazığ Province, a one-hour-drive from the site of his detention. Then, on 10th July, special forces carrying Kalashnikov rifles, opened fire on the funeral ceremony attended by hundreds of thousands of people.

This murder, which went down in history as one of the first murders by unknown assailants of the 1990s, also initiated a new historical period. According to some, this was the incident which heralded the systemic violence and abuse which was to follow.

However, for the Kurds, the repression began long before the 1990s and continues today. In 2025, that period provides a yardstick with which we now compare every other event or period. It has become a metaphor that splits our lives in two like a deep chasm and has indelibly inscribed itself in the mind of every single Kurd living today.

What was life like as a child in the Kurdistan of the 90s?

It was an exceptional time, with enforced disappearances, rape, village burnings, murders by unknown assailants, extra-legal executions, forced displacements, forced village guardianship, torture and the discovery of mass graves. Kurdistan was a place that was not recognised by the other regions of Turkey, in fact, it was not "visible" to the majority of Turkish people. It displayed all the characteristics of a colonized state. A community that had been declared "murderable" by the colonizer. On the other hand, the 90s was an exceptional time for the Kurds, in that it was a period when the uprising against state repression reached a mass scale.

Like many other Kurdish children, I experienced that abuse and violence first-hand. At Vedat Aydın's funeral, security forces fired heavy weapons at the crowd, killing dozens of people. I was 16 years old. That day, like many Kurdish youths, I decided to fight back. Most Kurdish children who witnessed that day went to the mountains, but I decided to stay in Diyarbakır and fight against oppression.

My first book, *That Day*, published by İletişim Publishing House in 2013, tells the story of that time.

Should more women have a voice in conflict resolution?

Of course. All studies show that women play a more constructive role in negotiation processes. It is possible to see this constructive role when we look at the presence of women in conflict resolution processes in countries with different geographical and cultural backgrounds, from Northern Ireland to Colombia, even the Philippines and Moro Muslims. In the peace process, which is a very male-dominated scene, women are making a difference by working hard. In referendums for peace agreements in countries like Colombia or Northern Ireland, women took to the streets and persuaded people to vote. They reached out to people that traditional parties could not reach, and they never lost contact with civil society. For example, they rewrote the peace agreement in simple words in Irish and English so that people could read it and distribute it to houses in neighbourhoods. They were very effective in spreading the peace process to the grassroots communities.

Again, the role of women is indispensable for the sustainability of peace. The community centres established by women after the peace agreements contribute to the sustainability of peace by bringing people from both sides together.

What are the dangers of social media for journalists?

Today, social media is a dangerous area for journalists in Turkey. On the one hand, it is the only channel we have left, but on the other hand, it's dangerous to use this form of communication because we are being imprisoned simply for our posts. For this reason, many journalists have left the profession.

The same thing has happened in the field of human rights. Especially after 2015, with the end of the peace process, the pressure on human rights defenders has increased tremendously. It has reached the point that to be a human rights defender has become synonymous with support for terrorism, treason, and espionage. Not only the judiciary and public authorities, but also the Turkish media have become an important source and instrument of these pressures. As human rights defenders, many of us have been targeted in the Turkish media, in various newspaper columns. We have been the subject of smear campaigns and hate speech. Civil society organizations and their employees have been subjected to various accusations, many civil society organizations have been closed down by emergency decrees, those which were not closed down have been branded as 'funders, agents, traitors, terror lovers', while civil space has been besieged and narrowed from all sides.

Today Turkey is a much darker country than it was twenty years ago.

Over the past few years, I have been sentenced to ten months in prison, detained three times, my house has been raided by police twice and the authorities have launched dozens of investigations against me. Now, I have to be extremely careful before tweeting or writing an article. How can I continue journalism and human rights advocacy in this situation?

I do not know the answer to this question. Thousands of journalists who live in countries with authoritarian governments and in conflict zones similar to mine are also struggling to find the answer. Journalists who are trying to raise their voices from Afghanistan, South Sudan, China, Vietnam or Eritrea are undoubtedly having trouble conveying their messages to the capitals of their own countries. A few years ago, I met a journalist from Ethiopia. He told me he was afraid to even go out and see his mother and he was staying in a house close to the airport so that he could leave the country at any time.

Often these local journalists are unable to make their voices heard by their own people or by the journalism organizations in their own countries. But they are the ones who feed the most famous journalists of the world with their local news from the most extreme places. Local journalists all over the world are not only invisible but also extremely vulnerable to all kinds of threats and pressures, especially if they live in conflict areas. I am one of the lucky ones despite all my experiences. Some Kurdish journalists have spent many years in prison for writing a single piece of news. There are so few organizations in the world today that advocate for their rights and freedoms or hear their voices and make them heard.

Journalism is already a risky profession in authoritarian countries, but if you do local journalism in small cities and conflict zones, where you can be easily found, and where you cannot hide in the crowds like in big cities, this risk grows in every sense. You live under physical, social, economic and psychological duress. You feel a huge sense of loneliness...

As a local journalist I was relatively lucky because I was able to establish relationships with international organizations, unlike most. The support of international organizations working on human rights, journalism and freedom of expression has been a protective shield for me in many places. If I am still free today, if I still live in Diyarbakır, where I can report and still hug my children, the most important reason for this is the solidarity of those international organizations.

I believe that we need to increase this solidarity. If it is very difficult for local journalists to reach the ears of people in big cities, is it not time for these organizations to reach out to local journalists and establish solidarity mechanisms accordingly? I know that I am free today due to the help of this solidarity, I am at home today thanks to this solidarity. Reporting our news in Brussels, Paris, Berlin, New York, Geneva, or London can affect our freedom. Then it follows that these reports from conflict zones should be multiplied. News organizations have to find new ways to reach us. We have to establish mechanisms to act fast to get the news out without waiting for solidarity campaigns launched by local journalists and rights activists to emerge. Political pressures and judicial harassment have brought many journalists and human rights defenders to the crossroads. If we do not increase international solidarity for freedom of speech and support for dissenting voices, many of us will perish. Dictators will prevail, and the truth will be left in the dark.

The world should hear our voices. We need to hear from you, too.

NURCAN BAYSAL

Nurcan Baysal is a Kurdish human rights defender, journalist and writer. She was born and grew up in Diyarbakır. She has worked for poverty and development programs at the United Nations Development Programme and various other non-governmental organizations. Following the ISIS attacks in 2014, she volunteered for the establishment of Ezidi camps in Northern Iraq and Turkey. Baysal is a founder of the Diyarbakır Institute for Political and Social Research (DISA), the Development Centre Association in Diyarbakır and the Platform to Save Women Kidnapped by ISIS. She is also one of the Middle East advisors of the Global Fund for Women and the Urgent Action Fund for Feminist Activism. Among her books are three non-fiction works, *O Gün (That Day), Ezidiler: 73. Ferman (Ezidis: The 73rd Decree), O Sesler (Those Voices-Diyarbakır: A City Under Siege*, published online in English by 60pages, a book of short-stories, *Yok Zamanı (The Time of Nothingness)* and a research she co-authored with Şeyhmus Diken, *Kürdistan'da Sivil Toplum (Civil Society in Kurdistan)*.

Since 2013, Baysal has been featured as a columnist in various newspapers and media outlets. Her articles focus on human rights violations, poverty, refugees, humanitarian issues and the Kurdish question. She is a member of PEN Turkey and an honorary member of English PEN.

Baysal won the Women's World Summit Foundation (WWSF) Prize for Women's Creativity in Rural Life in 2010 and the "Turkey's Changemakers" award in 2012 for her work in poverty alleviation. In 2017, she was awarded the "Brave Women Journalists Award" presented by the Italian Women Journalists Association. In 2018, she was named Global Laureate for Human Rights Defenders at Risk by Front Line Defenders. She also received the Deutsche Welle Freedom of Speech Award in 2020.

SASKIA BINET

Everyone has a voice in a literal sense, but metaphorically speaking there are some voices that are taken less into consideration in conflict contexts. Would you say this is the case for women in fragile and conflict affected areas?

Everyone has a voice, but it's how those voices are being heard. How are you designing the spaces for those voices to be heard? How are you creating spaces for inclusive and sustainable conflict transformation? Since the passing of the Women, Peace and Security Council Resolution 1325 in the year 2000, there's been an institutional mandate that highlights the critical role of women in peacemaking, conflict prevention, peacekeeping, peacebuilding, humanitarian action and post conflict reconstruction. Guided by the pillars of prevention, participation, protection and peacebuilding and recovery, there has been a push to increase women's participation at the negotiation table and in peace processes. However, women's meaningful participation at the negotiation table continues to remain limited, despite women's visionary leadership and action within peacebuilding and peacemaking. And when they do enter the political negotiation space, the question remains as to whether their demands are being transferred into action. Do they have agency over the peace process, and are their initiatives in conflict transformation – often groundbreaking and visionary – being fully recognised?

The UN Security Council Resolution 1325 was an important step, and we have to thank the women who pushed for that Security Council resolution to be passed, that progress is really from their work. But now it's about translating the institutional commitments into action, and showcasing the unique peacemaking models women have been pioneering within conflict resolution, prevention and conflict transformation.

What do you do, as Middle East and North Africa coordinator?

The role focuses on supporting inclusive peace processes and women's participation in peacebuilding and peacemaking, including with different women's movements and civil society organizations. A large aspect includes how to translate these normative commitments into operationally feasible solutions to influence peace processes. The role also supports in providing analysis, helping identify entry points, blockages and spaces for innovative and feminist peacemaking efforts. It's important also to document different mediation approaches that are being prototyped across different settings and to undertake analysis and comparison between these approaches. In the face of increasing conflict and a lack of implementation of mandates on inclusivity in peacemaking, it's critical to surface innovative methods to bring the end of conflict, that women are developing.

What do you find to be the most challenging aspect of your work?

Some of the most challenging pushbacks currently are perhaps the difficulty in translating demands for inclusive processes and peacemaking into action, and the backlash to gender equality on a global level alongside increasing conflicts. Inclusive processes, inclusive of provisions for gender equality and the participation of youth is an integral part of peace. However, the pushback to gender equality is strong and organised. So, if there is a backlash to gender equality, and a lack of an inclusive political process – that is a challenge to sustainable and positive peace. That's something that different peacemaking actors, including the women's movement, have to face on a day-to-day basis.

How does that backlash manifest? What happens?

The backlash occurs on multiple levels and is multi-dimensional. Firstly, on a political level there can simply be a lack of political will towards increased participation in a peace or political process. It can also manifest in a legal perspective. So, for example, the passing of discriminatory laws, and the shrinking of civil society space. It can also happen on a social norm perspective. For example, it's more difficult for women to access public spaces, online and in-person because they'll face a smear campaign when they speak out. It can happen that they face actual violence and harassment, often following years of threats that they receive. So, it's really multi-dimensional.

You work with Syria and Yemen, I imagine those are two very different countries. The challenges of navigating peace in both contexts must also be very different?

Of course each country has their own unique contexts and histories. But there are commonalities in different contexts. The first one is the backlash and anti-gender equality movements and how this affects the attainment of peace. We see in research that sex and gender inequality drive both civil and interstate conflicts. Violent conflict can increase gender inequality. But also feminists have long theorized how gender inequality can also be linked to an increased likelihood of violent conflict, for example, linking the privileging of certain masculinities and patriarchy with the probability of increased violent conflict.

There are other commonalities to focus on as well because if we start to look at everything that it's contextualized, it's much more difficult to come up with broader solutions. And one such commonality is shrinking civil-society space. Civil society is extremely important to develop mechanisms for accountability and a movement for peace. A shrinking civil society limits the ability for human rights defenders to speak out without reprisals, especially in a context of growing online violence.

Civil-society spaces have an important role in peace negotiations, especially in that they can bring accountability and legitimacy to a peace process. They can work outside a peace process to address the root causes of violence. They can organise mass action and push forward peace processes to make sure there's advancement and call out the conflict actors to come to the table to negotiate. With the shrinking of civil-society space, that will have a long-term impact on possibilities for peace.

In areas of Yemen, for example, there's a huge crackdown on civil society. There continues to be unlawful restrictions and arbitrary detentions of civil society and human rights defenders – including women, and especially women who have been calling out for the end of discriminatory laws and the suppression of rights. But we also see the results of organized women's movements in pushing back against this, and the importance of sustaining their work in calling out this kind of discrimination.

Part of your work included designing feminist mediation projects and providing technical expertise on feminist peacemaking and peacebuilding. What does feminist peacemaking look like?

There isn't one definition of feminist peacemaking and mediation, but a core tenet is that traditional methods of peacemaking that seek to find mutually acceptable agreements between conflict actors have not incorporated the demands, approaches, and strategies of different actors, including women and youth for feminist peace.

The first pillar of feminist peacemaking centres on participation, that broader participation at the negotiation table is both a right, and an effective way of delivering mutually acceptable agreements. But it's also beyond participation. Within the conflict resolution and peacebuilding sector, there's been a recognition that women's voices need to be at the table. However, this continues to be separated from a substantive and holistic interpretation of what participation means, in which actors have the space, resources, and power to create structural transformation, and reshape institutions and society into one that can foster sustainable and positive peace through democratic and inclusive systems.

Feminist peacemaking also explores the role that women have as being mediators themselves. This obviously includes within mediation teams, but also recognising that different women's organizations and movements have been designing innovative peacemaking models and parallel processes. Tired of stalling processes and negotiations, women's organizations and feminist actors have instigated different peacemaking practices. These include designing problem-solving workshops at different tracks, using their unique positioning to convene different actors that may not have come together before, and influencing parties through mobilizing their own networks that reach diverse groups and actors. Women, working as insider mediators, have also worked to consolidate different positions within different negotiating parties. Therefore, feminist peacemaking recognises the unique and innovative initiatives that women are leading, taking place not only at the track 3 and 2 level, but also at the track 1 and 1.5 level, and recognises there are different practices to convening, facilitating and designing dialogue processes that fall outside of traditional peacemaking efforts.

Secondly, gendering peacemaking and feminist peacemaking means increasing the substantive representation of policies prioritised by women actors within negotiations and agreements. So, although not all women or gender-equality advocates will believe the same thing or will be aligned, there are a number of issues that are important for setting a precedent to participation, and laying the foundations of an equal and rights-based society. For example, within negotiations and political settlements: what kind of constitutions, power sharing agreements, decentralization, federal arrangements are women advocating for? It's not only about having women at the table, it's about also designing political solutions that will have gender-equal and gender-transformative results within them.

Furthermore, it's not only about incorporating the political representation of women into agreements into negotiations, it's about incorporating this into all levels and stages. For example, are ceasefire and security arrangements, plans for the future allocation of natural resources, designs for a future political economy and a roadmap towards transformative justice designed in a way that will have gender-equal and gender-transformative results?

Thirdly, feminist peacemaking looks to unpack whether different actors have agency over the design of the processes and negotiations they are taking part in. For example, women may be included in a process, but feminist peacemaking also questions to what extent do those participants have power and agency over the process.

Feminist peacemaking also includes the incorporation of women and gender-responsive actors by the mediator, at least in processes that include a third-party mediator. It emphasises that the mediator has a responsibility of seeing who is in the room, who is talking more, who has the space to talk more, alongside supporting civil society and women's political actions outside of official peace processes.

That's obviously the goal, but what are the challenges that are preventing that?

First of all, in order to incubate these different and new peacemaking models, women's movements need to be resourced. They are already organised and well connected, but they need the space to deliberate on these things in order to design these solutions. It's not to say that those solutions are not there. But the other actors who are organising will be funded, they will have the space and agency to put forth their own solutions.

Funding these civil-society organizations, and these women political actors is a challenge. Furthermore, within the funding landscape, also, it's easier to fund women's civil-society organizations, and less so women political actors in peace processes, because women political actors are having to navigate a multitude of identities. If you push them into a kind of civil-society role, it removes their agency to be political, but it's easier to fund in terms of NGOs, in terms of the different funding institutions.

So, you do see one of the challenges also is that there's less of a space for women's political voices, and there's more of a space for them to lean to other identities, such as their work as humanitarian leaders. Furthermore, the mediation work that women can work around can be informal, or it's track 2, track 3, and so it might not be as easily recognised. Sometimes that means that they might not be considered as mediators, decreasing their likelihood to be invited to formal dialogues.

It sounds like it creates a bit of a paradox in the sense that the aim of this kind of organization is to give women a voice, however, when they have less of a political voice, they're more easily funded.

Yes, it does. It probably relates to the different understandings of what makes up civil society in the broader society, whether this includes, for example, women leaders that end up being active politically or even elected. One of the questions for an NGO is, "Are you associated with a political party?" This is understandable. But at the same time, identities are multidimensional, and that doesn't always fit with the system. Women leaders can be involved in humanitarian projects, be active in the community and end up negotiating ceasefires or access to water. Women political actors can be deeply connected to civil-society movements, working to represent different substantive policies. The identities are multidimensional and for some reason there is more scrutiny on what women represent within processes, than there is for men, and this translates also to funding.

Is that the biggest challenge to involving women and to make them more active participants in the peace processes?

I don't think the challenge is to make women more active, they already are, and are ready to be leaders within peace processes. The biggest challenge that remains probably is still the pushback to participation.

While peacemaking actors have developed guidance on gender and mediation and how to make this not only focused on quantitative representation, but also about the power and structural systems of the peace process, it's undeniable that participation remains low, especially in formal processes.

Before focusing on the participants, there needs to be focus on the mediators themselves, and the structure of the peace process and the actors there. The biggest challenge I've heard is that 'now is not the time'. Especially in the peacemaking spaces, and peace processes, this is a very sensitive time, in which conflict parties can and do pull out at any time. There's a perception that widening the circle of participation beyond elite actors or conflict parties could jeopardize the peace process, which translates to a hesitation about bringing other actors, including women, to the negotiation table.

Firstly, this ignores the fact that women also can be part of negotiating parties, and part of conflict parties or their associated political wings, and it is important not to essentialize women that they're all peacemakers. But also, it ignores the fact that not setting a precedent of participation from the beginning increases the difficulty of not only including women but the substantive areas they want to be addressed within the process, or the structure of the process itself. From the beginning, you need to think about how to make this process inclusive.

And this hesitation, around the sensitivity of processes, can translate to a lack of implementation on women's participation. Are third-party mediators including women into the formal process, having consultations with women, and communicating how they will integrate the outcomes of the consultations in the process and providing them regular opportunities for exchange? Are teams ensuring that they themselves are gender-balanced? Do they have the right technical expertise on the mediation team to do gender-sensitive conflict analysis?

Another challenge is violence against women peacebuilders and peace-makers. This is on the increase due to a variety of reasons, which makes women claiming space in public arenas more challenging. Also, women peacemakers and peacebuilders are working against the interests of powerful actors who often don't want peace. They will be at risk, and the risk that they face often is particularly gendered. It can be exacerbated by legal systems or oppressive authorities, online and offline.

Lastly, the question of agency in a given process is a particular challenge. At what stage are women being brought into the discussion? There's an element of path dependency. Maybe in the initial negotiations, say, there is an agreement to only discuss certain matters, and a particular area of concern like transformative justice will not be discussed. At a later stage, a participant to the process may raise that they wanted to include a topic that was not initially agreed on within the agenda. But the design of the peace process does not allow her to do that. So not having a say on the design of the peace process is a challenge as well.

Part of your work also relates to ending violence against women. What are the main issues there? What are the main obstacles?

Ending violence against women is linked to conflict resolution and conflict transformation because it's important to ask what violence are peacemakers aiming to end with conflict resolution and conflict transformation because violence also includes violence against women during peacetime. It's key to sustainable peace. It's always been something that's interlinked, and many feminists frame it as a continuum of violence across wartime and peacetime.

I find this quite interesting because very early feminists have linked peace with the status of women in society. The link between ending violence against women and developing sustainable peace has been made for a very long time. Now there are different kinds of indicators to measure women, peace and security and sustainable peace. For example, the Georgetown Institute for Women, Peace and Security produced a women, peace and security index. Within that, one of the indicators is intimate partner violence, linking ending violence against women with sustainable peace. Ending violence against women and conflict resolution are deeply connected.

In relation to this, armed conflicts often have gendered consequences. What are the specific gendered impacts you have observed, and how do you address them in your efforts to identify and implement solutions?

Power dynamics are always exacerbated during times of armed conflict. This will have different impacts on different genders, young people, persons with disabilities and also those in the LGBTQ+ community, which is often forgotten. Gender shapes how one experiences conflict, but also shapes conflict and peace itself. It's important to know that gender exists in an intersectional manner with race, class, age, disability and economic dimensions, which will also affect how people will be impacted by armed conflict.

One of the most focused on gendered impacts of armed conflict includes sexual and gender-based violence which disproportionally affects women and girls, perpetuated by state, non-state and criminal organizations. The 2023 UN Secretary-General report on conflict-related sexual violence links growing militarization and the proliferation of illicit arms to increasing levels of sexual violence. The report also flags how women who are working to represent people who are affected by sexual violence are often then harassed and targeted themselves, especially in ungoverned digital spaces.

Protracted conflicts also have gender dimensions. The destruction, especially in populated areas, of environment and critical infrastructure deeply impacts women in civilian populations. This is often coupled in areas of weak state capacity. As such, it is becoming more and more apparent that the gendered impact of armed conflict has a deep effect on all aspects of women's lives, especially their work on social reproduction.

According to research by Lingham and Johnston, 'social reproduction includes the biological reproduction, unpaid production of goods and services, and social provisioning, such as voluntary work to maintain communities'.[1] It's this idea that what women are producing, not only family and labour, but social production, and that conflict will affect their ability to deliver this or they will have to do more of this kind of work. It's very important to measure the kind of work women are doing in all aspects of life, and look at how conflict affects this, both aiding and hindering their ability to do it.

That also links to peacebuilding work because women can do peace-building work in a variety of settings, in more formal spaces and in their communities or in their homes, or with their immediate families. This is not always measured or captured in traditional interpretations of peacemaking. When working to end violent conflict, conducting a gendered analysis and amplifying the voices of those engaged in this work – including those involved in social reproduction – are essential for fully understanding the gendered impact of conflict.

I came across a UN Women report indicating that restrictions on women's mobility can undermine their decision-making authority, even if they hold positions of power. What impact does this have on their role in conflict resolution?

This comes as a result of a multitude of things. The first way will be official, legal discrimination. There might be rules and regulations that obstruct women's ability to move freely. The second way will be social

1 Jayanthi Thiyaga Lingham and Melissa Johnston, "Running on Empty: Depletion and Social Reproduction in Myanmar and Sri Lanka," Antipode 57, no. 2 (2024): 494–514, https://doi.org/10.1111/anti.13016.

norms. For example, it might not be acceptable for a woman to move around freely. They might by law be able to, but they will face backlash, people spreading rumours about them, online violence, pictures taken of them on their own, for example. They may face physical violence. This is something we see increasingly. There is also the impact of security risks resulting from conflict itself which hinders freedom of movement.

Women's freedom of movement is always very important to look at when you start to demilitarise zones and have ceasefires. People say that a certain area is safe to walk around and one of the questions women ask is "Is it safe for a woman to walk around?" This deeply affects the space and ability for women to have economic decision-making and to live their lives freely. Peacebuilders and mediators need to be very mindful of how to push back against these limitations to the freedom of movement, because their own perceptions on how to provide solutions are not always ones that may be most suitable. It is the reality that, for example, women travelling to a political dialogue might not feel safe to travel alone, or may have to travel large distances.

Organisations who support peacebuilding and peacemaking have to think very carefully. Rather than saying, "It doesn't fit with our standards of independence if you can't travel alone" or "We don't want to pay for someone to come with you," they need to listen to the voices of women. Sometimes, they might need to support them to be accompanied by someone, whether it's a friend or a family member, because it would be a risk on that woman's life, and then that woman would not be able to attend the process otherwise. Alongside supporting women's groups who work to push back against the structural legal and social norm limitations, navigating participation requires careful consideration centring the voices of women affected in the creation of solutions.

You have frequently highlighted the issue of online violence. In which contexts is it most prevalent, and how does it typically manifest?

There have been a lot of reports from countries with ongoing conflict that have online violence, and it often occurs to women who are visible in public or decision making spaces. Whether they are human rights activists or women who are political activists, women in the media will receive threats, hate messages, comments on their body, on the way they look. Often this is very delicate because they could report it on a social media platform, but the kind of threats they receive might be quite contextually and culturally specific.

For example, a woman may be seen and documented with attire that she chooses to wear in a particular setting (for example with friends or family). In the public arena she may not choose to wear such attire or it may not be as socially acceptable. Someone may spread images online, and should she try to report it, social media sites may fail to understand why, in this instance, this would be part of a smear campaign or considered a threat. But for her in that political space, it could constitute a threat.

For some time, and still today, digital spaces lack adequate reporting mechanisms to address the various forms of online violence that women face in different contexts. Social media sites may not always have the staff who speak the language of a particular context or understand the nuances. There is a shift now, and a big push towards digital peacebuilding and people are looking also into how to use online spaces to bring women into decision-making spaces as well. As everyone says about technology, it's a double-edged sword. It's the people who design these spaces who either work on replicating the power dynamics in life or can work to transform them into something better.

It's also a matter of cultural sensitivity then?

Absolutely. Content moderators need to speak languages and understand the different contexts. At the beginning when social media sites were expanding rapidly they had limited content moderators to monitor all the reports they were receiving. What you see is that the use of social media snowballed so fast that the safeguarding responses around it could not keep up, especially globalized safeguarding responses in which contextualized conflict analysis can be done.

Maybe there is space for AI to provide solutions. AI can help detect trends and online drivers of conflict, and that is something that should be regulated. Technology can provide further solutions for this, but definitely, I think in terms of moderation of dialogue online and being able to report very contextualized threats, there's a huge gap.

There is increasing recognition of the role that arts and culture can play in conflict transformation. How do you see music contributing to peacebuilding efforts?

Music can be an incredible tool to express yourself in a non-violent way and has the power to bring people together, creating shared spaces for connection and dialogue. While music can also be used to reinforce divisions, its participatory nature – especially in communal forms like singing – can foster unity. Most people have a voice, most people can sing, and so this, by default, makes the use of singing an activity that can unify people, making it an accessible tool for collective expression.

Have you incorporated music into your peacebuilding work?

Yes, in certain contexts. I once worked on a mediation effort bringing together women from two conflicting communities. A key dialogue session had broken down, and despite attempts to restart communication, tensions remained high. In the free time that followed, I shared some of my own musical background and sang. While this wasn't a formal intervention, it created a different kind of space – one that allowed for a moment of connection beyond the conflict. These kinds of cultural and artistic approaches can open the door for future dialogue and peacemaking efforts, even when formal processes stall.

Saskia Binet is an inclusive peacemaking practitioner currently working as a Middle East North Africa Coordinator at the Women's International League for Peace and Freedom. She focuses on supporting inclusive peace process and women's participation in peacebuilding and peacemaking in Syria and Yemen. She supports peacemaking efforts by women's organizations and movements working to identify entry points and spaces for innovative and inclusive peacemaking activities. Previously, she worked at UN Women, including on Women, Peace, and Security in Libya, providing technical guidance and programme management on women's participation in peace processes across different tracks. Having collaborated with a variety of actors including civil society and women's political movements, government stakeholders and subnational actors, UN agencies, funds and political missions, she also provides guidance in translating inclusive peacebuilding and peacemaking priorities into resourced and operationally feasible programmes.

CAROLINE BROOKS

Can you tell me about the work you currently do with Amnesty International?

I'm a senior advisor on organizational development and conflict management at Amnesty International. The job is a global role, and it involves working with Amnesty's national entities globally. It involves supporting the movement (which is what we call the global amnesty) in conflict management and things related to wellbeing and organizational development. The focus is really on the internal dynamics across the movement – internal conflicts and crises – but they are often very much linked to external conflicts and what's going on in the wider world as well as the internal dynamics.

Which countries have you been working on?

So, I have not been travelling to, but I've been working with and supporting national entities in the Asia-Pacific region over the last year or so: South Korea, Japan, Malaysia as well as working with colleagues in France, Mexico, Taiwan, Côte d'Ivoire, Israel, and a few other places. My role is really as an advisor to support the national entities.

After your studies, you moved to Jordan and you worked in the humanitarian response to the war in Iraq. Can you tell me a little bit about that?

This was around early 2010. I joined a humanitarian aid organization. I was based in Jordan in Amman, but most of the team was based in various locations around Iraq. We were working on the ground and delivering different aid to Iraqi civilians. My role was as a reporting officer. It was actually like an internship position, a stipended position on a fixed term contract. I think it was six months.

My role was to collect all the data from the field, from the people who were there, to put it into different reports for donors, for internal reporting and so on, and also to attend the UN cluster meetings, many of which were happening in Amman. Then part of my role was also to help develop programmatic work for the organization. That was a pretty short-term thing. I think I was there from January to April, 2010.

What were the challenges that you faced?

It was fairly chaotic, if I'm honest. When I reflect on where I was, as well, I was completely fresh out of university, so I had very limited professional experience. When you go into an environment where there's a lot more experienced humanitarian folk doing the work, it's not an environment where the people have a lot of time to introduce you to things and get you up to speed. So, it was really a learn-by-doing, a kind of baptism by fire experience; I just had to figure out what's going on here and find out where do they need support and how can I help?

I would say personnel-wise, it was very stretched. At the same moment that I joined, there was the earthquake in Haiti, and my direct line manager was deployed there to respond to that crisis. I was essentially left without anybody to manage me in this country I'd never been to, in a context I'd only sort of peripherally worked in and known about. I had studied it, but I hadn't been so close to it before. Then, obviously figuring out the UN system as well. Although I was working for an independent NGO, the UN was one of the main interlocutors. It was a pretty challenging development experience. And it was also pretty challenging being in Amman for a while and navigating that as a lone female. There were a lot of challenges and stresses that came with that.

Could you elaborate on this?

It's not very usual for women to be by themselves and to go around by themselves. That came with quite a lot of negative attention, which was very stressful for me. It limited my ability to explore and feel like I could navigate the city by myself. So, that was a big adjustment. But I had some great colleagues in the office. Although they weren't working directly with me and couldn't line manage me or give me any sort of professional direction, it's always good to have those colleagues there.

In terms of what was happening in Iraq itself, my insight into that really came through the people who were working there, and I'd be receiving their updates, receiving their reports. I do remember that when some of my colleagues came out of Iraq to spend some time in Amman, I remember noticing a lot of high anxiety, and understandably so. A door would close a bit loudly and everyone would jump out of their skin, some of those sorts of things that come from living on edge for such a long time.

I also got an insight into the humanitarian aid sector in general when it started to shape my views about where I wanted to work and how I wanted to work. That experience showed me, actually, I'm not sure this is the sort of place I want to stay for very long. It's a great short-term experience. It's great to learn so much. I definitely want to remain engaged in this part of the world and in these issues and in these contexts. But where? Not sure. I started to have all these questions, which is normal when you're starting out and trying to find your way in things as well.

When you were at International Alert, did you work in Syria?

I was the Syria programme manager for International Alert for seven years, 2015 to 2022, and I was working on various different things with regards to the war in Syria. Much of the work that I was involved in and helped to develop and deliver was multi-track peacebuilding and diplomacy work. So what that meant, in practice, was that I worked very closely with civil-society networks both inside and outside Syria, as well as the grassroots activists involved in different sorts of peacebuilding initiatives within Syrian communities. And then I linked those up to the political processes that have been going on for the last number of years within, for example, the UN and EU.

The work was to connect all those dots and do step-by-step peace-building work from the community-based initiatives, to the regional and national, and then to the international policymaking. Our strategy around that was developed with our Syrian partners. The work evolved quite quickly.

As you can imagine in a context like Syria, a five or ten-year plan is not really that feasible, especially in the earlier years of the war where it was just so unknown what was going to transpire and how things were going to go. We had to have a very agile approach, very much building on partnerships, networks, and defining a role for ourselves as an org-anization external to the context, which was really in support of the great peacebuilding work that the Syrian Civil Society was and is doing. We had to shape ourselves to be service providers in that sense, rather than leading because we're outsiders and had to define a useful role for ourselves in consultation with our partners.

What was the contact with civil society like?

It was great. There were so many people who are eager to work together and with us to engage on the topics and to build the dialogue spaces, to work on the strategies and to do the advocacy, to be involved in research and to collaborate. I never felt that was a hard thing for us to be able to do. It is hard operationally because you have to be so sensitive to the politics of the situation, to the conflict dynamics. You have to really tread carefully and be aware of where the different stakeholders are coming from in terms of their opinions and experiences on the conflict and how they see the future of Syria unfolding.

If you don't come with that lens of sensitivity to the conflict, you can quite easily become somebody that people don't quite trust, which is absolutely essential to have in order to do anything. Even if people aren't agreeing – and have very different views about what the future of Syria might look like and what has already gone on – having that foundational relationship base, partnership networks, trust and respect across the board just helps facilitate all of those very difficult conversations and very difficult spaces.

It was also great to see, especially with our partners, the development over those seven years to where they really didn't need us anymore. Our partnerships still remain because we are both evolving and changing the way we're doing things. It was a really great and a positive experience.

I suppose the frustrations come (and we could see it from time to time in the different workshops that we were running and in the advocacy that we were doing), we could get very fatigued in a conflict context, which is still incredibly difficult, still not resolved, where millions of people have died, been displaced, and been dispossessed. Everything with the war or moving forward on initiatives that people believe in, the politics of it and how that's changed.

When you've got, especially young groups, youth networks who are putting out really great work, it's trying to connect with that political level, maybe sporadically or in an ad hoc way. It can be quite frustrating because you think, this needs to add up to more than the sum of its parts. And you question, "Is this the right way?" These are questions you should be asking, but it's quite frustrating when you think "Well, all of this work, what's the impact?" But it was a great experience working with civil society and it was really rewarding.

While in Syria, you also worked on a research project titled "Why Young Syrians Choose to Fight: Vulnerability and Resilience to Recruitment by Violent Extremist Groups in Syria". What led you

to this research project and what were your conclusions?

That research project was part of a larger program of work, which was funded by the UK government in 2016. What we were interested to know was what are the push and pull factors for young Syrians to join armed groups inside Syria? We did qualitative research in a number of different locations because what we were also looking at was, does peace education, which was the other part of the program, have any impact on vulnerability or resilience to recruitment? We found that there's a number of different factors that were driving the recruitment.

One of the reasons was the desire for revenge against the Assad regime. That was a driver in terms of wanting to get revenge for the death of one's family or friends, for example, so a strong motivating factor.

The other one was economic reasons. At some point, the armed groups in different areas were one of the only sources of decent employment. That was driving some recruitment as well. The collapse of education facilities was another contributing factor because the collapse of normal infrastructure such as good schooling can make young people and children vulnerable to recruitment. Schools provide those sorts of safe structured spaces for children, so when they're not functioning, there's a vacuum. We really boiled it down to drivers that are looking to meet basic human needs. These psychosocial and socioeconomic factors were very strongly present amongst the people we interviewed.

We didn't focus too much on recruitment into ISIS. That was partly because of the sensitivities around researching that, in terms of access and safety, but also because a large amount of the ISIS fighters were foreign fighters. We were much more interested in young Syrians in different parts of the country.

We also spoke to people who had left armed groups, people who had gone and come back, people who are now living outside of Syria, but who either were part of armed groups when they were inside Syria or knew of people and their journeys into and out of armed groups as well.

How do you keep young people from being recruited in a world with social media where communication has never been so easy?

When we looked at it in our study, it was really around the enabling environment that children and young people were in. So, a war context leaves children vulnerable because of all of the effects that I've just described. In the absence of a political settlement and peace, that's the elephant in the room. The big overriding context is that there are consequences, multi-generational consequences to these wars and acts of aggression and violence and the environments that they create. That was the big picture stuff.

But then we did find that on a more micro level, the presence of more positive adult role models was a big factor that helped in the resilience part of it. Establishing the education spaces, whatever they would look like, whether formal or informal, where children could still be in that learning environment, and have positive choices given as well. Then, there was alternative means for families to make a living because one of the big drivers was needing to make a living. So, there's all these sorts of different strategies. What we didn't find, at least amongst the people that we interviewed was that there were very strong ideological or religious reasons . It wasn't the 'cause' that was the main driving factor. It was these more prosaic kind of things, "I need to survive, I need to make a living. I also want to be part of something".

More practical reasons?

Practical, yes. That's not to say that was the whole story, but amongst the people that we were interviewing, that seems to be a large part of the story. I think it's also worth bearing in mind how context changes over time. So, if we were to go back and do the same study today, we might find different narratives. Especially for people who've been part of armed groups, then left, "what was the reintegration like?", or "was there anything to reintegrate into?"

An important thing to keep in mind when we're talking about these results is that they are snapshots in time and that context and conflicts change, as do dynamics. What we discovered, because we worked a little bit with a social psychologist in this, is that whilst I say it's really important to situate in context, on the other hand, there are some common themes that you can see in international literature and trends.

For example?

So, the motivation around the desire to serve basic human needs as being a main driver. The things that we've just mentioned as well, they're factors that have shown up in other research in other contexts. So, we were able to use that as a frame of reference as well.

Do you feel like the revenge for something that happened in their family was also a big factor in your findings?

We were doing research in opposition areas, and what really couldn't be understated was the desire to get revenge against Assad's forces, who had killed family and friends. That I do remember came out really, really strongly in the report. It was giving people a sense of motivation, purpose, and reason to join armed groups. We did another study a couple of years later, which was around the gender dynamics of recruitment into armed groups. That also came up again, and that cohort included adults as well.

You've also worked in Iraq and Afghanistan. You've said before that work gave you different skills and perspectives. Can you explain how?

I joined the Iraq and Afghanistan Control Risks team in 2010, just coming out of that period from Jordan. It was a team that worked on political, security, and reputational risk. They have different parts of the consultancy business, and I was working in Iraq and Afghanistan where lots of clients needed both physical protection and information about the contexts in order to make decisions and strategies. That gave me a whole range of skills because it was a corporate environment. So very different to an NGO space.

It was also another experience where the learning curve was steep. You're part of a global organization, but very focused on specific things. I think it also gave me my first management experience. A few years into my time there I became responsible for a team of 12 analysts in Iraq – all of whom were 10 to 20 years older than me, all of whom were ex-military men. That was a first management experience for me. So, my skin had to toughen up quite quickly in that environment.

But I also had in my first couple of years there, a very brilliant team, a very close-knit team. There were only four of us who were doing specific work, and we had a very good manager who taught me a lot about leadership, about how to take care of your team, just by his example. That's also a skill that I've seen in action and been able to reflect on, and that you can apply to any context.

There were some very difficult political situations, both internally and externally that needed to be navigated because we'd be interacting with the authorities in Iraq and Afghanistan. That is really a skillset that's very important for working in conflict contexts, in very diverse environments with multicultural teams.

At the end of the day, you're working for a company. You've got all of these things to balance. Then very practical skillsets to learn like complex project management and client handling and business development, which are really transferable everywhere you go.

You had to learn to navigate all sorts of things on your own?

It was difficult. I think my answer 15 years ago would be quite different to today. You have to get a big picture view. What is going on here at the big picture level? What are the dynamics that I need to be aware of? You have to do your own context analysis of the environment that you're entering into. You have to do your own actor mapping and analysis. These are all basics in the peacebuilding and conflict transformation world. Now I apply that to new situations. So, if I were to go into the same kind of environment, I would do that same analysis. I would then build my allies. I would have people who I know I can reach out to for advice. This was a phrase an old line manager used with me ages ago, "It's evolution not revolution." Sometimes when you come into a new organization or a new team or a new environment, and you see things through a different lens than people who have been there for a while, or you just bring a different lens on things anyway. You can have lots of ideas, you can see where things aren't working and you can see what needs to be done, but not everyone's going to be ready for that.

So, you have to do that foundational work first and you have to build those relationships, build the trust, build the credibility within that space and then you can start introducing ideas. You can start building on what already exists. And although that might be a slower build, it's probably going to be more successful. It also meant that I had the time to grow into a space, grow into a role, test my assumptions.

Before, when I was a lot younger, in the posts I was mentioning to you, I would think like I was in my mid-twenties. When I became the manager of the team in Iraq, I was 25 or 26. I wasn't fully ready for that role. I didn't put myself in the best position to succeed there in a way that I would have wanted to. It's important to be really clear and upfront with whoever is your line manager, your team, about your barriers: "This is what's going to be a struggle. Here's where I need your help. Here's where

I think we're going to be okay." It's important to have those conversations early and often. I assumed at the time this is just how it is. This is just what managing a team is like. It's supposed to be this hard and it's supposed to be this lonely, having all of these problems that you have to deal with all the time. Now, I see that was quite naive.

Do you have any thoughts on the two big conflicts going on, one in the Gaza Strip, another one between Russia and Ukraine? Any thoughts on how those can be navigated and what will happen?

That's a huge and difficult question. Sadly, what we can see in both contexts – but I think most acutely in the Gaza context – is that violence will breed more violence, and that will be the case for many more generations. Approaches that are based on the annihilation of an enemy, the eradication of people, never lead to peaceful outcomes. They will never lead to reduced violence. It will only take us in the opposite direction. We're right in the middle of the war in both contexts. At that point, it's actually really hard to talk about dialogue, about peacebuilding, and people will question peace for whom and at what cost and at whose expense. They're obviously completely legitimate questions to ask.

If I reflect on my experience working with Syrians and in Syria, it gives me a lot of hope and confidence that there are networks, pockets, groups of people who are working extremely hard for reductions in violence and ways out of things. That's not to minimize any need for justice, for accountability, and for that to happen at the levels it needs to happen at, internationally as well as locally. What we can say for sure is that it will be a very long process; it will be multi-generational. The impacts of today's violence didn't start today, of course; they have decades of history behind them. That means that there are cycles of violence, which are yet to be broken.

You also have extreme power imbalances in both contexts. That's something which makes any sort of ceasefire negotiation and what comes next also very challenging to navigate.

CAROLINE BROOKS

Caroline Brooks is an experienced peacebuilding and conflict transformation practitioner. Currently, she serves as a Senior Advisor at Amnesty International, advising on conflict transformation, crisis management, wellbeing, and organizational development. Before joining Amnesty, she was the Syria Programme Manager at International Alert, focusing on multi-track diplomacy and inclusive peace processes. Caroline is also a fellow of the OSCE's inaugural Women Peace Leaders Programme, which promotes women's involvement in mediation. Her career includes work in political and security risk consulting, particularly in Iraq and Afghanistan. Caroline has been deeply involved in Syrian civil society, working with activists, diplomats and communities affected by conflict. She has worked directly with children impacted by the Syria conflict in Lebanon and Turkey. Outside her professional work, Caroline volunteers with animal rescue organizations. She emphasizes the importance of community-driven solutions, learning by doing, and building lasting connections to foster peace and inclusion.

LATIF FAYAZ

You worked as a language assistant and senior military administrative assistant. Can you tell me more about how your career has progressed?

I had the privilege of serving with the United Nations Assistance Mission in Afghanistan (UNAMA) for nearly 15 years, where I gained invaluable experience in both humanitarian and political affairs. In 2018, I transitioned into the political arena by running for a parliamentary seat representing the Kabul constituency. After this, I joined NATO/RS as country advisor to the Senior Civilian Representative Office in Afghanistan, a role that further honed my strategic and diplomatic expertise. I also continued my academic involvement as a part-time university lecturer, while actively engaging in various political and social initiatives within Afghanistan.

What led you to work with UNAMA?

Working with UNAMA as a prestigious UN organization was a privilege. I encourage everyone who has the qualification to be a member of such an organization. I joined the United Nations Assistance Mission in Afghanistan (UNAMA) at the end of 2003 as secretary and language assistant for the Military Advisory Unit. This unit, composed of international military advisors, played a critical role in providing technical, military, and strategic advice to the UN Special Representative of the Secretary-General (SRSG) in Afghanistan. Additionally, it facilitated communication between the UN and both the coalition forces and the Afghan National Security and Defence Forces. The overall aim of the unit was to provide military-related development to UNAMA leadership through bridging engagement and collaboration with ISAF/RS and Afghanistan National Defence and Security Forces (ANDSF) on military and security matters.

In my role, I was responsible for providing translation and interpretation as well as providing administrative services, while also attending meetings with senior military advisors and the military advisory unit team at HQ, regional and provincial level. My tasks were varied, including providing military development advice and conducting assessments to support the Senior Military Advisor Unit, thereby enabling the military advisors to fulfil their responsibilities effectively.

As a translator, what were the primary challenges you faced? I can imagine that, in a conflict setting, even nuances such as tone and other subtle details could pose significant difficulties.

The role came with numerous challenges and risks, particularly for those of us working alongside international uniformed officials. In the public's perception, uniformed personnel were largely seen as American, and there was little distinction made between the military advisors operating under the UN mandate and the international forces engaged in combat against terrorism and insurgency.

This meant that, despite our different roles, we were often grouped with the broader international military coalition, which made us vulnerable targets for insurgents and terrorists. From their perspective, we were perceived as supporting 'infidels' and, therefore, viewed as legitimate targets to be punished according to their interpretation of Islamic principles.

The situation was further complicated by the fact that we did not have any formal protection from international military forces. As civilians, we were travelling with the military, attending meetings, and participating in missions to visit regional and provincial offices. Despite our civilian status, we were seen as part of the military effort and, consequently, viewed as targets by those opposing the international presence. It was, indeed, a highly challenging and perilous environment.

You were not perceived as an intermediary, but rather as someone who had chosen a side. Can you elaborate on that perception?

Indeed. From the insurgents' perspective, we were viewed as far worse than the military forces themselves because we were providing critical information, reports, and intelligence regarding terrorism. Naturally, the insurgents did not refer to themselves as terrorists, but rather as jihadists. This perception extended beyond just me – it affected entire families.

In Afghan society, identity is not solely defined by the person or individual, but by your entire family and extended network. As a result, the families of interpreters and advisors were often targeted by insurgent groups, adding another layer of danger and complexity to our roles.

You mentioned that you were treated as a civilian with no protection?

In Afghanistan, the UN adheres to a strict code of conduct which designates all UN staff members as civilians, which prohibits you carrying any weapon. Even the military advisors, despite their roles, did not have personal protection weapons, because that would have been in contradiction with the UN's values and principles. This policy became particularly problematic during the rise of "blue-on-blue" attacks in Afghanistan, where even allies sometimes became targets due to infiltration by insurgents posing as Afghan National Security Forces.

What were these "blue-on-blue" attacks, and how did they affect your work?

"Blue-on-blue" attacks occurred when insurgents infiltrated Afghan National Security Forces and attacked coalition forces, often using tactics that made it difficult to distinguish between the enemy and allies. I personally witnessed these tensions during visits to military camps where the situation escalated, and it became evident that insurgents had posed as Afghan soldiers to create confusion and initiate hostilities.

For interpreters and non-armed military advisors, such incidents created immense challenges, as our ability to move freely and access key meetings with the regiment, the divisions, the commanders and HQ leadership became severely restricted. We were forced to adhere to heightened security protocols, which, in turn, limited our operational capacity.

In a conflict situation, how do you manage miscommunication, especially given the high stakes and tension? Did you ever experience such situations?

One of the worst things I've ever experienced was during the protests in Mazar-i-Sharif. Demonstrators, upset over the burning of Qurans, stormed the UN Assistance Mission office. Among the crowd were insurgent groups who seized weapons from security guards, ultimately leading to the deaths of five UN staff members, including one of my close colleagues, a military advisor.

This tragic event left a deep impact on me. It was one of the most difficult times that I have endured, and it underscored the immense risks we faced while trying to carry out our duties.

Did you work as a translator while serving as an administrative assistant?

Indeed, each of my roles was deeply interconnected. Translation and interpretation were integral parts of my responsibilities, even while serving as the senior administrative assistant for the Military Advisory Unit. Similarly, when I joined NATO as a country advisor, I continued to provide translation services for the Senior Civilian Representative's office.

What kinds of translation work did you do with the UN, and how did that contribute to your role?

My translation work was diverse, encompassing both military and political contexts. I provided interpretation at various levels – from group discussions and workshops to high-level meetings with military leaders, ministers, and parliamentarians.

For example, I have attended meetings with a senior military advisor, parliament speaker, ministers and provided translation to a UN senior representative in Afghanistan. I translated military documents, security documents, and military-related code of conducts, procedures, policies, and legal documents. For texts that were longer, technical or legal, we had a language unit, but as part of the Military Advice Unit, we translated documents that were specifically related to the military. My translations played a critical role in facilitating clear communication between international and Afghan counterparts, ensuring that complex security and political matters were properly understood.

More recently, you served as a country advisor for NATO in Kabul. Could you tell me a bit about this?

This work was more political in nature. This was because I was responsible for providing the office of Senior Civilian Representative of NATO in Afghanistan with essential information regarding Afghanistan's political, cultural, and social landscape. That included the performance of Afghan institutions, civil societies, and political parties.

The Senior Civilian Representative was NATO's highest-ranking civilian official in Afghanistan. He was engaging with Afghan officials, such as the Presidential Office, the National Security Advisor, the Vice-President' Office, Parliament speakers as well as the political parties' leaders and influential members.

My role involved providing translation during sensitive discussions, often with high-profile officials whose meetings were covered by the media. The Senior Civilian Representative (SCR) met with political leaders in Afghanistan, which meant information about it was published on the media. And for example, a meeting with a National Security Advisor of Afghanistan would be on the national TV channel.

This made my work particularly delicate, as insurgent groups, including the Taliban, were aware of my involvement. They knew my face and my name. My association with NATO and working with the Senior Civilian Representative Office as part of the Resolute Support Office in Afghanistan, especially in the context of combating terrorism, made my position extremely precarious. This eventually led to the Taliban coming to take Kabul on the 15th August 2021. I left Afghanistan the same day the Taliban came.

When you were working with NATO, did you have much interaction with the civilian population?

When I was working with the United Nations Assistance Mission in Afghanistan, the nature of the job was more military as we were mostly engaged with the military and security institutions of and coalition forces in Afghanistan.

In contrast, the NATO engagement with Afghan society was much broader. NATO's Senior Civilian Representative Office's involvement extended beyond just military support to include political engagement with Afghan society, civil society groups, and political parties. As a result, I had more direct interaction with the Afghan people, helping facilitate dialogue between the international community and Afghan leaders.

How did NATO's approach differ from the UN's, and how did this affect your work?

NATO's role in Afghanistan was multifaceted, as they were not only a civilian entity but also a military force directly involved in supporting the Afghan government and defence security forces. By contrast, the UN primarily served as a facilitator, working to mediate between the international community and Afghanistan.

The war in Afghanistan started in 2001. You started working with the international entities in 2003 and continued until the end of the war in 2021. How did the evolution of the war impact your

work throughout the years?

The war in Afghanistan profoundly affected my work and my personal journey. The presence of the international community in Afghanistan had a huge impact on the different layers of Afghanistan's society, especially on the youth and minority groups. There were a lot of changes.

When I first joined the UN in 2003, I had just graduated high school. By the time I left in 2018 and had registered as a parliamentary candidate, I had earned a master's degree in Political Science and International Relations and had also been teaching at university level. Throughout this time, Afghanistan underwent significant social, political, and economic changes. The war certainly took its toll, with countless lives lost and an escalating insurgency.

But there was also hope, particularly among the younger generation who envisioned a democratic future for Afghanistan. Tragically, the fall of Kabul on the 15th August 2021 shattered these dreams. It was a real catastrophe for the Afghan people and, I believe, will have far-reaching consequences for the world in the years to come. These fundamentalist terrorist groups do not have any principles or boundaries. They don't respect anything.

When you ran for parliamentary office in 2018, what motivated you?

I had a dream, and my candidacy in the 2018 parliamentary elections was driven by a deep desire to pursue this dream. I wanted to offer the younger generation of Afghanistan – a generation that transcended ethnic, religious, and tribal divisions – a chance to shape their own future. I envisioned a more united, democratic Afghanistan, one that could sustain itself even after NATO's and the United States' eventual withdrawal. This was the reason why I registered as a candidate – my campaign was rooted in this hope, and I believed that change was possible, despite the challenges.

Had you been elected, what kind of change would you have pursued?

My vision for change was twofold: both in terms of domestic and foreign policy. Domestically, I sought to establish and form a parliamentary group which united Afghanistan's various ethnic groups to act together towards common goals. I wanted to tackle corruption while promoting good governance, ensure that the Afghan government would be held accountable for its actions and that the nation's political processes would be transparent and fair.

In terms of international relations, I was looking to make a more realistic definition of Afghanistan's national security. I wanted to work towards constructive negotiations with the Taliban, in an effort to preserve the democratic foundation of the political system in Afghanistan that had been made. Ultimately, I sought to safeguard Afghanistan's democratic foundation – something I viewed as the most critical element for the nation's future. During this time I was presenting these policies on different social media platforms and on the television.

Reflecting on your career, is there any situation you wish had ended differently?

This is a difficult question for me. A very hard moment for me was in 2021, when I was working with the SCR office, and a message was conveyed to them that the international community decided to withdraw from Afghanistan without considering on-the-ground realities. The decision to leave Afghanistan, regardless of the conditions, undermined everything that had been built over the previous two decades – immense financial investment, and the sacrifices of around 6,500 Afghan National Security Force members who were killed in the fight against terrorism.

So, I went from advocating for the international presence in Afghanistan to then suddenly having to just pack and leave. Right now, the students I was teaching Politics and International Relations to, the girls, they cannot go to university. They can't even go to public gatherings. How can we even imagine that after 20 years in a democratic system and society, suddenly, a group comes and denies everything? They deny the dignity of human beings, they deny the basic and fundamental rights of women, the foundational rights of ethnic groups.

Right now, the ethnic group that I belong to, the Hazaras, are subjected to genocide acts. They are killed in the mosques, in the schools, in the hospitals, on the streets. The Taliban do not even know the person they are going to kill, they only know their ethnicity. Because they are Hazaras, they have to be killed.

What could have been done differently to avoid the situation that Afghanistan finds itself in now?

The international community should have made it clear to the Taliban that the people of Afghanistan, especially those who supported the international presence, would not be abandoned. The withdrawal should have been contingent on real, substantive change in Afghanistan, not a hasty departure that left the country vulnerable to extremist forces.

Do you believe AI and robotics will play a significant role in future conflicts and territorial expansion?

I recently read a book titled *An Army of None,* which explores the future implications of technology, robots, and AI in warfare.[1] The book references an incident during the conflict, where insurgents used young children as unknowing instruments in their attacks. A group of international military forces was deployed in a specific area near the Pakistan border and the author describes how a young shepherd girl came first which was then followed by an attack by the insurgents. The girl had a tracking system and was an instrument at the hand of the enemy. So the question was whether they should act against her or not? But they decided not to shoot her.

The author posits that if AI-controlled robots were deployed in similar situations, their programmed response would be purely utilitarian, lacking the ethical considerations of human decision-makers. This raises profound questions about the autonomy of AI in combat and the potential consequences of allowing such technologies to make life-or-death decisions on their own.

What are you doing now?

I currently reside in Finland, a beautiful small country in northern Europe, where the cold winters contrast sharply with the warmth of the people who have welcomed my family.

I am pursuing studies in Business Administration, adapting to a new life and environment while helping my family adjust to the new environment too. Though it has been a challenge to build a new life after 40 years in Afghanistan, I remain committed to my dreams for the country. I continue to monitor developments in Afghanistan, hoping for the day when I can contribute to a better future for its people.

---

1 Paul Scharre, *Army of None: Autonomous Weapons and the Future of War,* W. W. Norton & Company,

Do you ever envision returning to Afghanistan?

Returning to Afghanistan depends entirely on the future circumstances of the country. Under the current Taliban regime, which shows no respect for fundamental human rights, particularly those of women and ethnic minorities, returning is unthinkable. However, should Afghanistan ever return to a democratic system that upholds the rights of all its citizens, I would gladly return.

Mohammad Latif Fayaz is currently the Director of the Hazara Cultural House in Finland. Previously, he has served as the Country Advisor for the Office of the NATO Senior Civilian Representative (SCR) in Resolute Support (RS) to Afghanistan. In his career, he has also worked as a political analyst, writer, and civil activist. Fayaz volunteered as a senior member of the Centre for Democracy and Development Studies (CDDS) from 2009 to 2013. Then, from 2016 to January 2021, he held part-time positions as a university lecturer at various private universities and institutes of higher education in Afghanistan. In 2019, Fayaz served as the Director and spokesman of the Security and Justice Presidential Electoral Team. He was also a parliamentary candidate for the Kabul constituency in the 2018 parliamentary election. He has held various positions, including senior administrative associate, and language assistant, with the Military Advisory Unit (MAU) of the United Nations Assistance Mission in Afghanistan (UNAMA).

PAULO GONÇALVES

Can you tell me what you did in the Portuguese Air Force?

I did several things over the course of almost 40 years of service in the Air Force. I started as an air traffic control officer. In that role, not only did I control the air traffic at the several air bases I was assigned to, but I was also in charge of the Air Traffic Services' Squadron. Meaning I was the commander of the staff operating at the control tower, radar, fire department and meteorology section.

Afterwards, I had another qualification, being specialized in Chemical, Biological Radiological, and Nuclear Defence. In that role, I was the officer in charge for CBRN defence of the air base where I was deployed. Later on, I had yet another role, being the air base's Protocol and Public Affairs Officer.

These last two roles brought me to participate in the first of NATO's CBRN event response team, dealing with strategic communication in case of an attack or an accident involving these kinds of hazards. Because my Air Force is a very small, but active one, I kept adding courses and operational qualifications to my CV, such as parachuting, combat information and peacekeeping.

That projected me to international missions in NATO, the European Union and United Nations. I served in many countries, but my most memorable overseas deployments were three UN missions; namely – UNAVEM II in Angola in 1992, UNPROFOR in 1995–96 in Bosnia/Croatia/Serbia and UNAMA in 2012–14 in Afghanistan. In all these three missions there was an armed conflict still ongoing, where we – the peacekeepers – had no peace to keep.

In Afghanistan, where I served for almost three years, and because of my experience in other operational theatres, I was invited to become an analyst of conflict situations for the United Nations. Therefore, it was no surprise when, after returning to Portugal, I was appointed to the NATO Joint Analysis and Lessons Learned Centre (JALLC), in Lisbon.

Just before I retired from the Air Force, with the rank of full Colonel, I became the Deputy Director of the Portuguese Air Force's Instruction Department, and finally the Commander of the Portuguese Air Force's Documentation Service.

In your experience, has conflict resolution changed over the years? How?

Not to be sceptical, but when I was involved in conflict resolution missions with NATO, the UN, or the EU, either in three civil wars or in other situations which weren't exactly a conflict but were definitely preparation for a conflict, I didn't see much of an improvement over the years. Specifically regarding the UN, very little has changed or improved.

My first UN mission – in Angola – wasn't really conflict resolution. It was more an attempt to develop a post-conflict resolution, which didn't work, and then the conflict restarted. Being an air traffic control officer, I was called to help organize the UN's aerial campaign for the Angolan elections. I experienced such surreal situations on this mission that I started drawing cartoons and writing a diary, which ended up giving rise to a book. Everything worked out really well in terms of the mission we had, but it was a tremendous failure in terms of conflict management by the international entities.

In what sense?

Because the war started again. There were ten more years of civil war after those elections. The war against Portugal in Angola (1961–1975) was driven by the Cold War rather than the majority of Angolans. The Portuguese "colonial war" in Angola was serious but localized. When Portugal left, its poorly managed decolonization handed power to one political party, sparking a civil war. MPLA, UNITA, and other groups fought, dragging all Angolans into a brutal conflict that nearly split the country.

Then, Angola started supporting a resistance group that was trying to bring down the regime in South Africa. Therefore, because Angola was hosting those guerrillas, South African forces moved into Angola to eliminate them, and that started an undeclared war between Angola and South Africa. Undeclared, but brutal. In 1991, no thanks to the UN, it was possible to sit all the people around a table and get an agreement.

In 1992, finally, we were involved in the Angolan elections. The electoral campaign went really well, but the UN didn't have the ability to manage the political problem in country. Those in power in Angola didn't want to let their power go, and those who wanted to get power didn't even consider another option but to win the election. The electoral process went really well, but it didn't count because they went back to war for ten more years. The UN had no means and no mandate to stop the war. The Senior Representative of the UN Secretary-General complained that she had to "pilot a jumbo jet with the fuel of a small Cessna."

The UN representatives faced significant challenges, including poor evacuation planning. In 1992, staff were told to buy their own tickets with cash in a war-torn country, making them vulnerable targets. A person with a lighter skin tone was already a target. Knowing that he had 2,000 or 3,000 US Dollars in his pocket, was a target-practising reward.

Shortly after the fall of the Berlin Wall and the collapse of the Soviet Union, the UN started to show that they didn't have the ability to do what they were created to do – which is to prevent a war from happening. The UN Charter states, "We the peoples of the United Nations are determined to save succeeding generations from the scourge of war." A failure. Why? Everyone knows why; it's the matter of the veto power, given to the five permanent members of the Security Council.

How do you think the role of the UN has changed over the years? What do you think makes the organization inefficient?

Throughout the decades, the UN has taken over many tasks and roles, where they are absolutely essential for international regulations and standards, humanitarian aid and social development. However, regarding conflict resolution – the primary reason it was created – successes have been far fewer than failures. I got to know the UN in 1992 when they demonstrated they were incapable of managing an internal and external conflict. The international powers did not provide the resources nor the mandate for their UN representatives on the ground to stop the local people from killing each other.

Right after that, there was the problem of Yugoslavia. The UN Charter has something called Chapter 6, a series of articles dedicated to maintaining peace among countries that had frozen previous conflict, but still face tensions. In these scenarios, the UN intervenes to maintain and solidify peace. Chapter 7, on the other hand, isn't really about maintaining an achieved peace, rather about imposing peace by force if necessary.

While the UN has the authority to politically declare peace imposition, it lacks the ability to enforce it. The UN does not have its own army and relies on countries to provide forces for specific missions. These forces don't train together, leading to issues like incompatible equipment. For example, in Angola, the Russian helicopters I used couldn't refuel with the UN's western pumps, so I had to use buckets. Similarly, soldiers from Bangladesh who were deployed to Bosnia without proper winter equipment suffered casualties due to the weather, not combat.

That was the UN in 1995, but honestly, not much has changed. Kalashnikov ammunition is not compatible with Portuguese or French rifles, meaning UN peacekeepers cannot share bullets depending on their country of origin. In fact, many lower-ranking UN contingent soldiers do not even share a common language, such as English. This is not the case in NATO. Member countries of the North Atlantic Alliance follow standardized procedures, use compatible equipment, and share common manuals. A Portuguese F-16 pilot, for example, can fly an F-16 from the Netherlands and communicate seamlessly with pilots from all NATO countries.

NATO has greater capability and effectiveness, but it's a defence alliance and lacks the mandate or political authority to interfere in other countries' conflicts. That's when we go back to Chapter 7 of the UN Charter. The UN can give a mandate to someone who has the capability they don't have but has the capacity to act the way they can't.

This happened in Kosovo, where the UN lacked air power but authorized NATO to intervene. Similarly, in Bosnia, the UN asked NATO to attack Serbian forces around Sarajevo to stop the war. These examples highlight the UN's inability to act decisively due to the limitations of its structure and mandates.

The Bosnian conflict, in 1995, was the culmination of the incapability of the UN. Peacekeepers didn't fail due to incompetence but because they weren't authorized to act effectively. The Security Council is dominated by the agendas of its five permanent members with veto power. In Bosnia, the UN Protection Force's biggest contributors were France and the UK, but the mandate was a Chapter 6 Mission. Neither warring faction had signed a ceasefire agreement, and the war was at its peak. The UN sent 30,000 peacekeepers, and I wasn't allowed to use a gun for self-defence because I was a military observer.

During the Srebrenica massacre, the Dutch Blue Helmet contingent had only light weapons against Serbian heavy-armoured vehicles. When the Dutch attempted to counterattack, they weren't authorized because counterattacks didn't qualify as self-defence. In the three years of the UNPROFOR mission, over 230 Blue Helmets died.

The UN mandate had many gaps, such as the lack of provisions for protecting civilians outside limited spaces or addressing rape as a weapon of war. Ultimately, the UN declared itself incapable of ending the conflict and requested NATO's intervention. US-led NATO airstrikes ended the conflict. Ironically, it wasn't even the UN that negotiated the ceasefire and peace agreement – it was the United States. The Americans brought the leaders of the warring factions to an airbase in Dayton, where they were effectively held until they signed the agreements. This demonstrated the ineffectiveness of the Security Council and its veto power in resolving conflicts.

What lessons has the UN learned from past failures in peace-keeping, and how have these lessons influenced its approach to handling conflicts and working with other organizations?

Yes, there are many parts where the UN has changed and improved. The UN learned lessons from Rwanda, Angola, and Bosnia. These lessons introduced the concept of "robust peacekeeping," also known as Chapter 6.5 of the UN chapter. It's a middle ground between traditional peacekeeping (Chapter 6) and Peace Enforcement (Chapter 7). For example, in the Central African Republic, the Portuguese deployed with peacekeepers and heavy weapons. They actively pushed back threats from rebels, earning praise from both UN leadership and locals. Other UN contingents, bound by Chapter 6, could not operate the same way. The challenge lies in translating lessons learned into mandates assigned by the Security Council. Knowing *how* to act is not enough; action is necessary.

The concept of "robust peacekeeping" was an improvement, and the UN introduced other advancements in their mandates. One was recognizing that when peace needs to be imposed, the task is delegated to regional organizations – NATO in Europe or the African Union in Africa. For instance, ISAF in Afghanistan was a NATO-led mission open to contributions from countries like Pakistan and the UAE, operating under Chapter 7. However, in Africa, regional organizations lack NATO's capabilities.

The European Union (EU) takes a different approach. I was a peacekeeper for the EU for a time. Politically averse to combat, the EU focuses on training locals through programs like "Train the Trainers." This is evident in Mali and Mozambique, where the Portuguese military instructs locals without engaging in combat. They provide intelligence and teach local forces to handle threats themselves.

That's what the Portuguese military assigned to the EU are doing in Mali, or in Cabo Delgado region of Mozambique. We deploy there, we share the military knowledge and intelligence, but we do not engage in combat situations. We inform the local police, or the army, where the terrorists are attacking the civilian population, and we teach them how to handle those situations. That's what the EU normally does.

The other conflict I was involved in with the UN was Afghanistan, where I dealt with the Taliban and insurgents for almost three years. The conflict dynamics there were unique – a street policeman by day could be a Taliban fighter by night. For Afghans, survival is the primary concern, and their loyalties tend to be more tribal than national. The environment was unsuitable for traditional peacekeeping under Chapter 6 and instead required robust peace enforcement under Chapter 7. Pakistan's involvement added further complexity, with allegations that its intelligence services were supporting the rebels. Once again, the UN deferred to NATO, which had the technology and resources to manage the situation.

Progress in peacekeeping has been slow. The UN is hindered by the veto card in the Security Council, but the organization remains essential. The UN regulates global systems beyond conflict resolution. UN agencies like the World Health Organization dealt with the COVID-19 pandemic and the UNHCR handles refugees. The UN has 97 permanent agencies. If they disappear, there would be a worldwide collapse. Only some countries will have conditions to survive.

But, again, that was not the main reason the UN was created. It was created for conflict resolution and in those terms, while there are five countries in the Security Council with veto rights, that will hardly be solved. While the veto right prevents wars among superpowers, it also promotes proxy wars and stalls resolutions. For example, the League of

Nations failed partly because all countries had veto power, leading major players like the US to withdraw because the veto right would interfere with their national sovereignty. A worldwide institution without the United States was simply condemned to vanish; and that was when the Second World War started!

So the UN addressed this by limiting veto rights to five countries: China, Russia, France, the UK, and the US. Portugal doesn't have a strong voice to claim that the veto right hurts our national sovereignty and the world conflict resolution. However, I am sure there will be a solution to the satisfaction of the superpowers and the rest of the world. It is a question of compromising.

As I often say in class, I don't believe we'll ever have a perfectly peaceful world. This is because, even to walk, we need to deliberately lose our balance, leaning in forward, in order to move ahead. If we are always perfectly balanced, we stay in the same place for all of our life. We only progress in unbalanced situations.

You wrote about a boy in Angola in 1992 who asked you for batteries to make moonshine. What's the relationship between the military and the population like, in conflict situations like that? What were the challenges?

The relationship between civilians and the military varies by conflict. In Angola, there were no issues with the population, as there were no colonization traumas. However, political leaders exploited situations to build narratives that reinforced their power. In former Portuguese colonies, there were no significant conflicts between locals and international forces.

That was not the case in the former Yugoslavia. Why? Because the UN headquarters was in Zagreb, Croatia. Croats expected the UN to take their side against the Serbs, while Serbs expected the opposite. The same applied to the Bosnian territory, with three ethnic groups, the UN's impartiality frustrated all sides.

In Croatia, the relationship between the local population and UNPROFOR was often poor. In Zagreb, locals provoked UN peacekeepers by speaking German, knowing most UN staff only spoke English. However, the Portuguese faced no issues; they were well-regarded due to Portugal's neutral history and lack of aggression in European conflicts.

Unlike others, the Portuguese could rent houses and interact freely, while some contingents faced hostility, even struggling with basic tasks like buying bread. Relationships depend on the country and the conflict.

In Afghanistan people are lovely, and even though they're afraid of the Taliban, and other extremist groups, they abide by the Pashtun code of honour. If a Pashtun says you're their friend, he would rather die than put you in danger. There were situations in which Pashtun villages were attacked by the Taliban only because they helped NATO forces with water and food. The Afghans are more loyal to their tribal structure then they are to their national institutions.

I also went to Ukraine, in other circumstances. Everyone says the Ukrainians are great fighters. They are! But that's because they're defending their home. When we're defending our own street, we're all great heroes and warriors. The backstage of the trenches is our own house, and our family is still living there. We become friends with anybody willing to help us, and foes to the ones that see our family perish without doing anything. Impartiality may be vital for political conflict resolution but doesn't always build connections with affected populations.

The problem of the Middle East is something else. The clash of cultures becomes incredibly relevant. Tribal leaders in places like Libya hold significant influence. Groups like Hamas represent concepts that cannot be destroyed through military action. You can bomb structures and people, but you cannot bomb concepts and hard feelings. That's why it depends on the country's culture, and on the conflict. It can't be generalized.

What impact does strategic communication have in conflicts such as the ones in the 90s – Angola and Bosnia – as well as the current ones?

These conflicts only happen because there are small leaders who want to become big leaders. That happens through the mobilisation of people by exploring their traumas. In the former Yugoslavia, some intellectuals told me that the Portuguese could never really understand what was going on there, because we are one single tribe within a specific territory, while in Yugoslavia there were several tribes in one territory. In the 1990s, I think that Portugal and Iceland were the only cases where there were no significant minorities in the country and the population was extremely homogeneous (that has changed since then).

Ethnic niches tend to form communities where people do not operate outside those communities. Integration with the host nation's population becomes an issue and tension starts to arise. As an ethnic minority grows, its needs and demands also grow, and that opens opportunities for ethnic representatives to become "cause leaders". The ethnic population needs to be mobilized to the streets' protest, and that's when the communication process becomes essential.

On the other hand, strategic communication must be used to resolve these types of conflict situations. Integration of different cultures can be eased with the proper communication tools coordinated in a predefined strategy.

In Afghanistan, we implemented a coordinated strategic comm-unication plan. Operators from public affairs, information operations, and civil-military operations all shared the same platform and message, broadcasting across various channels. In remote areas, we distributed hand-crank radios tuned to a single frequency, which broadcast vital information about minefields, water sources, medical facilities, and, of course, the messages we wanted people to follow, encouraging them to reject the Taliban.

We also engaged permanently with opinion leaders, influencers and journalists, in order to softly pass our message. But there was also the "Hard Way" to pass the message. That was the ISAF (NATO Lead forces) arena. For instance, the insurgency issue was normally dealt with by military kinetic – war type actions.

I'm going to give you an example of a STRATCOM kinetic action in Iraq during the coalition attack on Saddam Hussein's forces to encourage desertion. Two positions with good communication but weak air defence were targeted. A coalition fighter aircraft dropped pamphlets over those positions, warning of an upcoming airstrike with specific details. The strike was executed as announced, sparing communication assets so the Iraqis could report it. A few days later, a similar pamphlet was dropped over a strongly defended Iraqi position, which the coalition avoided due to high casualty risks. However, the Iraqis manning the stronghold surrendered without opposition due to the earlier strikes on weaker positions. That was strategic communication using lethal weapons to obtain a certain communication goal: "Give-up fighting"!

You have written about the relationship between the military and the media in zones of conflict. Has it changed? How?

The relationship between the military and the media has evolved, but much remains an illusion. Journalists may feel they have more freedom, but access to raw information is still controlled by factions. For example, in the Ukrainian conflict, the same event is reported differently by opposing sides, with each side controlling the narrative. Satellites have made a difference in observing the battlefield, but access to imagery is still controlled by state-sponsored entities. War has also become more sophisticated, creating a need for specialized journalists, but most are generalists, leading to reliance on commentators who interpret pre-filtered data.

Since I spoke several languages and had public relations experience, I was often tasked with handling media representatives during international missions. My main concern was ensuring that journalists didn't do the work of the military or vice versa. At times, I noticed journalists becoming overly involved in operations, losing their objectivity, and presenting biased reports due to limited access to only one side of the conflict. Naturally, soldiers wouldn't speak positively about their enemies, and there was no contradictory reporting.

The relationship between the military and journalists in combat zones is complex. In one of my books, I likened it to train tracks: two lines running parallel, always maintaining the same distance and direction. While they may appear to converge at the horizon, this is an illusion. Any deviation from their separation risks derailment.

There is a strong tendency for the military to take on the role of journalists, and when that happens, we move into the realm of psychological operations (or propaganda). While this is not necessarily a problem, as the military has its own audiences – whether internal or external – it is common to find military-operated radio stations, television channels, newspapers, newsletters, and internet platforms.

NATO-led forces have used various media engagement strategies in multiple operations. At the NATO Joint Analysis and Lessons Learned Centre (JALLC), we warned strategic communicators to be cautious, as major media agencies often arrived before the military, with their own contacts, communication channels, and agendas. In 1995, during the Bosnian conflict, I witnessed a CNN report from a cemetery filled with crosses. The reporter stated, "Behind me, you can see the graves of all the Muslims killed by the Serbs." However, Bosnian Muslims don't use crosses on their graves – those were recently killed Serbians.

Some journalists want to do proper impartial reportage, but they're not authorized to cross the battle lines by the opposing factions. If they really want to do it, they must do it alone, illegally, without any type of support, facing all types of threats, starting with the minefields they'll have to cross, to sniper fire because they are easily mistaken for being spies. During the Iraqi invasion, an American cameraman was killed when a soldier mistook his camera for a missile launcher. He wasn't registered with the coalition forces, highlighting the risks journalists face when working independently in a conflict zone.

In Afghanistan, international forces were authorized to use lethal force when threatened, even in cases like a child playing with a laser pointer, which could be mistaken for a sniper targeting device.

Journalists working outside military frameworks risk gathering biased information or facing serious danger. In Bosnia, an American journalist sought to cover the Serbs' perspective but was denied access and ventured without proper clearance. He disappeared, and I, along with a Russian colleague, was tasked with searching for him. He eventually bribed his way out, while we struggled to return to Sarajevo.

Covering military conflict outside the military framework is not advisable, but being embedded within a military contingent also has restrictions on information quality. The military will only let the media see what it wants them to see.

Do you believe climate change and desertification in Africa will lead to new conflicts, more refugees and migration? What are the risks?

There are two different aspects to your question – threats and Risks – and for both of them my answer is yes! Global warming is a threat to Africa and the rest of the world. In Portugal, it causes water shortages, the Atlantic archipelagos suffer from unusual tempests, and economic impacts, creating internal conflicts and social dissatisfaction.

I've worked with Professor Francisco Leandro on Brazil's surroundings. A country like Brazil, with the Amazon rainforest and its massive water reservoir are under threat due to reduced snow in the Andes, which feeds the Amazon River. If Brazilians migrate to Portugal due to drought, the country will struggle with housing and healthcare.

Global warming will also bring diseases, and the national health services are not prepared to deal with mass casualties. Even if there aren't migrations from Africa to Europe, Europe is not prepared in terms of emergency services for a great flood, much less for drought, which brings mosquitoes, which in turn bring malaria. In Portugal, during the times of the old regime, we used to take measures in the southern part of the country regarding the mosquitos that spread malaria, hence there were initiatives of pulverizing the fields near the Sado River (south of Lisbon). With the cessation of our African Provinces (colonies) that was stopped because of the transit of people and goods between the European part of Portugal and its African provinces. However, now, mosquitoes seem to have reappeared, because of global warming.

Migration from regions affected by global warming is a risk. Refugees flee conflicts and return when threats subside, while economic migrants seek better opportunities but often arrive illegally, leading to integration challenges. There are also "evildoers" trying to exploit those situations, marketing Europe as an easy to achieve paradise, and charging huge amounts of money to these desperate people, until they run into debt, sell what they have, and don't have, and become small criminals in their countries of origin, so they can pay someone to take them to Europe. The same thing occurs in the American continents.

Uncontrolled migration creates social tensions in Europe, despite the need for labour. Therefore, it seems there's a paradox in this situation. This is due to the negative perception that uncontrolled arrival of immigrants is having in much of the host (European) nations' population. Host nations struggle with integrating immigrants who form ghettos and maintain incompatible social systems.

Europe can avoid the migration "risks" by introducing proper measures, but the Africans cannot eliminate the global warming "threat". In fact, no country on its own can deal with the global warming threat. That is why it's called "global".

Global warming and its effects require global coordination, at the UN's Assembly. While technology exists to mitigate these issues, political will and private sector engagement are essential. The private sector must be engaged in this process. One must not forget that about one third of the 100 biggest world economies are not states but enterprises;

and enterprises seek profit not social satisfaction. There have been five mass extinctions on earth in the past. Is the planet now reacting to this exhausting period of human exploitation?

Do you anticipate artificial intelligence (AI), which is growing so rapidly, will be used to get resources such as oil and natural gas? Yes, I do, but I hope AI will offer better solutions for energy sources than oil and gas. In fact, I believe AI will dominate most areas of knowledge and development, even the arts – which worries me quite a bit. Let me give you an example: In 2021, I took an excerpt from my book about Bosnia, rewrote it, and entered a competition in Hollywood for the script of a short musical. I won the contest, and they turned my story into a musical, featuring an actor/singer performing the narrative. A composer wrote the melody, with my input to ensure the music aligned with the lyrics. It was a fascinating process, but also extremely demanding in terms of workload. We worked on the project online, between the United States and Portugal, for nearly a year – writing the story, composing the songs, and coordinating with the actor.

However, some time ago, a friend of mine did a similar thing in about 15 minutes, and he didn't even have a story to tell. He just gave instructions to an AI site and the final product came out in 15 minutes. Of course, it did not have the same quality as mine had, but nevertheless it was acceptable enough to entertain our guys during an afternoon gathering. Mind you AI is still learning, give it some more time and the quality of its products will be much higher.

I often say that most conflicts happen because there are small leaders who want to become great leaders. If they use artificial intelligence, they will be big leaders much quicker and with much more drastic effects. That's my fear. Artificial intelligence has the ability to solve conflicts, but I think it also has a great ability to promote them. AI has no ill-intent; people have.

Of all the conflicts you worked on, was there any that you would have liked to see end differently? I wish all conflicts had ended differently or had better outcomes. Unfortunately, most are resolved by third parties, creating artificial solutions that collapse when populist leaders exploit old wounds.

Western solutions didn't work in Afghanistan; I fear the outcome of the African countries governments' policies, which are not solving the poverty issues of their people and I am not convinced that the peace solutions introduced in the Balkans are strong enough to prevent the resurgence of those conflicts. There is peace, but most conflicts have just been frozen, not solved. Genuine good judgment and a willingness from all parties are needed to promote peace.

In one of my NATO missions in Lithuania, we were deployed to perform air policing over the Baltic countries, due to the Russian Air Force's permanent disrespect of those countries' airspace sovereignty. There were a lot of instances in the Baltics when we had to have "good judgement" in order not to engage the trespassing Russian aircraft, and so did they. Any harsh decision, as legal and just as it could be, would without doubt escalate the tensions between NATO and Russia.

All conflicts require good judgement and common sense from the parties involved. The problem is that you can't order a box of "good judgement", or "common sense", via the Amazon delivery system. In the military, we joke about our ranking symbols, because they are represented by stripes. The more stripes you have, the closer they get to the jugular vein in your neck. If you have a lot of stripes it may interfere with your ability to think properly. There's something called the "Peter principle," which says that people tend to be promoted to the maximum level of their incompetence. That's what happens in politics. There's a lack of good judgment when it comes to the needs of the local population.

When a volcano erupts, everyone gets very upset, people are evacuated, but no one is responsible for that accident and no one can control it. But the wars I witnessed happened not because of population demands or ideology, it was because of certain leaders' ideals. Mr. Savimbi wanted the diamonds in Northern and Eastern Angola, Mr. Izetbegović wanted to make Bosnia into something it had never been before, and the Taliban wanted Sharia law to be the rule in Afghanistan. There was no "good judgement", from those leaders. The UN's ability to act was severely reduced, because it was created to avoid war, not to resolve it. The UN will never have that ability while the veto is still in place. But please don't disregard the UN, because if the UN disappears there will be a major collapse in many knowledge areas of the world. The UN has evolved from the "saviours of humanity" into the "promoters of development".

What do you currently do?

I have been writing and illustrating books about my military experience, and about geopolitical aspects of the Portuguese-speaking countries (Angola, Brazil, Cabo Verde, Equatorial Guinea, Guinea-Bissau, Mozambique, Portugal, São Tomé and Príncipe and Timor-Leste).

Regarding the military experience, at first I wrote in English because I was under the impression that I would have a larger audience abroad. That wasn't the case, so I rewrote the books in the Portuguese language. Those books aren't exactly the same, because it's not just a matter of translation; I added new information. There's a book out about my mission in Angola, and two others about Bosnia. I have some writings about my mission in Afghanistan to publish later.

Regarding the geopolitics aspects, I'm collaborating with Professor Francisco Leandro from University of Macau in research of matters of geopolitics.

Meanwhile, I also became the Secretary-General of the Portuguese Air Force Veterans Association, where I have the pleasure to promote all kinds of cultural activities.

I left the Air Force's active duty due to a health problem. After having solved that issue, I thought it would be difficult for me to go from a very active life, into a very calm and steady life, staying at home and having nothing to do. But it turns out it's the opposite – now I have no free time.

AT THE HEART OF CONFLICT: TALKING RESOLUTION

Colonel Paulo Jorge Machado Dias Gonçalves is a retired senior officer of the Portuguese Air Force, were he served for 39 years. He operated in a myriad of functions and tasks, including international engagements in EU Forces, NATO and the UN. During his military career, Gonçalves operated in 25 different countries, in the American, European, Asian, and African continents, including three civil wars. He served as an air traffic controller, defence specialist on chemical, biological, radiological and nuclear weapons, strategic communicator, and performed conflict observation and analysis functions for NATO, EU and UN. He operated as an electoral support staff member, and program implementer for the United Nations Development Program and was an advisor at the UNAMA, making analyses and assessments on Afghan regional and national governance, in order to identify best practices. Before retiring from active duty, Gonçalves was the Deputy Director of the Portuguese Air Force Instruction Department, and the Head of the Air Force's Documentation Services. He lives in Lisbon – Portugal – and currently works as an independent writer and researcher on international relations.

MARIA HADJIPAVLOU

Tell me about your work with "Hands Across the Divide" and now with the "Gender Advisory Team".

I got into conflict resolution during my PhD years. I was a postdoctoral student at Harvard, so I was trained by Professor Herbert Kellman who was, at that time, doing a lot of work with Palestinians and Israelis and introducing a special methodology that was based on the theoretical underpinnings of the social-psychological aspect of ethnic conflict and international conflict. When I experienced these processes and this methodology, I realized that's what I wanted to do in Cyprus.

After I returned to Cyprus, when we established the university here, I became what my professor had called a scholar-practitioner. I was the first one to introduce this kind of analytic perspective and tool in Cyprus. Of course, it was a very challenging risk because it was the first time that an analysis was given from an academic with theoretical perspective looking at both sides' experiences, fears, pain, suffering, injustices done, historical grievances, and so on. I had a lot of reaction because of this analytic perspective, not by colleagues or academics from abroad, but by political conservative forces on the island and even academics from the University of Cyprus where I was teaching.

One way was to become an activist as well, and to become involved in civil society work. Much of my research from the early years was both theoretical and applied. With Hands Across the Divide (HAD) until then, we were not really looking at the gender aspects of the conflict, but a group of women from both communities started feeling that the gender aspect was very important, looking at our Cypriot experience, and especially the war experience, the displacement, and how men and women experience these social phenomena differently. So, we started getting together, and we had the help, at first, of the feminist and activist with sound theoretical background, Cynthia Cockburn. Unfortunately, she passed away. She was a great friend of mine. She became interested in Cyprus and, with her help, we established Hands Across the Divide. We organised first, a workshop in which women from Northern Ireland, from Bosnia-Herzegovina, from Israel and Palestine were also invited to share their experiences.

The general theme was "What Can Women Do in a Divided Society?" It was in 2001. We went to London because we couldn't meet in Cyprus. There was no free contact then; we couldn't have a space where we could work continually. In London, with the help of Cockburn and some other colleagues from the diaspora, we established Hands Across the Divide and collaboratively wrote the constitution, our principles, our values, and the kind of work we wanted to do. It was very difficult to register in Cyprus because of the non-recognition obstacle, so we registered in England at first.

Of course, later, in 2003, when we could meet across the divide, with the opening of some of the checkpoints across the green line, in the buffer zone, things became a little bit easier. It was the first independent bicommunal women's organization in Cyprus. Until then, we didn't have one. The activities of Hands Across the Divide initially had to do with both trust-building workshops, sharing experiences, street activities, and one of our issues was how to pressure the leaders on both communities to sit at the negotiating table and at that time, because we couldn't meet together, we would meet outside each leader's home and simultaneously express our desire and demand a solution. I published two academic papers on the work of HAD in international journals as well as research on women's experiences in all Cypriot communities.

What are the challenges regarding getting these two different communities talking to each other?

It's related to the political environment in which we work but also the international environment – how events in the region and in the stakeholders outside Cyprus, Greece, or Turkey for instance, or the UK, impact the life and work domestically in Cyprus. It's a series of challenges. One of the first was that by doing this bicommunal work, this peace across the divide, it was viewed as a threat. We were really taking a risk at the beginning. The Turkish-Cypriot leadership viewed these meetings as a threat to their political position that Greeks and Turks of Cyprus cannot live together.

So, by working together, by doing projects together, creating new alternatives to the official narratives, this was really breaking down these myths of Greeks and Turks not being able to coexist. On the Greek-Cypriot side, we were a threat especially amongst conservative and nationalist circles that we demoted the international aspect of the conflict, which was defined as a conflict and violation of international law, of foreign invasion and occupation of the island. By working together, it was perceived as undermining the international aspect. But we were saying there are multiple levels of work that need to be done, and one of these levels, yes, it's at the international level, diplomatic level, but it's also important at the societal level. Living separately now for half a century, a lot of social issues need to be addressed.

What kind of social issues?

Fear, mistrust, issues also of mutual understanding, of getting away from putting all the blame on one side, and saying "My side was really only a victim." This was one of our earliest and biggest challenges, especially as women, because we live in a very patriarchal, nationalistic, and militaristic environment.

What would a good solution for Cyprus look like?

A good solution is one that is mutually agreed by all interested sides. It will be one that will promote the federal spirit and values of coexistence, of cooperation, and of freedom from fear, as well as address the basic needs of people, like safety, security, and identity.

That's what we are talking about when we say bicommunal, bi-zonal federation, which means a central government with institutions that both communities will be part of. And then we have the two constituent States with their own autonomy in issues of culture, of development, and of local needs and competencies left from the federal level.

It will be a solution where we will all feel connected to Cyprus as our homeland and to our identity as Cypriots but also with different ethnic origins. On the island, there's not only Greek Cypriots and Turkish Cypriots, but also other communities: Armenians, Maronites, and Latins who also have rights and today the demographics have been changing and new communities are formed as well. The issue of citizenship is very important to be addressed in any future agreement or solution. Of course, gender equality should be part of the solution because the more gender equal a country is, the less prone to violence it will be. Gender equality, for me, is very basic to be ingrained in the future constitution and final agreement.

You've written about how Cyprus is a very patriarchal country. What impact does that have on the problem you're trying to solve?

We live in a culture of conflict. Us and them. Men and women, bipolarity. In a patriarchal society, usually, they're attributing different roles to men and women. This is becoming very sharp during the conflict and wartime. Men are being perceived as the ones who would go and fight, who would be also burdened with the duty to protect women and children. Women are viewed as the ones who will be protecting the family, the household, building communities after the war, and so on. This dichotomy really separates men and women and, therefore, leads to them experiencing war very differently.

We all know that in wartime, as in many conflicts, in Cyprus too, many women were sexually abused on both sides, especially young girls. Rape was very much one of the consequences, and this was an issue that was perceived as a shame issue, societal stigmatisation of these women, and they were silenced in it as in other conflicts as well. Only recently we started publicly talking about this issue.

Regarding nationalism, the roles attributed are very different as well. The women are viewed as the reproducers of the nation – to have more children, which is needed for the nation to survive and assert itself. This happens in many societies. The men are associated in nationalism with the state, where power lies, where it is the centre of decision-making.

Also, militarism is tied up in this. What is the masculine ideal: it's a man who is brave, strong, and courageous, who will fight and become a hero. But the woman who has been raped, humiliated, sexually abused – she is shamed by the nation. We don't give the same support and attention to the raped women as we do to the wounded men. What I am saying is that in conflict culture, patriarchy, nationalism and militarism reinforce each other. We need to work on all three levels for the conflict culture to be transformed into one of peace and gender equality.

What are the consequences of that cooperation between patriar-chy and militarism, and what does that mean for women's voices in a conflict situation?

It means their voices are not heard. They're marginalized, so that's why Hands Across the Divide, the Gender Advisory Team, and some other women's groups have been fighting to be heard because the Cyprus conflict is gendered and politics in Cyprus are a men's affair. But women need to be there. They have different views, different ideas to offer, different perspectives, suggestions and recommendations on the major issues under discussion at the negotiating table.

For example, how is governance viewed through women's voices? Women should be there. In a way, by promoting women's voices, we really unpack the issue of democracy. How does democracy work (or doesn't work) in a conflict situation? Why aren't women's voices heard? Why are they marginalized? Why are politics and negotiations concerned only with men's ideas and perspectives? We need to challenge that. As the Gender Advisory Team, we produced recommendations on all issues of the negotiations – governance, economy, property, citizenship and many others. We presented these recommendations to the negotiators and the international community and mention was made in the UN-Secretary General's reports on Cyprus but not much meaningful impact.

This is something we must really work hard for, there is research saying that when women participate in negotiations or the peacebuilding processes, the agreement reached lasts 35% longer than if women were absent. This tells us a lot about how patriarchal obstacles, which are, in the case of Cyprus, historical, social, political, psychological and structural, still hold women's voices apart.

What could women's voices bring to the conflict resolution process?

First of all, there is the big issue of security. In all conflicts, the issues of security and trust are very important. Until now, in Cyprus as in most conflicts, security has been dealt with in a very narrow, militaristic, and territorial perception and understanding, that is from a state-centric approach.We have six armies and seven flags in Cyprus. It's the most militarized place in the world, compared to its population. So, what does it tell us about militarism? We need processes of conflict resolution that are inclusive and transparent.

Women's presence and voices on issues of security will complement this discussion on bringing in human security, which deals with the everyday of people's lives. It is human-centered. Do people have jobs? Do they have safety in their neighbourhood? Do they have good education facilities? Good health services? Do they have clean air? Issues that deal with services for children and so on. This is human security. Why are they not talking about broadening the security issue when they are at the negotiating table? To this day, this aspect of human security in Cyprus' negotiations has not really been addressed, although we have been promoting it and making it a public issue.

You've written a lot about issues such as disappearances and people going missing for decades. What impact does that have in the negotiations and the conflict?

One of the most pressing humanitarian issues in conflicts is the fate of unaccounted-for individuals – those who were last seen alive but never returned. These individuals are classified as missing persons. In Cyprus alone, over 1,200 Greek Cypriots and around 600 Turkish Cypriots have been missing since the conflicts of 1963, 1967, and 1974.

This issue has often been framed in a way that feminizes pain and suffering, as if they are concerns only for women. On the Greek Cypriot side, women – daughters, sisters, and other relatives of the missing – have long stood along the Green Line, holding photographs of their loved ones and demanding answers. This began soon after the 1974 war, as families waited in vain for their return. By 1975 and 1976, it became clear that many were never coming home. Now, nearly 50 years later, the search for truth and accountability continues.

This issue was, of course, politicized, and it was used by the state very often and instrumentalised to promote the nationalist project which was to demonise the other and expose the brutality of the other. It happened on both sides, absolutely. Instead of addressing it as shared pain, which came later at the civil society level with a group called "Together We Can," which talks about that humanitarian situation, it was completely separate. It was us and them again. The Greek Cypriots did not know about the Turkish Cypriots' missing persons and vice-versa. For years. We really needed to raise this issue and these voices. This was a human right to know.

In the last few years, with the information coming again from people, citizens, given to investigative journalists, like Sevgul Ulutag, people would say where they saw there was a mass grave, and they would find different locations. With expert teams from the UN and third parties, they would start exhuming the bones. Now, there is still a process of identification. Relatives go and give blood to match DNA, and we have funerals on and off. This task should have taken place very early on. Not many of these families expected their loved ones were still alive. It was a trauma again. It's a big issue; there's collective trauma, and of course it hasn't ended. It's still going on. This is the other aspect of the gender considerations that we need to look into.

Has technology and social media impacted the way that the instrumentalisation you mentioned happens?

Yes, especially the younger generations use social media a lot to exchange information and to organize events and so on. We have now quite a few young people working jointly on issues across the divide, who share an interest in the arts, in the environment, in climate, in theatre or social issues such as domestic violence in LGBTQ issues. This is often helpful because the information is channelled through social media, and people gather very quickly.

This is very important for conflict resolution processes in Cyprus because it develops relationships, and in conflict resolution the relationship building is very fundamental. Bringing people together in conversation immediately humanizes the other. Through the other you learn a lot about yourself, and learning a lot about yourself and how you're perceived by the other, immediately develops a very different perception and eliminates a lot of the mainstream ethnic stereotypes that are usually engrained in the education system or in other politics. Social media play a very big role, and we had groups of youth for technology in the early years before the checkpoint openings. These are all mechanisms to promote conflict resolution and people-to-people contacts.

Is the education system promoting peace or, on the other hand, is each side pushing for the stereotypes?

Education is one of the mechanisms of every state to promote its own national identity, its own story, and its own selective glories and trauma. So, education can be a great mechanism for peace promotion and conflict transformation, but it can also be a conflict reproducer. The mainstream curriculum in Cyprus has been very exclusionary on both sides and also very one-sided, silencing many multiple truths and perspectives, giving only their own side, their own justice and victimhood, their own struggles.

There have been efforts by different civil society groups to change this. For example, many of my former students had established the Association for Historical Dialogue and Research, creating a multicommunal group for cooperation in the buffer zone. They do a lot of research on education, producing alternative materials for teachers and retraining teachers, especially history teachers, to bring in multiple perspectives to understand our situation in Cyprus, among other social issues. The struggle is how to make the literature and the cultural studies books as inclusive as possible, and to teach the students in high school what it means to have a critical mind and perspective, as well as how to look for different resources and empathize with each other's pain. At the same time, to teach appreciation of each other's talents, creative minds, and achievements, not just concentrating on what's bad about the others. Also, it is important to learn about other communities' histories and cultures like Armenians, Maronites and Latins.

In your experience with Hands Across the Divide and the Gender Advisory Team, how's the contact with the population on both sides like?

The issue of funding sometimes is a problem for us, as there is so little to produce materials or organize local events and training. We have been doing research at the same time, trying to see what women really think about the different issues. Our latest research that the Gender Advisory Team has engaged in, with participation of women facilitators from all communities, has been to use as our foundation some of the pillars from UNSCR 1325 on women, peace, and security.

We worked as a group of 14 facilitators for almost two years and then we went out into the communities and built networks with women there. We established a safe space and a trusting relationship by running dialogues. It's amazing the need on the part of women to share their story. They need to be heard and to have a voice in the different events and issues around them, be it at the local level, the community level, or at the national level.

One aspect was how to raise consciousness of their right to participate, to be visible, and to run for office in the local government so that they have a say when structures are built in their community and how money is allocated. One way of transferring what I said about starting to develop this new consciousness is to build networks and safe spaces for these voices to emerge and create spaces for empowerment.

I remember in one of the villages we went to, one woman was 90 years old and told me, "You came here, and you gave us a voice." She had waited all that time to have a space to talk about her own experiences and needs, like the fact that there is no bank in the village, no doctor, no facilities. These are some of our activities to open issues that are not very often addressed by the mainstream political elites, even by women. We have 56 MPs in the Greek Cypriot House of Parliament, only eight of whom are women. On the Turkish Cypriot side, with a total of 50, only around nine are women. They're not aware of all these complexities and realities in the non-urban areas.

At the Gender Advisory Team, we want to raise these voices, we want to make women's needs louder in order for policy makers to address them and gradually bring a better life to these women, increasing social and political change at the gender equality level as well.

Cyprus is an EU country, so is Greece, but Turkey is not. Does that impact the conflict resolution somehow? Does the EU intervene? Should they do more?

Cyprus joined the European Union in 2004, despite being an island that was not unified. This was a key opportunity to resolve the division and reunite the island before joining the EU. However, the acquis communautaire (EU law) does not apply to the Turkish Republic of Northern Cyprus, which is considered illegal by the international community. It is only enforced in the southern part of the island, where the Republic of Cyprus, governed by Greek Cypriots, has been in operation since 1964. In the north, it is Turkey that is really dictating all the policy of the administration there, and Turkish Cypriots are suffering limitations in their freedom or decision-making. The isolation of Turkish Cypriots is due also to occupation and to the embargo that was imposed because of the war and the illegal state that was declared in 1983 by the Greek Cypriot Government. There's a big dependency in the north of Cyprus on Turkey. All the economic assistance and their exports are via Turkey.

The Turkish Cypriots voted overwhelmingly in 2004 for the Annan Peace Plan and one of the reasons was to disengage from Turkey.

Now, the EU has had an office in Cyprus since 2005. They also allocate annually an amount of euros to the Turkish Cypriot community, to address issues of infrastructure, peacebuilding, reconciliation, and harmonizing policies. I think that was very good, and it should continue. But the EU could do more on the issue of the peacebuilding processes, especially in terms of preparing our communities, on both sides, for a solution and to build a culture for a solution. That means looking at how our mass media work, how, in the south, the church narrative is coming out in our education and other institutions. We have to revisit a lot of these narratives if we want to revisit the bigger goal for a culture of solution in Cyprus.

The EU can help with that, because of the values of the European democratic institutions. There's still a lot of work to be done. For us, I think it would make a big difference if those values were also applied in Cyprus, especially on the issues of reconciliation and the present global challenges that we are all affected by.

Do you believe issues such as global warming, which affect both communities equally, have an impact in the process of reconciliation? Can working together to tackle the global problems help with reconciliation?

Absolutely, because it's a shared interest. It's not our or their issue; it's a common issue. Unless we cooperate, we are both going to lose. In that respect, now we are promoting a lot of these issues. Environmentalists protest at the digging of quarries in the Pentadaktylos mountain range in the Turkish Cypriot side which creates flooding when it rains. There's no resistance, and it floods villages and streets. It's making people's lives very difficult. The same is happening in the south with flooding and deforestation, and fires.

This is a shared environmental issue and, as we mentioned earlier, it would also help cooperation, while building relationships of coexistence. That could happen through different organizations, NGOs, with EU funding and support. I think, by sensitizing the local communities and changing our lifestyles and becoming much more respectful of the environment and of our species here – Cyprus could really be extremely beautiful, with a healthy environment to enjoy, without all the tall, unregulated buildings and the destruction of the environment that has come along with that.

There are two huge conflicts currently going on, between Russia and Ukraine and in the Gaza Strip. Can they have an impact on how the international community looks at the situation in Cyprus?

Of course. We are not a very urgent situation, compared to these conflicts, especially the invasion by Israel in Gaza and the continuing of all the losses of innocent people, women, and children. This is going on and on. For us, it's next door; it's only half an hour's flight to Tel Aviv. We live in a very precarious and insecure region. This should make us even more determined to reach a solution here, where there are no killings or violence. People started, in a way, getting used to the status quo, but the status quo is never stable. It's continuously changing.

The UN Secretary-General has sent his personal representative here to explore possibilities for restarting the negotiations, and she has already visited Athens and Turkey. She is going to the EU and the UK to gather information. She will then make an evaluation and come back to the island in the first two weeks of March to consult with the civil society and hear more perspectives and voices before she makes a decision about whether there's ground for the resumption of negotiations. We have an opportunity and we really should embrace it. We are interdependent in Cyprus. We are not separate communities. If we remain separated, we both lose, continuously. It's a zero-sum game if the separation continues and we want a win-win result.

Maria Hadjipavlou is a distinguished scholar and practitioner in gender and conflict resolution. She was an associate professor at the University of Cyprus (1995-2013), where she pioneered courses on gender and conflict resolution. A feminist and expert in her field, she has taught internationally, including a popular course on 'Conflict Resolution Theory and Practice' at Bogazici University in Istanbul. As a visiting scholar at Columbia University (1996-97), she co-founded the Center on International Conflict Analysis and Resolution with Andrea Bartoli. She has also been a post-doctoral fellow at Harvard University, where she contributed to the Program on International Conflict Analysis and Resolution. Maria has founded or co-founded several NGOs promoting peace and reconciliation in Cyprus, such as Hands Across the Divide and The Peace Center. She has trained women globally on gender, peace, and conflict resolution for organizations like UNFPA and WINPECE. Her book *Women and Change in Cyprus* (2010) is widely referenced in the field.

JOHN HOLMES

You were awarded the Military Cross. Can you tell us what that was for?

I was a platoon commander in the Scots Guards at the time, and we had responsibility for West Belfast just after internment for four months – so from about August 1971 until December of that year. It was a time of huge unrest. The battalion took high casualties, five dead and more than 30 seriously wounded. It was a very active time from the terrorists' point of view. My company was stationed in Ballymurphy, and had responsibility for Ballymurphy, Whiterock, and Turf Lodge, which were all Catholic areas – Republican areas.

On this particular evening, a large crowd of about 350 people gathered at the Turf Lodge roundabout, which was a bypass going around the housing estate itself. But it was a favourite place for protesters to gather. I was sent with three men – there were four of us altogether – to watch events at the roundabout, not to interfere at all. We were on operational patrol, sitting in a hedge about 150 metres back from the roundabout, up on a hillside, just reporting back on what was happening.

After about an hour, two Ferret scout cars drove up the road towards the roundabout. They obviously had no knowledge and hadn't been warned that there was a large crowd waiting for them up ahead. They saw the crowd and did three-point turns to head back. Unfortunately, the rear wheels of the lead Ferret scout car, in doing a reverse for the three-point turn, went over the embankment, and it bottomed out. It couldn't move any further. The other Scout car moved off. We were left with a scout car and 300 screaming Republicans.

The commander of the scout car, it's a two-man crew, opened the turret, stood up, looked around, and immediately slammed it shut again as the 300 people milled around wondering what they were going to do about this scout car. It was clear that they were going to do something pretty drastic; they had the wherewithal. They couldn't have pushed it further, but they could set it alight. They could certainly, one way or the other, kill the two soldiers inside. There was no time for reinforcements or anything like that. This was all going to happen very quickly. Reinforcements would have taken 30-odd minutes to get there. So, I did the obvious thing, or the only thing, which was to yell to my three compatriots, "Follow me".

We rushed down through the field to where this was all taking place, fired some shots over the head of the crowd, and then laid into them with our rifle bats. As it happened, I think they thought there were more than four of us. The crowd scattered and withdrew under gunfire from the nearby block of flats. They had friends up there who were in a position to give covering fire. And, after a couple of minutes, there we were standing alone in the middle of the road having gotten rid of the crowd. We got the two Ferret people out of the armoured car and reinforcements arrived. It became rather a long evening of one thing or another, but that's what happened.

That's being at the right place at the right time and having the courage to deal with the situation.

It was one of those times when you either do something or you do nothing. There's no compromise. The extraordinary thing was the three soldiers followed me. It was clearly a mad thing to do. When I said "Follow me", they knew exactly what was going to happen and they followed. That's priceless.

While you were serving in Northern Ireland, did you believe that, at the time, a negotiated settlement was possible?

I think everyone realised that a negotiated settlement of some kind was the only way forward. This is sovereign territory. I don't think there was ever any feeling that the Republicans could win secession in any way like that. Negotiation was out front from the start. You only need to read the political side of what was going on at the time to realise how determined some politicians were to get a political settlement. It was drummed into us, as soldiers, that we were supporting a political process. We were in support; we were not the lead.

In terms of conflict resolution, in practice, do you think that what you were taught in the military differs from what you've experienced over the course of the years? If so, how?

It's actually a very good question, because our training for that deployment in 1971 was based on colonial-type thinking. How did we control crowds and rioters in the colonies? In those days, a body of soldiers would march down the street with signs or posters and things; they'd hold their rifles. Eventually, if the rioters didn't withdraw, one would be shot. That's how things were done in those days. That was our training for Northern Ireland, in June/July of 1971. Completely and utterly, no context with what it was actually like.

But, to be fair to the army, that's how they had been trained and they handled themselves well in colonial situations like that over the years. We didn't know any better, and it was radically different once we got there. One adapted, and I think the great thing is that the British Army adapted very quickly, because it's no easy matter to adapt to policing your own streets. Particularly, you might say, in a Scottish regiment, which has strong ties with Ireland, family ties, and all that sort of thing. I think over successive years, the British Army excelled at handling those sorts of circumstances and learning when to become involved, learning how to deter and learning when to leave well alone, because we were in support of the civil power, and we were never allowed to forget that. That is always a very useful mantra if you're a serviceman. If you know that you're in support of civil power, it conditions how you react. Without that political overview, that's when I think excesses can occur.

You served as Director of UK Special Forces for two critical years, from 1999 to 2001. What were the missions that you are the proudest of, or that are important for you?

The highlight, although that's not quite the right word, is operation "Barras" in Sierra Leone for a whole raft of reasons. I can't remember the day of the week it started, but my immediate superiors were travelling. The soldiers were taken hostage, I think it was a Thursday or a Friday. I was a one-star officer, but I worked with the Chief of the Defence Staff, who was a four-star officer, through an appointment called DCDSC. The chain of command went one-star, three-star, four-star. And my three-star and four-star were both away. It was very foggy, and neither could get back. It was left to me and my immediate circle to get things going.

We not only did that, but were exceedingly well-supported by, for instance, the Royal Air Force, because it was clear that helicopters would be required. There were none in Sierra Leone at that time, or not the right type. And by the end of that day, the RAF had three Chinooks just about to take off to fly to Sierra Leone, which they duly did. That was very much a catalyst for everything that followed.

Can you recall any regrets about that mission, something that you wished you would have done or the setup that it would have been different?

The SAS units involved nicknamed it "Operation Certain Death" because it was a very bold plan, which succeeded. It's unusual for a director to deploy on an operation. Normally, a director would be back in London, with Cobra advising the Chief of the Defence Staff. But it was very clear to me from the outset – and I had been to Sierra Leone in the months previous, so I had a good understanding of how it worked – that the troops on the ground would need top cover down there. However, it transpired that this was going to be a very complicated operation, both militarily and politically.

You can imagine what the consequences would have been had the kidnappers taken their hostages, retreated further into the jungle, and we'd lost them. I mean, huge political implications there. That was very clear from the outset. Hence, my taking the decision on day one: myself and my little headquarters will go down there, and we will be the conduit for the commanding officer who will control the ground forces and make the plan and lead the assault and all that sort of thing. We will be the intermediary that interfaces with the Chief of Defence Staff and the politicians back home. That worked very well.

Every day, I'd talk to the Chief of the Defence staff and the thing went on and on. It was day eight or nine, we were getting concerned that they might move and, in our daily call, which was about midday Sierra Leone time, General Guthrie, Chief of Defence Staff said, and I will never forget the words, "John, this cannot be allowed to continue".

I knew him well, and I knew exactly what he meant. It had to be sorted. The assault was launched at first light the following day. But I'll never forget. He was a very political general. But if you knew him, his heart was always in the right place. He was absolutely right. If they had moved their position further into the jungle, it could have gone on for weeks or months, with all the political ramifications that would involve.

So, Operation Barras was my highlight, if you like, as director. We lost a soldier and people were killed. So, I don't mean it in a triumphant sort of way.

Do you think it is acceptable, and to what extent, for a country to deploy drones or special forces in foreign countries to go after targets? And I'm thinking about for example, when the US sent special forces to kill Osama Bin Laden.

I think that's a very legal and constitutional issue. Some countries will find as America does, that they can do that sort of thing. Whereas other countries, I think, would be shy of it from the legal standpoint. It's not really my side of things. What I would say as passing comment, is if you're going to do that sort of thing, it must succeed. There is no halfway house.

If it succeeds, then you can demonstrate you've taken somebody out who deserved to die for whatever reasons. If it doesn't succeed, it's going to be messy. Innocent people will probably get hurt. To date, America would appear to have gotten it right. Whether the UK would be prepared to do that sort of thing, I have no idea. I suspect not. Because there would be constitutional legal-type issues that the government of any hue wouldn't particularly care to deal with. And after 9/11, you know, who can blame the Americans?

Do you think mediations and diplomacy are important to resolve a conflict?

I think, ultimately, use of the military can only be in support of the political scenario, whatever it is, in that particular country. If you lose sight of that, then you will have enormous problems, because ultimately, all conflict is politically based. There's no grey area. You might not agree with the harsh opinions sometimes, but they are political opinions. And so they can all only be solved politically. Military solutions, by themselves, rarely succeed. In fact, I can't think of one that has succeeded in the long term.

From your experience in conflict zones, what are some of the highlights in terms of the negotiations being successful?

The war in Dhofar was concluded by military means very much in support of the political party of the Sultan at the time. It's a long time ago, so I'm not sure if you know a lot about Dhofar, but it was a communist insurgency against the then Sultan, who was an old-fashioned despot effectively, and took little interest in Dhofar, which is the southern province of Oman.

Hence, the insurgency.

It was resolved very effectively by carefully controlled military action, internationally. British forces, Iranian forces (funnily enough), Baluch battalions, and Omanis, from the North. But they were very much in support of the political process. I had two tours out there and I would say categorically, it was the victory of politics, supported by the military, but it was a political solution. And it's worked, Dhofar is now a thriving, rich province of Oman.

Politics is not a short-term solution. Politics needs time to build, to coalesce, to come together. It's very easy, in the military, too early on in a conflict, to dismiss the politics as ineffectual or whatever. The mere fact that there are politics is a good sign. How you bring it all together. And what's going on in Israel and Gaza now, is a prime example. You might argue that politics has failed there, to date. But what is going to solve the problem? It's not the military. It can only be a political solution.

What do you think about the value of private armies in conflict?

I think it's a very complicated question to answer, to be honest. The academic answer would be private military companies acting in support of the legal government of a country are probably a good thing, because they will be given jobs that the regular forces are unable to do, whether for resources or whatever reasons.

Of course, nothing is that easy in the private security world. Because you could argue that the Wagner Group, in support of five sub-Saharan governments, is doing exactly that. But it's not a good thing because it's fleecing the country of its reserves; it's a law unto itself, and is essentially sustaining dictators in power.

There's a spectrum...?

Take the American invasion of Iraq, the second Iraq War, as it were. I was advising a private military company. We arrived in Baghdad a week after the American military, along with a few other security companies. We were immediately embraced and made part of the security structure because the American military did not have the numbers and the wherewithal to do everything.

We were given, I remember, responsibility for securing various parts of the oil industry, which was important to the country, not only to the Americans, so that these installations weren't pillaged and destroyed, but were kept relatively safe. In those circumstances, private military companies do a very good job and an essential job. But we were very much part of the American military legal piece. There was no opportunity to be independent and quite rightly so.

How are the private military forces used to combat terrorist groups such as ISIS?

I think you've come back to the legality of the whole thing, really. Not surprisingly, with my background, I wouldn't consider doing anything that was outside the legal envelope. Private military companies should always operate within that legal envelope. That envelope will differ from country to country and differ from situation to situation. I don't think there's a one-size suits all panacea there.

Should private military companies be governed?

There are lots of grey areas. The aid agencies in particular normally have a view that all private military companies are murderers, robbers, et cetera. We want nothing to do with them. They ignore the fact that quite often it's those companies that allow them the versatility to distribute whatever aid it is that they've got. I mean, you've hit the nail on the head, really, because you've been referring to private military companies. Private security companies wouldn't have such a ring about it.

A lot of these companies are just security companies. They're not guarding nightclubs in London, but they are guarding government buildings in wherever. I think one has to draw a line between the two. To me, a private military company is one that does military things as opposed to security things.

Do you think it's possible to resolve conflicts in places like Yemen and Sudan through negotiation?

There are some countries in this world where ending violence and ensuring a democratic way forward is very difficult. In empire days, the British had a very good way of dealing with parts of the world that they couldn't contain. They just marked them on the map as tribal areas.

If you go back through the history books, some of the biggest tribal areas were in Afghanistan and Yemen. I've got friends from those areas, and some parts of their societies are, I believe, probably irreconcilable. But setting those sorts of countries aside, I think any country that has undergone some form of democratic, liberal government at some stage can always be brought back in, but it's a political process.

Recently there was news that the Wagner Group had split – some were in Ukraine, others back in Africa. What impact are they likely to have on political situations in Africa?

You have to park the Wagner group. At the end of the day, it's, I don't know, 10,000-odd mercenaries. The scale of things in Ukraine is such that they are incidental as to how things will turn out militarily. They do their bit. Yeah, the media, I think, unwittingly, focused on them too much after the failed coup – or whatever it was.

At the end of the day, it goes back to what we said at the beginning of the interview. There's got to be a political process, and that means engagement with Russia. Now, the present government in Ukraine rules that out. I would suggest that going forward, it will have to change its stance on that. That doesn't mean giving in to Russia. It doesn't mean ceding territory to Russia. It does mean talking to Russia.

Ukraine is lucky to have the support of the international community, although not so much in its provision of arms and ammunition now, which is vitally important. But going forward, it is the international community who will somehow broker some sort of ceasefire and an end to hostilities.

One could well imagine parts of Eastern Ukraine that are currently under Russian occupation, perhaps being put under a UN mandate of some kind. I don't know.

My point, though, is they will have to talk. All we're seeing, at the moment, is both sides trying to get themselves in a position where they would hold the whip hand at any subsequent negotiations. I don't see either side getting to that point, certainly this year. We shouldn't lose sight of the fact that, ultimately, the longer it goes on, so Russia's strength will increase. At the end of the day, it's all about resources and manpower. The West would have to change its involvement in the long term in order to deter Russia, because Russia is getting stronger. Ukraine, I would suggest, is holding its own, but holding its own only.

Looking at the broader realm of your work in the intelligence field and investigative work. What are the biggest challenges?

In fact, I do very little really in that field now, although I'm still consulted with sometimes. I have some very different interests now. All I'd say there is that I've been lucky to have a very interesting career, both militarily and as a civilian. There are parts of the world that I've been to as a civilian that I'd never go to in the military at all. I've really enjoyed it, but I am better placed now as a consultant with a lot of experience. My strength now is to be able to stand back from situations and give advice based on experience.

How do you think AI will impact the future in terms of the potential military capabilities?

Good militaries are best placed to differentiate between the pros and cons of artificial intelligence because their lives depend on it. That's a statement of the obvious, I know. But it's right that civilians are easily swayed by technical progress. Militaries are much slower to embrace technical progress because lives are at stake. More than lives: policies, and all sorts of things.

It's a slow-moving edifice, really, the military, in any country. It's well placed being a slow-moving edifice to differentiate between the pluses and the minuses, but also in terms of becoming involved in conflict. Of course, some of the great technical advances in the world have come directly from conflict.

I would expect that to be the same in AI, and I suspect the origins of AI lay somewhere deep in the militaries of America or wherever. But I'm not being critical of the civilian world. It's the civilian world that embraces these things quickly and takes them forward, and is able to, if it doesn't work, reject it and move on to something else. But I think there will be ups and downs with AI in the civilian world. We invented it, we can control it. I don't think it's a demon at all. But there again, I would say that – I'm old.

With climate change and the increasing desertification of the Middle East – all the natural causes that give rise to conflict – how do you see that playing out in Africa and the Middle East?

More of the same. Your question is very political because it's all about politics at the end of the day. Climate change will have dramatic effects in some parts of the world, and the world as a whole must be aware of that and be prepared to assist. But when you look back at the Middle East, there aren't many countries with a 500-year-old history there. In fact, very few. Egypt, Oman, Iran – if we go that side of the Gulf, that's about it, really. It's still quite a young area politically.

Do I believe in global warming? Yes, I do. But I also believe that the global community is capable of dealing with it, and that common sense and in all these things will normally prevail. Even the Chinese will realize at some stage that opening a new power station every month is probably not helpful.

Major General John Holmes joined 22 SAS Regiment from the Scots Guards in 1974. He subsequently enjoyed a full UK Special Forces career including serving as the Special Operations Liaison Officer at the British Embassy in Washington DC, running the Special Forces Policy Desk in the UK Ministry of Defence, commanding 22 SAS from 1989 to 1992 (a period which included Gulf War 1), commanding the UK Airborne Brigade from 1993 to 1996 and subsequently serving as Director of UK Special Forces, during which time he commanded Operation Barras in Sierra Leone in 2000. He opted for early retirement in 2002 and completed Project Unicorn, a counter-terrorist study for the Metropolitan Police and in 2003 he joined the Board of Erinys International. Subsequent to Gulf War 2 he was instrumental in creating a 15,000-man Oil Protection Force with its own air wing for the Coalition Provisional Authority. He resigned from Erinys in 2008 to concentrate on other projects.

COREY LEVINE

What first inspired you to pursue a career in human rights and peacebuilding that would take you to various conflict zones? Can you share an early experience in your career that shaped your approach to this work?

That's an interesting question. I wouldn't say there was a single moment of inspiration – it was more something I fell into. But I've always felt drawn to supporting those on the margins of society, people who, through no fault of their own, lacked the privileges I had as a white, middle-class Westerner.

One defining moment for me was watching the war in Bosnia unfold on television. It was the first war I remember seeing broadcast in real time, where human rights violations were happening right in front of our eyes. It was shocking. Later, I had the opportunity to go to Bosnia myself, and that experience changed everything.

At the time, I had been working in Prague. I moved to what was then Czechoslovakia in the early 1990s, just after the fall of the Berlin Wall. I think it was 1991 – that really dates me. I was working for a trans-European NGO called the Helsinki Citizens Assembly, and I was sent to Bosnia on their behalf.

Like in many war zones, the banking system had collapsed, making it nearly impossible to get funds to the organizations we were supporting. One of those organizations was in Tuzla, a city fighting to remain multi-ethnic despite the ethnic cleansing happening all around it. The mayor was determined to keep Tuzla a place of coexistence, and local NGOs were working hard to support that vision.

But without access to funds, they were struggling. The only solution? Deliver the money in person.

And so, my first real job in this field was as a money mule. I smuggled $20,000 in cash from Prague into Bosnia, traveling to Tuzla to hand-deliver it. I remember thinking, *Well, this isn't your typical nine-to-five job.*

That was probably the moment I realized this was the kind of work I wanted to do. More than anything, that experience shaped my worldview. I saw firsthand the incredible humanity that can exist in the midst of inhumanity. I spent days traveling alone, trying to get through Croatia and then into Bosnia. I took buses, hitchhiked, hired taxis – whatever it took to get there. Along the way, I met the most extraordinary people, people who, despite the war, showed kindness, resilience, and generosity.

That lesson has stayed with me ever since: in times of crisis, ordinary people are capable of extraordinary courage. Some rise to the occasion, while others exploit the chaos. That contrast is something I have seen time and time again in conflict zones around the world.

What made you want to work in Afghanistan, and what was your first impression of the country when you arrived in 2002? Has it changed over time, and if so, how? Describe your role and your initial expectations – how did those expectations align with the realities you encountered on the ground and evolve over time?

Once again, it wasn't that I actively sought out work in Afghanistan – the opportunity simply presented itself. At the time, I was working as an advisor in the peacebuilding unit of the Canadian International Development Agency (CIDA). When the Taliban fell and the international community began its engagement in Afghanistan, I was sent there to assess how Canadian tax dollars could best be used to support peacebuilding efforts.

With no formal Canadian diplomatic, defense, or development presence in Afghanistan at that time, I had the rare opportunity to explore the country freely. I spent a month traveling across Afghanistan – visiting Mazar-i-Sharif in the north, Jalalabad in the southeast, and several other regions. The only major areas I didn't visit at that time were Herat and Kandahar.

My first impression was that Afghanistan was a country deeply scarred by decades of war – about 40 years at that point. Yet, what struck me even more was the optimism among the Afghan people. Despite everything they had endured, there was a genuine sense of hope – a belief that this could finally be the moment for change.

That initial experience set my expectations: I saw a country ready to rebuild, and I believed that the international intervention could help steer Afghanistan toward stability. However, over the next twenty years, I watched how everybody got it wrong. What started as a hopeful intervention gradually unraveled into failure, leading to the tragic return of the Taliban in 2021.

At the beginning, it wasn't obvious that things would go off the rails, but within a couple of years, the cracks in the approach became clear. And from then on, I had the dubious privilege of witnessing, firsthand, the systemic failures of the international effort in Afghanistan for the next two decades.

After my first mission for CIDA, I returned to Afghanistan several times, working with different NGOs. Eventually, I was hired by the United Nations Assistance Mission in Afghanistan (UNAMA) – the civilian peacekeeping mission.

At first, I was seconded to the Afghanistan Independent Human Rights Commission, serving as a technical advisor on women's rights. Later, I became the Gender Advisor for the mission, reporting directly to the Special Representative of the Secretary-General. I held that position for about a year and a half before returning to Canada.

Over the next decade, I continued my engagement with Afghanistan in various capacities. In 2008-2009, I worked again with UNAMA, running a political rights monitoring project. After that, I worked with Amnesty International, where I conducted a report on the growing threats against women human rights defenders. And then, in 2020-2021, I returned to Afghanistan as part of UN Women, where I was seconded to advise Afghan women parliamentarians. My role was to help them develop a roadmap for addressing women's issues, including peacebuilding, economic empowerment, and political participation. I left six weeks before the Taliban takeover in August 2021.

After I left Afghanistan in July 2021, I started receiving frantic messages and calls from Afghans I had known for years – friends, former colleagues, and especially the women parliamentarians I had just been working with. They could sense the end was near, though nobody realized how quickly it would happen. They were desperate to escape.

At the time, the Canadian government had already announced a program to support Afghans wanting to leave — primarily those who had worked with the Canadian military. But Afghan women parliamentarians argued that, while they hadn't worked directly with Canada, Canada had funded their participation in public life – particularly in politics and governance. They felt they had a legitimate claim for assistance.

When the Taliban officially took over on August 15, 2021, the floodgates opened. I suddenly found myself immersed in assisting evacuations, working non-stop to help Afghans at imminent risk – not because I had planned to, but simply because it was the right thing to do.

Since then, my life has been consumed by this work. It wasn't a calculated decision or a career move; it was simply a response to a need. The same instinct that first led me into this work – what can I do to help? – is what has kept me in it. I've never spent much time strategizing my career path; instead, I've always followed the need and done whatever I could to assist. That, I suppose, is the common thread running through my work.

Why are you risking your life helping Afghan women escape life under Taliban rule, and what made you decide to become a voice for Afghan women? Was there a particular moment that defined this choice?

Honestly, it wasn't something I planned or consciously decided – it happened in real time as the situation unfolded. It started with people texting me, sharing their fear and desperation, telling me about the horrors they were facing. Many of them were complete strangers, reaching out because they had nowhere else to turn.

I remember thinking, how could I not at least try to help? I was sitting in the comfort of my own home while they were facing an immediate, life-threatening crisis. So I started doing whatever I could from a distance.

But at a certain point, things got stuck. The initiative I had been working on with Afghan women parliamentarians – helping them escape – was facing obstacles, and I realized that if I really wanted to make a difference, I needed to go back to Afghanistan and help in person.

It wasn't an easy decision, and I understood the risks. But it felt too important not to go back. When you know you have the ability to help, when people are reaching out in fear for their lives, you don't stop to weigh the pros and cons – you just do what needs to be done. That's what has kept me going, and it's why I continue this work.

In your fieldwork, you often operate in challenging environments that require navigating complex situations. How do you apply conflict resolution or mediation skills, especially when engaging

with individuals who may be responsible for human rights violations against women?

This is such an important question. When working in complex environments, you inevitably come face-to-face with individuals who are responsible for human rights violations. One of the most critical things to understand is that, in order to make progress, you have to set aside your own personal politics and judgements.

It doesn't help to go in with an aggressive or confrontational approach, berating people for their actions. The reality is, those individuals are often still in power, and if you want to assist those at risk, you have to be willing to negotiate with them. The key is to stay focused on the larger goal rather than getting caught up in personal feelings toward the individuals you're dealing with.

What I mean is, it's not about the specific person sitting across from you – it's about what you're trying to achieve. You have to be able to engage in conversations with people you would never want to socialize with, people whose actions you deeply oppose, while maintaining a sense of openness.

For example, if you have thousands of internally displaced people in urgent need of shelter, food, and protection, you will need to negotiate with those in power to get them the assistance they need. No matter how much you may resent or oppose their actions, they are the gatekeepers to critical resources. That's the reality you have to work within.

In my work, I regularly engage with individuals who have either ordered human rights violations or carried them out under someone else's command. Navigating these conversations requires a strategic mindset and a great deal of restraint. The only way to successfully negotiate any kind of support for those in need is to remain engaged, open, and as non-judgemental as possible – at least in the moment. It's not easy, but it's necessary.

What tactics have you seen used by insurgents or terrorists involving women and children, and how has that affected your work and advocacy? How did you cope?

That's a really complex question. What I have seen most often is the aftermath of these tactics – whether it's sexual violence, displacement, ethnic cleansing, the use of child soldiers, or human trafficking. I've seen the impact on individuals, families, and entire communities.

The tactics used by insurgents and terrorist groups are rarely just about harming an individual. Their purpose is far greater – they aim to break down families, destroy communities, and dismantle social structures. That's the larger strategy behind these violations. Witnessing these effects has only strengthened my sense of urgency for advocacy. It has reinforced my belief in the importance of mediation, even with those responsible for these atrocities, because finding solutions requires engagement – even when it's difficult.

Coping is another challenge altogether. Everyone copes in different ways, and like many others in this field, I haven't always coped in the healthiest ways. I've learned that acknowledging those struggles is part of the process, but I also work actively to develop healthier coping mechanisms.

One of the most important lessons I've learned is knowing when to step away. I used to spend prolonged periods in war zones, but I've since realized that staying too long can lead to a point where you're no longer able to function effectively. I've made a conscious decision to limit how much time I spend in high-intensity conflict areas, recognizing that sustainability in this work requires balance.

It's essential to have a support system, to take care of yourself, and to give yourself breaks. It's easy to feel like you need to take on everything, but no single person can carry it all. Change happens through collective action, and for individuals to be part of that change, they have to take care of themselves first. That's something many of us forget, but it's a crucial part of staying in this work for the long haul.

It can be difficult for the international community to grasp the challenges faced by women in Afghanistan. What is commonly misunderstood about the experiences of Afghan women, and how do you bring awareness to those so far removed from the situation?

One of the biggest misconceptions, not just in Afghanistan but in conflict zones in general, is how women are perceived. Women are often grouped together with children, and both are seen primarily as victims. While it is true that Afghan women and girls are living under the world's only gender apartheid regime and face extreme oppression, what is often overlooked is their agency – their resilience and their ongoing acts of defiance, no matter how small.

In the first few months after the Taliban takeover, women were out on the streets protesting. But as it became too dangerous – with women being beaten, arrested, and even disappeared – they had to find different ways to resist. Some turned to social media as a platform for protest, while others took to more discreet but equally powerful forms of resistance.

Every day, Afghan women are finding ways to push back against the system. Some are trying to earn a living to support their families despite restrictions, while others are running underground schools to educate girls, keeping alive the progress made during the period known as the Republic – the time between 2001 and 2021 when the Taliban was not in power. These acts of defiance don't always make the headlines, but they are happening all the time.

The international community tends to focus on the Taliban's oppressive policies, and while it is crucial to address these human rights violations, it is equally important to highlight the resilience and rebellion of Afghan women.

To bring awareness, I engage in public speaking, write articles, and share these stories whenever possible. My goal is to show the complexity of Afghanistan, not just the suffering, but the strength and determination of its women as they continue to fight back in ways that the world doesn't always see.

Can you share a story from your time working with Afghan women that highlights both their challenges and resilience?

When I was in Afghanistan a year ago, I met some truly incredible women who were not only trying to support themselves but also finding ways to help others. One woman, for example, had received funding from the UN and used it to teach other women poultry farming. She distributed chickens and a rooster to a group of twelve women in her village, all of whom were either widows or had no male relatives to support them.

Even though she herself was not allowed to officially run the organization, she found a way around the restrictions. Her brother and husband became the public faces of the initiative, handling negotiations and paperwork with the Taliban. Meanwhile, she was the one actually teaching these women, most of whom were illiterate, how to become self-sufficient.

I met another woman who had started a restaurant exclusively for women, employing only female staff. It became a rare space where women could gather freely. The Taliban largely left them alone, occasionally checking in to ensure no men were present, but for the most part, they were able to operate. I'm not sure if that would still be possible today, but at the time, it was a small victory.

These are just a few examples of the ways Afghan women continue to resist, adapt, and survive under an impossible system. Their creativity and determination don't take away from the cruelty and brutality of living under gender apartheid, but they do prove that even in the worst circumstances, they find ways to fight back.

What was the most difficult decision you faced in Afghanistan, and how did you navigate it? Is there anything you wish you had done differently?

There were many difficult decisions I faced in Afghanistan, but one that stands out was when I was working as a gender advisor with the UN. One of my colleagues in a field office brought me a case of a young woman whose life was in immediate danger.

She had been secretly involved with a young man, despite having been promised in marriage to an older man, which is a common practice in Afghanistan. When her family discovered the relationship, they killed her boyfriend and were preparing to kill her as well. In many parts of Afghanistan, as in other parts of the world, the concept of honour and shame is deeply ingrained, and in these situations, it is always the woman who is blamed. The way to restore family honour is often through an honour killing.

She came from a powerful family, but she had managed to go into hiding. She found temporary refuge in the home of the provincial governor's family, and his assistant reached out to the local UN office for help. That's when the case came to me.

I had no idea what to do. There was no official system in place to help her, and seeking assistance through formal channels could have easily led to her being found and killed. I turned to a colleague at UNHCR, and together, we quietly negotiated behind the scenes with another country's UNHCR office. In an operation that was entirely off the books, we managed to get her out of Afghanistan. That country later accepted her as a refugee, and she was able to rebuild her life there.

It was a difficult decision because we used *only* back channels, and while it saved her life, this is not a sustainable or scalable solution. You can't handle every case this way. It was kept completely quiet, and while I don't regret the decision itself, I do wish I had been able to address the larger, structural issues that create these situations in the first place.

Helping one person is important, but unless we work toward broader systemic change, we won't make a lasting difference. That's what weighs on me the most – not just the individual cases, but the realization that for every person saved, many others remain trapped in the same cycle.

What is the most significant change you've seen in Afghanistan over your 20-year engagement? Do you think it's sustainable, and how has the role of women evolved during that time?

The most significant and most sustainable change I have seen is the transformation of women's roles in Afghan society. Even though the country has now reverted to a draconian system under Taliban rule, the fact remains that Afghan women and girls have been educated, have gained empowerment, and have learned tools for self-determination. Once that genie is out of the bottle, it is incredibly difficult to force it back in.

The stories I shared earlier – about women resisting in small but powerful ways – illustrate something that didn't exist when the Taliban was first in power. Women today have experienced a different Afghanistan. They have lived in a world where they had education, careers, and a voice, and that awareness cannot simply be erased. However, sustaining this change depends on the international community's willingness to support these acts of rebellion and resistance.

If we fail to do so, these hard-won gains will be erased within a single generation. Women and girls are now being forced back into purdah, confined from the time they reach puberty until old age, silenced and made invisible. The international community made real, tangible changes in Afghanistan, but those changes are at serious risk of being wiped out.

I appreciate the ongoing efforts to hold the Taliban accountable under international law. Cases being brought before the International Criminal Court (ICC) and the International Court of Justice (ICJ) regarding the creation of a gender apartheid state are crucial. We need those legal precedents in place for the future.

But the question remains – what does this mean for Afghan women right now? It's hard to say whether these legal efforts will make any difference in their immediate lives because we are dealing with a regime that has no respect for international law.

That's why we need to find other ways to support Afghan women. Their resistance is still there, but without international support, it is at risk of being crushed. The world cannot turn its back on them now.

When the Taliban regained control over the country, how did that impact your work and your perspective on international intervention? Were there moments when your outlook on the global community's role in Afghanistan fundamentally changed? What do you see as the future for women in Afghanistan if the current political situation persists?

My outlook on the global community's role in Afghanistan had already changed long before the Taliban regained control. Within two years of the initial international intervention, I could see that they were making the same mistakes that I had witnessed in other conflicts.

From the very beginning, the US and its allies empowered the wrong people. Their approach was simple: anyone who had opposed the Taliban was seen as an ally. But many of those very individuals were warlords and powerbrokers who had played a direct role in leading Afghanistan into decades of conflict. There cannot be true justice without accountability, and that was never properly addressed.

We saw something similar in Bosnia, where some of the deep-rooted local conflicts could be traced back to unresolved issues from World War II. Afghanistan was no different – historical grievances and cycles of violence remained unaddressed, yet the international community failed to recognize that. While Afghans themselves bear some responsibility for their country's downfall, I would argue that much of the failure – perhaps three-quarters of it – can be attributed to the way the international community handled the intervention.

As for the future of women in Afghanistan, if the current political situation persists, their rights will continue to be systematically erased. However, the knowledge, education, and empowerment that Afghan women gained over the past 20 years cannot be undone entirely. Women are still resisting in small but significant ways. The challenge now is whether the international community will step up to support them or allow their struggle to fade into the background.

What role do you think the international community should play in supporting Afghan women and peacebuilding initiatives moving forward? At the local level, do you believe there is a local nonviolent path forward, or does the context necessitate other approaches?

There always has to be a nonviolent path forward. That being said, I am not someone who believes that nonviolence is always the only way to address conflict, especially when violence is being imposed on people. However, if there is going to be true peace, it cannot be achieved through violence. Sustainable peace built on violence never works in the long run.

The problem with international interventions, including in Afghanistan, is that they are often top-down. The international community comes in with big plans, imposing their own structures rather than supporting organic, locally-driven initiatives. But real change has to be built from the bottom up. There is absolutely a local, nonviolent path forward, but it is extremely difficult to pursue when dealing with an authoritarian regime like the Taliban.

This raises a difficult question – how do you support local, nonviolent initiatives when an authoritarian police state is in power, especially one that is also under sanctions? Most Afghans, particularly women, believe that international support for Afghan individuals and communities is still necessary because the humanitarian crisis is so severe.

Of course, some of that aid will inevitably fall into the hands of the Taliban – that is the reality of working in a country controlled by an authoritarian regime. This is similar to the challenge of negotiating with human rights violators. There is always a risk of legitimizing them by engaging, but the bigger question is: what is the ultimate goal? If withholding aid means that millions of people starve, is that really the right choice?

I firmly believe that while morals, ethics, and politics are important, the realities on the ground require us to make hard choices. If you focus too much on ideological purity, you risk losing sight of the broader goal – helping civilians survive. The more international actors engage with and support Afghan civilians and local communities, the more empowered they become to resist and create change from within.

That being said, engaging with Afghan communities does not mean recognizing or legitimizing the Taliban. There is a clear distinction between supporting aid and development inside the country and empowering the Taliban through diplomatic recognition. Some countries have failed to make that distinction – Japan, for example, recently hosted Taliban leaders who were on a no-fly list, treating them as legitimate state authorities. That is not the path forward.

The international community needs to find ways to provide aid and assistance directly to Afghans without legitimizing the Taliban as a governing body. That is the challenge. And while I don't have all the answers, I do know that complete disengagement is the wrong approach. The worst thing the world can do is turn its back on Afghanistan and leave its people to suffer in silence.

You've worked with organizations like the UN and Amnesty International. What have been the most effective strategies for advocating women's rights in Afghanistan?

There is an important role for both intergovernmental institutions like the UN and NGOs like Amnesty International, as they each have distinct but complementary functions. The UN operates at the governmental level, engaging with institutions to support, advise, and strengthen them. This kind of diplomatic and structural engagement is key to ensuring long-term policy changes and institutional reforms. However, organizations like Amnesty International are equally important because they mobilize grassroots activism, which is critical for holding governments accountable and raising global awareness.

For example, when I was conducting research for Amnesty International, my report was tied to a larger advocacy effort that included diplomatic engagement, public awareness campaigns, a documentary film, and a photography exhibit that toured internationally. This combination of strategies helped bring global attention to the issues Afghan women were facing.

One case that stands out is when Amnesty highlighted the story of a Mullah who had raped a three-year-old girl. Amnesty launched an international campaign demanding justice, making it their "case of the month" and urging people around the world to email Afghanistan's Ministry of Justice. The response was overwhelming – hundreds of thousands of people sent emails demanding accountability, and the volume was so massive that it crashed the Ministry's email server.

At one point, I was in a meeting with officials from the Ministry of Justice, and the deputy minister asked us to tell Amnesty to stop their advocacy. He said, "We've got the point, but please ask your organization to back off. We will pursue this case."

That moment demonstrated just how powerful grassroots activism can be. While high-level diplomatic engagement is necessary for shaping policies and institutional change, public pressure from global activism can force governments to take action, even when they might otherwise resist. Both approaches are necessary, and when they work in tandem, they can be incredibly effective in advocating for women's rights.

Did the use of private military contractors in Afghanistan help or hinder peacebuilding? How do you view outsourcing conflict resolution to private entities? Given the strides under international law to regulate private military contractors, do you think these regulations are effective? How can they be improved?

One of the main reasons Afghanistan ultimately failed after 20 years was that the international community empowered warlords who maintained their own private militias. While there was talk of disarming them and integrating their forces into national security structures, in reality, very little was done. These warlords continued to operate independently, undermining national institutions and governance.

One example from my early time in Afghanistan stands out. I met a warlord who gave me his business card, which identified him as the commander of a military campaign in southern Afghanistan. His private militia controlled a significant portion of the region. At the same time, he was appointed as a representative to the Loya Jirga, the first Afghan assembly that was tasked with selecting representatives before official elections were held. Later, he became the governor of his home province, where I met him again.

He took me to his private landing strip, which was later discovered to be a hub for smuggling antiquities out of the country. When I asked him how he funded his private militia, he simply said, "The Americans." I asked whether it was from the military or development agencies, but he didn't know. All he knew was that once a month, someone arrived at his compound with a trunk full of cash because they saw him as a useful ally against the Taliban.

The result was entirely predictable. As governor, he ruled his province like a personal fiefdom, completely disregarding national institutions. Corruption thrived, governance collapsed, and when he was eventually fired by the president, his province was one of the first to fall to the Taliban. His dictatorship and lack of cooperation with national structures created so much instability that the province was left defenceless.

Another example involves a UN fact-finding mission sent by the Office of the High Commissioner for Human Rights (OHCHR) to investigate the role of private militias in Afghanistan. The team went to meet with the American ambassador, but the US had outsourced much of its security to private military contractors. These contractors, who controlled the outer perimeter of the secured area, detained the UN fact-finding team. They searched them, searched their vehicle, and tied them up. It took direct intervention from the ambassador to negotiate their release. If that intervention hadn't happened, I'm not sure what the private security firm would have done with them.

This shows how little institutional control existed in Afghanistan. The president was often referred to as "the mayor of Kabul" because his authority rarely extended beyond the capital. Warlords, militias, and private contractors operated autonomously, making governance impossible.

From my perspective, outsourcing conflict resolution and security to private contractors is dangerous. International law has made efforts to regulate private military forces, but those regulations remain largely ineffective. The problem is not necessarily a lack of laws – it is the lack of enforcement.

As someone with a master's in international human rights law, I firmly believe in the necessity of legal frameworks. The real challenge is not just drafting laws but ensuring they are implemented. The international legal system has been systematically weakened for years. Certain states, including democratic ones, have flouted international law with no consequences. Israel, for example, has consistently ignored international rulings, yet the global community has taken little action.

This is the crux of the problem. If there is no real enforcement, then international law is meaningless. The United States, for example, has refused to sign on to the International Criminal Court (ICC), and even those that do are often unwilling to recognize its authority. If powerful states refuse to be held accountable, how can we expect laws governing private military contractors to be effective?

Sure, these regulations can be strengthened, but without real enforcement mechanisms, they will remain ineffective. If the global trend continues toward authoritarianism in democratic countries, we will likely see even further weakening of the international system. At this point, I am not very optimistic about the future of international law, particularly when it comes to regulating private military forces.

How do you define "peacebuilding" in today's world and who are the key players? What does the term mean to you personally, and how does it manifest in modern conflict zones?

To me, peacebuilding is not just the absence of war, which is often how peace is traditionally defined. Instead, it is about building a sustainable peace – one that is rooted in strong, legitimate institutions that people trust and are willing to engage with.

For real peacebuilding to happen, national and regional institutions must be seen as legitimate by the population. If people do not view these institutions as fair and capable of governing their lives, then peacebuilding simply does not happen.

The key players in peacebuilding include a wide range of actors at different levels:

Civil society at the local, national, and international levels plays a crucial role. Civil society organizations help hold institutions accountable and ensure that they remain transparent and responsive to the people.

The international community, including the UN and bilateral organizations, has a role in supporting, advising, and strengthening national and local institutions. This can happen through diplomatic, development, or even military engagement, but only if it is done with the goal of reinforcing local governance rather than overriding it.

The people within these institutions are also critical. Are they willing to engage in a way that supports development and governance, or do they undermine it through corruption?

Corruption is one of the biggest obstacles to peacebuilding, and Afghanistan is a prime example of how it can destroy any efforts toward stability. Corruption was a key factor in the collapse of Afghanistan, and the international community largely turned a blind eye to it. There were numerous anti-corruption commissions and initiatives, but they never truly tackled the root causes.

At its core, corruption thrives in environments where poverty is endemic and accountability is lacking. If development efforts do not reach the grassroots level, and if local power imbalances are not challenged, then peacebuilding remains impossible.

To me, peacebuilding is not just about negotiating ceasefires or reducing violence – it is about ensuring that people have a system they can believe in, one that allows them to build a stable future. Without that, any peace will always be fragile.

Is there a systematic approach or framework in peacebuilding? If so, how does this guide the strategies, interventions, and outcomes in conflict-affected regions?

You have to start with local community buy-in. Without it, there is no sustainable peacebuilding. Peace cannot be imposed from the top down; it has to be built from the ground up. It also has to be inclusive, meaning that all ethnic and religious communities, men and women, and all segments of society must have their voices heard and included in the process.

Too often, inclusion and grassroots peacebuilding are just lip service. In practice, they are rarely prioritized. The international community tends to throw money at the problem, believing that financial investment alone will fix things. But unless they are willing to do the hard work of engaging communities and recognizing that peacebuilding is a long-term process, the efforts will fail.

Building institutions takes years – often generations. It is not something that can be accomplished in a one- or two-year project cycle. Yet time and again, the international community approaches peacebuilding as a short-term endeavour, expecting quick results.

One of the biggest mistakes is the belief that holding elections automatically leads to stability and legitimacy. In Bosnia, in Afghanistan, and in many other places, the international community pushed for elections as a milestone of success, assuming that once people voted, the country would be on the path to democracy. But elections alone do not create functioning institutions or ensure public trust in governance.

Western capitals want to see measurable outcomes, often within the short timeframe of a funding or project cycle. But peacebuilding does not work on a six-month timeline. It might yield real results in 25 years, but not in six months. If there is no patience for long-term investment, then the entire approach is flawed from the start.

Did you have any mentors/people you looked up to in this field? Did/do you engage with fellow conflict resolution specialists? If so, who and how?

The people I looked up to in this field weren't necessarily conflict resolution specialists. Instead, they were diplomats or grassroots activists who approached their work with commitment and integrity and were unafraid to challenge those in power when necessary.

One person who stands out is Richard Bennett, who is now the UN Special Rapporteur on the situation of human rights in Afghanistan. He was my boss for about a year when he led the Human Rights unit for UNAMA. I watched him work to ensure that any activity, event, or program was genuinely owned by Afghans. He made sure their voices were heard, that there was real buy-in, and that efforts weren't just imposed from the outside.

He was able to negotiate with key stakeholders with both integrity and respect, but at the same time, he never hesitated to call out corruption, political shortcuts, or expediency when they were getting in the way of long-term engagement. Too often, international interventions prioritize short-term political wins over meaningful, sustained efforts, and he was one of the few people willing to push back against that.

Another person who comes to mind is my UNHCR colleague who helped me get a young woman out of Afghanistan, despite the personal risk involved. She was willing to put her job on the line to do the right thing. Those are the people I admire most – those who don't just follow protocol but are willing to take real risks to ensure that their work has integrity and impact.

Having worked in multiple conflict zones, what common lessons have you observed about the role of gender and women's rights in conflict?

One major shift I have observed over time is how women are viewed in conflict zones. When I first started working in this field, women were largely an afterthought, often lumped in with children. That has changed, and it is now recognized that women and girls face distinct challenges separate from those of children and youth.

However, as the language around gender has developed, it's also become easier to pay lip service without doing the actual work. There has been an explosion of gender advisors and specialists in organizations like the UN, but the presence of these roles doesn't necessarily translate into meaningful change. Women are still excluded from key areas where they need to be included – particularly in leadership and decision-making spaces.

Women are often hired into roles related to human rights and development, which are considered "softer" areas, but they remain underrepresented in the upper echelons of power. While this is beginning to shift, it is still very much a male-dominated space at the highest levels. Looking at who is placed in leadership and decision-making roles is critical to understanding whether real change is happening.

Another issue is the siloing of gender programs. When gender is treated as a separate category rather than fully integrated into broader policies and initiatives, it can have a detrimental effect on the inclusion of women's rights in governance, security, and peace processes.

Language is another major challenge. Many of the terms used in international gender discussions – such as "gender mainstreaming" – do not have direct translations in local languages like Dari, Bosnian, or Krio. In many communities, the concept of "gender" is misunderstood, often interpreted as an effort to give women special privileges at the expense of men. This kind of miscommunication can create resistance and backlash, making it harder to implement meaningful reforms.

This issue is not limited to conflict zones. Even in places like the United States, we see political backlash against gender-focused policies when they are perceived as being imposed from the top down. In conflict settings, this kind of externally driven, Western-centric approach can be especially damaging.

To be effective, gender-related efforts need to be rooted in the realities of local communities. Instead of imposing terminology and frameworks that may not resonate, the focus should be on understanding existing gender dynamics and working within those structures to empower women in a way that leads to real, sustainable transformation rather than simply displacing existing power structures, which will inevitably lead to backlash.

How do you approach training soldiers and officials on sensitive issues like conflict-related sexual violence?

When I worked in Mali, I served as the international humanitarian law, gender, and human rights advisor for a European Union military training mission of 550 personnel. I was the only female civilian on the team, and part of my role was to develop training for Malian soldiers on key issues such as international humanitarian law (the laws of war, including the Geneva Conventions), human rights, women's rights, and conflict-related sexual violence.

Sometimes, I conducted the training sessions myself, and I have to say, the soldiers taught me far more than I taught them. What I quickly realized is that our international humanitarian laws are outdated. They were designed for a different era – where two opposing forces met on a battlefield – rather than for the kinds of conflicts we see today, where civilians make up the vast majority of casualties and where non-state actors often play a larger role than national armies.

Many of the Malian soldiers were poorly equipped, often illiterate, and sent into incredibly complex combat environments. During training, they would raise difficult but valid questions about the realities they faced in war. For example, when I explained the legal prohibition on targeting civilians, they asked, "How do we know who is a civilian and who isn't? The enemy dresses as civilians, they attack us and other civilians, and then they disappear into the streets again. What are we supposed to do?"

Another common concern was the prohibition on attacking schools and hospitals. They would say, "What if non-state actors have taken over a school or a hospital and are using it as a base? If we cannot target them there, how do we defeat them?"

These are incredibly difficult questions, and to this day, I still don't have fully satisfying answers. The laws of war assume a certain structure that no longer exists in modern conflict.

That being said, these justifications can also be exploited. The same argument – that militants operate from civilian areas – is used by governments to excuse bombing hospitals and schools, as we've seen in conflicts like Israel and Palestine. So while it is true that non-state actors exploit protected spaces, it is equally true that this rationale can be used to justify unlawful civilian targeting.

When it comes to conflict-related sexual violence, the issue becomes even more complex. Sexual violence has been used as a weapon of war for centuries, not just as an attack on individuals but as a tool to destroy entire communities. It is one of the most effective ways to break social structures, instil fear, and control populations.

Addressing this issue in training is difficult, but it must be done. The best approach is to frame it within the broader discussion of rights – the rights of individuals, the protection of communities, and the responsibilities of armed forces under international law. Soldiers need to understand that conflict-related sexual violence is not just an unfortunate by-product of war; it is a war crime, just as much as targeting a school or a hospital.

While we have made significant progress in strengthening the legal framework around this issue, there is still much work to be done. What we need are not more gender advisors, but more prosecutions and accountability. State and non-state actors alike must understand that engaging in conflict-related sexual violence will result in serious consequences. Without real enforcement, the laws remain just words on paper.

What advice would you give to those entering the field of human rights advocacy, focusing on women's rights in conflict zones?

I think this goes back to the challenge of working in conflict zones where you often have to negotiate with individuals who are human rights violators. One of the most important things to remember is that you need to check not only your politics at the door but also your assumptions.

Too often, I have seen advocates enter the field believing they already know what is best – what should be said, how issues should be framed, and how advocacy should be conducted. But the reality is, you are not the expert on someone else's life. The people whose rights you are advocating for are the real experts. They know what they need, and they should be the ones setting the priorities. Your role is to amplify their voices, not dictate the message.

Successful advocacy requires consistency, transparency, and communication in a way that is understood at every level – from grassroots communities to top diplomatic circles. Messages should be clear, concise, and compelling. Advocacy is, in some ways, similar to advertising. You need to persuade people to care about an issue, to take action, or to provide support. And to do that, you have to frame the issue in a way that resonates with them.

This is particularly true for women's rights, which can be more controversial in many societies. You cannot rely on language or frameworks that are unfamiliar or alien to the communities you are working with. You can't bring high-priced advisors (although I have been one myself) who don't have an understanding of what's really going on on the ground. You need to ensure that what you're offering is going to be something that the individual, the group, the institution that you're advocating to wants to buy into. It's as simple as that.

Unfortunately, high-level advisors, no matter how experienced, often lack a real understanding of what is happening on the ground. It is critical to ensure that advocacy efforts align with what the affected individuals and communities actually need and want, rather than what external actors assume is best for them.

Ultimately, advocacy must be something that decision-makers, communities, and institutions can buy into. If they do not see the value in what you are advocating for, they will not engage. Advocacy is not about imposing ideas but about finding ways to make people want to be part of the solution. It is as simple as that.

Corey Levine is a human rights and peacebuilding advocate, researcher and writer. She has spent more than 25 years working in conflict areas, including Bosnia, East Timor, Iraq, Kosovo, Mali, Palestine, Sierra Leone, Sri Lanka and Ukraine; and has worked with both non-governmental and intergovernmental organizations. She has also taught at the UN University for Peace in Costa Rica, the Kofi Anan Peacekeeping Centre in Ghana and Carleton University's Norman Paterson School of International Affairs in Ottawa. In March 2002, she travelled to Afghanistan for the Canadian International Development Agency in order to determine Canada's peacebuilding support after the fall of the Taliban. This began a 22-year and counting, engagement with the country. She is the recent recipient of the King Charles III Coronation medal and the Wallenberg-Sugihara Civil Courage award for her work in assisting Afghans at-risk.

SIMON MANN

Why did you decide to join the army?

I think I was about 14 or 15, and I needed to do something. I had a first cousin who was one of the very first people in the Special Air Service (SAS). He was a bit of a hero of mine and a bit older than me. So when I found out what he was doing and how it all worked, that's what I wanted to do.

In your career, what kind of missions did you undertake and is there one that you're most proud of?

Well, I was in the British Army for 12 years altogether, and I went to Northern Ireland five times with the British Army. I did five tours, and that was just basically Northern Ireland. Not very exciting, but quite hard work. Northern Ireland was not pleasant because of the political and social situation. I'd say it was more like dangerous police work as much as it was soldiering. We were shot at, occasionally. We did shoot back even more occasionally.

Most of the time it was pretty boring, pretty dangerous, and very routine. It was mainly patrolling. Obviously, doing that with the SAS was a step-up in terms of excitement because we were in plain clothes. We were closer to doing things – at least I hoped.

Then, Angola was where we started. I was there because I was with an oil and gas company. This is all in my book, but we were there on a gas project, and we got attacked basically by the National Union for the Total Independence of Angola (UNITA), who decided that they were going to go back to war.

They did so against all the treaties and promises that they'd made and signed. The United Nations and the international community accepted the results of the November 1992 election, so it should have been a peaceful transition. That election was the result of a huge effort going back to the Crocker plan to get everyone out of Angola. Because as you probably know, Angola was the worst of all the proxy wars of the entire Cold War.

When I say it was the worst, it was statistically the worst, in the sense that there were more tanks destroyed, more aircraft destroyed, more this, more that, more the other thing. It was a real war and horrible for the people of Angola. It came almost as a part of their war of independence, and by 1992 when the election that I've just referred to took place, they had been at war for 30 years. So my partner Tony Buckingham and I, we were both just horrified that UNITA had taken this position and action.

In fact, I had met General Zavimbi, the head of UNITA, shortly prior to the election when I saw him with Lord Steele, the senior UK liberal politician. We saw Zavimbi, and he said, "Look, guys, I promise you that whatever happens at the election, we're not going back to war." And he did go back to war.

At that point, we decided that we would fight back. They captured our operating base at a place called Soyo, on the mouth of the river Congo. Our men there had to flee for their lives.

Our equipment had been captured and our business was now in grave jeopardy. We thought we were totally justified in fighting back. I mean why should we accept that kind of thing and why should the people of Angola? So, we suggested to the Angolan government that we would retake Soyo. They were a little bit surprised but quite quickly agreed that this was a possibility.

We then went down to South Africa where, because I'm half South African, I knew the right people, one of whom was Eeben Barlow, who had a dormant company called Executive Outcomes. We asked: Will you be our subcontractor? We were an oil and gas company, so we thought we'll get those guys to do it, like they are a drilling contractor. And that was the beginning. It wasn't actually the beginning of Executive Outcomes because Eeben had already formed it, but it wasn't really doing anything. We brought the contract from Angola, which was the beginning of Executive Outcomes as a serious mercenary outfit.

We had a victory at Soyo that was a great success. The Angolans were thrilled, and they asked us if we would help them with the broader war, which they were, at the time, losing. We thought about it very hard from all sorts of angles and decided that we would help them. That then actually led to the ceasefire, which really signalled the end of the war. In terms of the war being won, it was largely Executive Outcomes that achieved that, obviously, together with the whole Angolan armed forces. We were very instrumental in that and that was an amazing thing to do. I'm proud that we basically ended a war. I said, "Look, the way to end this war is to win it." That's obviously not exactly everybody's step one in the peace book, but the poor Angolans had been through many, many steps in the peace book already.

The UN was utterly useless. Somebody needed to take charge of the situation. You had a classic problem where UNITA were never going to be strong enough to take Luanda. There were four million people in Luanda, and they were all armed. They were not going to take Luanda. At the same time, the MPLA government, who were in Luanda, only owned the major cities. They were never going to have the strength in the countryside. I mean, 80% of the country was UNITA. So, that's the whole tragedy in Africa, often.

I don't want to sound trite, but the wars are badly organized. They don't have the logistics, and they don't have the real material capability. So then, the war just drags on and on. Look at the DRC today. They've been messing around there. For the people, it's the worst possible situation; they've just got this endless war. Anyway, so I'm proud of that. We ended it, and at the same time we got involved with Sierra Leone, which was a much lesser conflict, but we also helped to bring that to an end.

Then, we were told we were getting too big for our boots, and we should all pack up.

Do you think that the Bougainville crisis could have been resolved without violence? Going into it, what were you thinking?

It was resolved without too much violence because we didn't get to carry out our operation. If you remember, we didn't get that far. But our thoughts were that, as far as we could tell, the Papua New Guinea government had made many efforts to resolve the problem. Okay, they may not have been very clever, but they had made many efforts. The Bougainville side had killed a couple of policemen, a couple of soldiers, I think.

We sort of felt that if this had been an island off the coast of the UK, would it be legitimate for the UK government not to let that go? Yes. Is it legitimate to use force if the people there have used force against our own troops? Yes. So, we didn't see any political big issue, really.

We acted like the police in a way, and we actually saw it more as a kind of police action than a military one. But on the other hand, we knew that the people there were armed. It's a bit like throwing somebody out of a nightclub. You're much more likely to hurt somebody if you're not very strong. If four really good bouncers throw out one drunk, the drunk isn't going to get hurt, nor are the bouncers. If one bouncer tries to throw out a drunk, it's a fight, you know what I mean? And anyone can get hurt.

It's better to be certain. And we were, in no way, able to be certain. You probably know what happened, that we actually didn't do it because there was an attempted coup against the government. Nothing to do with us, and everyone was arrested and sent away. I wasn't there at the time. I was in South Africa because by then we had started a company called Diamond Works, and I was told by the others in the company that I had to run Diamond Works and not go to Papua New Guinea. Our mining manager had been killed and someone had to take over. So, I got the job knowing nothing about mining.

Would replacing Obiang as President have fixed Equatorial Guinea's problems? Could it have led to a non-violent solution?

The President who we were dealing with before the attempted coup was pretty reasonable. He had his head screwed on, more or less. That doesn't really answer the question, but I think the answer is I don't know. The Wonga coup, as it became known, seemed to be based on getting ownership of natural resources in specific areas – in this case, natural gas and oil.

Do you think that's a valid reason for a regime change?

Well, no, I don't. In fact, that wasn't the plan. If you look at who owns or who are the operating companies for Equatorial Guinea, none of them are Equatorial Guinean. That was true before the attempted coup. So the licenses wouldn't have changed had we been successful. The people who are there now would have had the same blocks, the same licenses, the same terms and conditions. It wouldn't have changed.

What have you learned from any unsuccessful military action?

You could use the word failed. It's fine. I am a very minor amateur mountaineer. I've done quite a bit. But if you get me to lead a mountain expedition, whether it goes well or whether we fail, do not expect me to turn around easily. So and so has hurt his foot, and the avalanche conditions are a bit dangerous, and the weather forecast isn't good. I would just say, "Well, we're here to climb the mountain, not worry about this kind of stuff."

Mountain leaders of that sort can get into terrible difficulties. I knew we were pushing the boundaries very hard because we had to, otherwise we were going to have to cancel the operation. I didn't want to do that. Undoubtedly, there's no question I should have cancelled the operation. ties. I knew we were pushing the boundaries very hard because we had to, otherwise we were going to have to cancel the operation. I didn't want to do that. Undoubtedly, there's no question I should have cancelled the operation.

In your military career, what was the most difficult decision you had to make and why?

Well, the most difficult decision was to go or not. Should we pack it in, or should we go for it, and I made the wrong decision.

Did your involvement in private military action change your perception of the world?

I don't think so. No. I think if you've been a soldier for 10 to 12 years, then your mindset, your view of the world, I don't think it's going to change if you join a Private Military Company (PMC). However, there are certain things that you have to get your head around, such as you now need to make money rather than just spend it. So yes, that's a difference. And some people don't really make that transition very well. If you're in the army, there is no commerciality. You have no idea how much your tank costs or how much it costs to run or anything like that.

I mean, you probably do if you go to staff college and they'll teach you, but it doesn't naturally come into your head because it's not part of the equation. You've got a job to do, and you've got to do it. In the army, people just say, it's a big firm. It doesn't matter if you just crashed a Land Rover or something. That's too bad, we've got another one. Whereas in private military contracting, suddenly everything is affected by the bottom line. Actually, that's a very difficult equation to manage because military decisions, which very often can be life and death, don't become easier if you also have the commercial prerogative going on.

I can give you an example. In Sierra Leone, we had two MI17 support helicopters, and the guys were desperate that we should have a third. The argument was that if one's down or one's busy and there's a casualty, we may not have medivac capability and someone might die. Now, a new helicopter, I think, was going to cost at the time something like $300,000 and $50,000 a month to run. And that's coming straight out of our pocket. We had to say, "No, you've got to make do with two." They were expensive enough. So, it's a very tricky argument, but I would say that in terms of answering your question, your view of the world is the same. But, if you go into a PMC as opposed to the army, you've now got to put on another couple of layers in terms of the things that didn't happen in the army. The whole money thing, the PR thing, all those aspects suddenly are now additional layers of complexity.

In fact, a lot of mistakes that get made in the PMC world happen because the people in that world are used to operating and thinking as a part of this very big machine, and suddenly it isn't there. You were Special Forces. Wow. You used to parachute, you used to jump at night into the sea and into the mountains. You guys can walk on water. I don't think so.

But anyway, if you're lacking the infrastructure that is around you when you're doing those things in the army, it's a very different story because where is your back-up? Who's packing the parachutes? Who is doing all the logistics and the service support that we just took for granted? If that helicopter comes down, even from mechanical failure, how are we going to get everyone out? Where is the Quick Reaction Force to do a search and rescue, possibly in enemy territory? And I mean, that sort of stuff gets really expensive.

We can take it back to the climbing analogy. Let's say in the British Army or in the American Army or any other army, if you are Special Forces, you are meant to be special. So that then introduces a sort of 'Gung ho' belief: "Well, we can do it. We can do what you have to do."

I remember we were in a Puma helicopter in the RAF and the pilot turning around saying, "You've got too much stuff on this helicopter. It won't fly." And the SAS troopers, myself included, looked at the pilot and said, "Just pedal harder." And the pilot said, "It's physics. This helicopter can't take off with this weight on board."

We're used to pedalling harder and getting the stuff up the mountain, just through determination. But pilots don't have the same outlook. I'm both a pilot and an SAS trooper, so I understand the constant conflict between physics and the determination to get the job done.

Is private military action a valid method of conflict resolution or a last resort?

A last resort isn't a method. A last resort is the last resort. First, I think any soldier knows very well that violence is the last resort. We don't do violence unless it's absolutely necessary. I mean we're not there to do it because we feel like it. When I was in the SAS's anti-terrorist team, we had hostage situations. And we knew that we would not be used unless every possible other way had been exhausted.

It meant just waiting and waiting and waiting. We would wait forever. If there's a hostage situation and stronghold, we'll just sit it out if that's the way. The trigger for us was if the terrorists started killing a hostage or hostages. Once that starts, then violence is permitted because under common law, it's self-defence and under self-defence, you are allowed to defend other people. So, violence is justified at that point.

Soldiers really do understand that very well. There are a lot of people who have a really romantic notion of war, unfortunately, but anyone who's been in one knows there's nothing romantic about it at all. Violence is absolutely the last resort.

I think people do sort of get muddled up with this, but you can have an armed private security company in many parts of the world. Your use of violence and those weapons will be covered by a set of rules, which will be basically all about self-defence – and only self-defence.

Now they could be, let's say, something like Aegis or Blackwater in Iraq. They're a private military company, and the people in it are probably all ex-soldiers, but not necessarily. They will fight, defensively. For example, they're there to escort the ambassador from here to there. If they get ambushed along the way, they are going to fight. But that again is different from, if you like, what I would call the mercenary band like we had in Executive Outcomes.

We didn't say we were going to secure anything. We were asked to help them win the war, and we said we would. And I became a General in the Angolan armed forces and all the men in Executive Outcomes were signed up into the Angolan armed forces and we were there to fight. We weren't there to protect things. We were allowed to take offensive action on our own initiative.

In my mind it's pure semantics, but you can have a Private Security Company, you can have a Private Military Company, and then you have something else, which for the sake of argument, let's call it a mercenary band. They're mercenary soldiers, they are there to fight the war, they're not there to secure things. That's a very important differentiation because if you take that last step, then I think you have to be part of the armed forces of that country because, otherwise, what is your moral and your legal position? It's very dodgy.

If I'm not a member of the armed forces, and I go on an aggressive mission and I kill somebody, I can be accused of murder straight off by that person's family, for example. What's your legal basis for doing that? You have to be able to say, "No, well, I'm actually a member of the armed forces. In the 17th, 18th and 19th centuries, they dealt with this by the Letter of Marque. A ship could sail under a Letter of Marque, which meant it was a king's ship, even though it wasn't part of the navy. The Letter of Mark, if you were captured, was the difference between being hung as a pirate or being treated as an officer.

If you lost the Letter of Marque, that would have very severe consequences. That takes us straight into one of your other questions, and it doesn't really matter whether you're PSC, PMC, mercenary band, or regular soldiers. If you commit an atrocity, it's an atrocity. What's the difference? It isn't about what label people are sticking on you, it's about what you do. Your actions are what matter.

What do you see as the main sort of challenges in conflict resolution, whether we talk about Africa or other regions, and have they changed over the years? Has it become more or less challenging with technological, political, and military developments?

That's difficult to answer, really. Obviously, the technological challenges do change things. Humans are very complicated, aren't they? Is it more complicated now because everyone knows what's happening? It's very hard to hide things now, and I think that's probably a good thing in terms of conflict resolution, because it's hard to do things in secret. People are greedy for money. People are greedy for power. They always have been. Things are going to happen because of greed. Now, if it's all going on in the dark, all sorts of things can happen that the world doesn't know about. That's getting harder and harder and harder.

It was very interesting for us in Angola. Remember, we're talking here about a long time ago. Our involvement with Angola was sort of 1993 to 1997, and our involvement with Sierra Leone was like '94 to '98. They overlapped, but there was a huge difference in that with Angola, it was sort of like, "Where is Angola?" Most English people have absolutely no idea where it is. It's huge and very wealthy and important, but people in the UK just don't know where it is. And it's not important to them. It's Portuguese-speaking. It's another planet.

When we were operating in Angola, we were operating on a massive scale. We had over a thousand men of ours in action at one point. No press, nobody even slightly interested, nobody pitched up in Angola. People knew, in certain quarters, what was happening, but that's it.

However, Sierra Leone was a much, much smaller affair. We only had 100 men there at the most at any one point, and there were UK press coming all the time.

I know some of them who are still friends, and they were sent to find out about us. They were sent with a very negative brief. Find out who these people are and what they're doing. They're mercenaries and this and that and the other thing. And we were confronted by that. It was weird that it happened in Sierra Leone but not in Angola.

Did it help either way?

No, it didn't make any difference. It was just a nuisance, really.

Africa is one of the continents that's been greatly impacted by climate change. Do you think that the desertification of countries is going to lead to increased conflicts?

Large-scale hardship makes the security situation more dangerous, because when people get desperate, they will do desperate things. There is a creeping desertification in the South of the Sahara Desert and the Sahel, which has been going on for a long time now. That region is particularly vulnerable, and it's very volatile at the moment. Mali, Niger, Chad, Burkina Faso – those countries are all in a state of turmoil with IS, Al Qaeda, Boko Haram, and all these organizations.

For those organizations, the Sahel is easy because the hardship is there, the life is so hard for the people and the governments are so weak. If I'm a JNIM commander and I go to see a headman of a village, it's very easy for me to say, "Look, we can pay your young men, give them something to do, build a mosque, build a clinic, build a school." We offer that, and they will accept. But why wouldn't they? I would if I was the headman.

Every time we see the government, it's just rape and pillage. It's bad army, bad police, bad government if we see them. So why would I not go a different way? I'm putting it in a very simplistic way, but that's what's happening on a daily basis all across the Sahel now. The desertification – the Cain and Abel lines – is moving. The Sahel is where those lines meet. It's where Islam meets animalists and Christians. It's where Arab Nilotic people meet African people. So, it is a line of great natural flux. Not necessarily friction, but change and movement. It's dangerous. The climate issue is going to make it a lot worse for a lot of people. It will make it a lot more dangerous.[1]

Are groups like ISIS and Al Qaeda getting stronger there?

Those groups have stated that they see Africa as their great play. They can see it. What our reaction should be, I don't know. It's difficult because we are not perceived well. We have to deal with all the neocolonialism, neo-imperialistic, the 'you're only here for the oil' stuff.

Do you think individuals with some monetary funds like Elon Musk and Ali Khalil should interfere in political conflicts?

Look at, for example, Wagner. Most of Wagner's revenue comes from oligarchs who want to defend their natural assets in the country. Of course, that's a very short step from, "Well, we'll defend you if you give us the natural assets."

In a way, we did that in Sierra Leone. We got a very fair wind getting the Koidu Kimberlite. We still had to go through all the normal procedures and everything else, but there was a lot of goodwill behind our bid for the Koidu Kimberlite diamond mine.

Now, that came about because we had not been paid, and we had basically helped them win the war. The Koidu Kimberlite was a known world-class diamond mine of immense value. Was Sierra Leone able to develop that on its own? No, not a chance. Would a Western company spend the $50 million, $100 million required to develop the mine and get it going? Yes, they would. But political risk and security are top of the agenda, so how are we going to achieve that? Immediately, you're into a chicken and egg situation.

It doesn't take the brains of an archbishop to work it out, that an entrepreneur will put in the $100 million, but he is going to sort the security out for you too. And the quid pro quo is that he gets the concession. Now, that is a very dangerous path if you think about it because you're very

---

1 Since this interview was conducted in December 2023, the Sahel region has experienced a surge in extremist uprisings and military coups, alongside escalating attacks by the main two groups of Al-Qaida-linked Jama'at Nusrat al-Islam wal-Muslimin and the Islamic State in the Sahel..

close to allowing a corporation to declare war.

Morally, it's an absolute minefield. But these are the realities. You have to be very careful if you're a stock exchange-listed company to get close to that sort of situation where you say, "We'll hire a PMC for your security if we get that gold mine." And that may not even be legal. So the conundrum remains.

This happens in the DRC, for example. You can have a gold mine there, and people do, if they have an army. There are Western companies running proper gold mines in the northeastern DRC, but to do so, they have to have all the licenses from Kinshasa, knowing full well that Kinshasa has no power whatsoever over the warlords and what's going on around the mine, up where the mine is. So another deal has to be done with the warlords.

You can argue it both ways. On one hand, yes, that's actually good for the Congo and for the local people because it is some work and some money, because otherwise they're not going to be there. But then it's just a constant war going on.

The moral arguments behind all of this are very difficult. If someone says, "Simon, what do you think?" I'd say, "I think it's much better if government troops sort this out. And if government troops can't sort it out, then allies should, but with regular troops." In the absence of that, then PMCs are going to step in. They're going to fill the gap. I don't think that's the best way of doing it; it should be done by local troops suitably trained, equipped, and helped by whoever (preferably by sovereign states). War and fighting should be done, if it's going to be done at all, by sovereign states. It's fine having a PMC guarding the ambassador or the embassy, but PMCs as serious military actors are not the best solution.

People have said to me, "That's really weird that you're saying that when you did what you did." But if I'm walking along and I see a house on fire, I will try to help the house-owner. And if the house-owner says, "Well, we've got a hell of a house, a hell of a fire here, can you help me put it out please?" I will say, "Well, yes, I can bring in my men and my firefighting equipment, but then you're going to have to pay me because they cost money."

So we can put the fire out, but I think that a municipal fire brigade is a better solution. The trouble is that the official fire brigade, especially if it's the UN, is useless. It's hopeless, and we've seen it many times. It's very good at administering itself, it's very comfortable, but because of the mandate they are given, it's normally impossible to stop the fighting. They're not allowed to shoot at anybody, and they're not allowed to do this and that and stuff, which makes getting the job done very difficult.

One thing I think you should be clear about is that PMCs are not the right people to do conflict resolution. PMCs can come in and act as the policemen to enforce a conflict resolution, but it's a bit like a hostage situation. We have professional negotiators. They are not part of us, and it's the politicians who are going to decide when to use us. It shouldn't be us that decide because there have to be these sorts of silos. Otherwise things get very out of balance.

For example, if we're thinking of a theoretical conflict, what are we going to do to resolve it? Well, don't immediately send in a PMC. Think about it. Negotiate. The negotiators, the people who could negotiate a conflict resolution, are not going to be the PMC guys. They won't be. It's a different mindset. You go back in history. That's why we have diplomats. Soldiers aren't diplomats. Sometimes we are asked to be diplomats, but it's not what we're good at.

Which leads to the last question. When you were in prison in Zimbabwe and Equatorial Guinea, did the British ambassador play any role in helping to get you released? And in general, do you view ambassadors as useful, as someone who plays an important role in getting hostages and prisoners out?

The British government was very much *not* involved in getting me out of prison. Or if they were, it was so far behind the scenes that they were invisible. That's the first point, and I'm certainly not complaining about that. Second, the British consulate, their responsibility is to look after you as a British citizen in prison, not to say whether you should be in prison or not. Just to ask, "Are you getting your letters? Or are they starving you to death? Are you being tortured?" and all that. So, when I was a prisoner in Zimbabwe and Equatorial Guinea the consular service was fantastic for me. In fact, in Equatorial Guinea, they had to fly from Lagos to see me because there's no embassy in Equatorial Guinea. The consular service was really good. But the ambassador, he represents the government. He has to be kind of a figurehead. Stand apart.

There have been situations in Africa where the consular office was closed for the weekend, and it was impossible to get somebody out of the country until Monday. Is this your experience too or are there behind-the-scenes movements that can happen over the weekend?

I think we're all a bit spoiled. I always look at things from a historical perspective. If you're doing stuff overseas, you've got to be very careful how you do it. If you want a sort of instant response to a problem, hire people who will get you that, locally. The embassy couldn't do it. They don't work like that. It's not really their job. For example, they will not even give you legal advice. They won't even tell you which lawyers to use. And I understand why they have to be like that now. At the same time, obviously, all sorts of things can be going on behind the scenes, and there's a lot happening that we don't know about.

Simon Mann is a British former SAS officer, mercenary, and co-founder of Sandline International. Educated at Eton, he served in the Scots Guards and SAS, later launching IT businesses in combat intelligence and electronic security. Rejoining the British Army for the Gulf War, he served under General Sir Peter de la Billiere. Mann co-founded Executive Outcomes (EO), playing pivotal roles in the Angolan and Sierra Leone civil wars, supporting UN-recognized governments to victory. He also founded DiamondWorks PLC, listed on the Toronto Stock Exchange. Sandline became known for its involvement in the Papua New Guinea coup and the "Arms to Sierra Leone" scandal. In 2004, Mann led a failed coup in Equatorial Guinea, resulting in imprisonment in Zimbabwe and Equatorial Guinea, with a 34-year sentence. Pardoned in 2009, Mann has since shared insights into his life, the coup attempt, and international geopolitics through memoirs and public speaking.

PATRICK MCGRANN

Could you tell me about your role as program director for Voices from the Void, and the work of the organization?

For the past 20 to 25 years, I have worked in development, humanitarian relief, and conflict zones across the globe, focusing on fragile and challenging environments. My experience spans collaborations with the US government, various UN agencies, and numerous international development and humanitarian organizations. While I have learned a great deal, I have often been frustrated by the lack of transparency in addressing the issues and the problematic track record within the industry.

During the COVID pandemic, some colleagues and I, who shared similar frustrations, launched a research collective in southern Colombia. My focus has been examining the impact of the 2016 Colombian Peace Accords. We chose Colombia as our base in the hope that this peace agreement would fare better than others in history. Our work revolves around education, rural development, and other sensitive issues, with a specific emphasis on elevating marginalized voices in Colombia. We engage with communities and stakeholders that many others avoid or choose not to engage with publicly.

Which marginalized communities are you reaching out to?

Traditionally, the United Nations and other stakeholders do not consider youth, particularly students, as active stakeholders. Instead, they are seen merely as beneficiaries. Our approach, however, starts from the ground up. In Colombia, we primarily engage with young people, especially those around the age of 15 – the point at which many drop out of formal education to enter illicit industries like narcotics production or illegal gold mining. These activities are often perceived as offering better prospects than formal education or legal careers.

We begin with the youth, then involve teachers and parents. Over time, our scope has expanded to include former combatants and individuals operating within the informal or 'grey' economy, such as those working in prostitution. Recently, we completed a significant research trip along Colombia's Pacific Coast, where we worked with illegal gold miners. On one occasion, a Colombian government delegation arrived near our location and advised us not to disembark from our boat, citing safety concerns. Despite their warnings, we had a productive and fulfilling experience. Such incidents are common as we strive to engage with communities that others are often reluctant to meet.

What do you do with those communities?

In many of these communities, people are often excited by our approach. When we arrange visits a month in advance, they frequently ask, "You're really coming just to listen? You're not here to take something from us, impose anything, or exploit our situation?" And we confirm, "Yes, we are here to listen and amplify your voices to a broader audience."

For instance, we are currently working on a short film about gold mining and education along the Pacific Coast. In the past, we have engaged in art projects, photography, and other creative endeavours, depending on the local context. However, the core of our work is always about listening – truly understanding and sharing the experiences of those we engage with.

I understand that you have worked in Colombia, but where else have you worked?

I have been in Colombia for the past three years, working both during and after the COVID pandemic. Before that, I spent roughly four years in North Eastern Nigeria, responding to the Boko Haram crisis, collaborating with organizations like Anti-Slavery International, Mercy Corps International (funded by Shell Oil), and the US State Department, which financed my work with Anti-Slavery International. Prior to my time in Nigeria, I was conducting doctoral research out of London.

I have also worked in Somalia, though my focus was largely on Gaza. Over a span of about ten years, I split my time between Gaza and the broader region, maintaining a primary focus on Gaza itself. Before that, I was involved in the Iraqi response following the US invasion, largely based out of Jordan. My earlier work also took me to Peru, Bolivia, and Italy. These are the primary locations, though there are many smaller assignments I've undertaken along the way.

Each country undoubtedly comes with its own set of challenges, but was there one you found particularly difficult to navigate?

Headquarters – it's always the headquarters. Interestingly, the more adverse or underdeveloped the community, the easier the work can be, because expectations are so much lower, and the people are incredibly grateful. Honestly, I'd rather be in the most remote, under-resourced area imaginable than at a UN office.

When I worked with the UN in Rome, it was an amazing experience, but I distinctly remember the petty squabbles over things like how many windows each office had. One office had two windows, another had three.

I'm showing my age here, but I remember a world summit on sustainability in Cape Town. Many of my colleagues refused to go from Italy to Cape Town because all the business class seats were booked. That became a huge scandal.

For someone like me, that kind of attitude is more challenging than any disease, arrest, or other hardships. It's difficult to grasp that people earning $250,000 a year would complain about something as trivial as how many windows they have when there are much bigger problems in the world. On the flip side, one of the most rewarding, eye-opening, and energizing experiences has been working with communities whose expectations are minimal, but whose gratitude is boundless.

You've already mentioned that your work heavily emphasizes the role of education in conflict situations. What do you believe the role of education should be in such contexts?

Many people argue that education is the most powerful weapon we have to combat conflict and violence and make the world a better place. From an idealistic standpoint, I agree with that. But in practice, theory and reality often diverge significantly. I fully support the idea that education should empower young people, providing them with the tools and frameworks needed to resolve conflicts and improve their lives. But, unfortunately, that's rarely the case. More often, education becomes a political tool rather than a solution.

I've worked extensively in Colombia, Nigeria, and Gaza, and I've seen how much money – typically around $3 billion – is poured into educational assistance aimed at stabilizing fragile countries. Yet, if you look at the statistics, you'll see a clear correlation between how many of these conflicts collapse within a decade and the fact that we're currently facing 55 or 56 ongoing conflicts or wars. The number is at an all-time high and continues to trend in the wrong direction.

Despite this, education is still widely cited as one of the main tools for resolving these issues. But honestly, forgive me for saying this, but I have to ask – do these people really understand what they're talking about? Have they seen the realities on the ground?

We've conducted polling across Colombia, where about 20% of the peace accords focus on rural development and education. Many insurgent groups like The Revolutionary Armed Forces of Colombia (FARC) and The National Liberation Army (ELN) agreed to the accords, but one of their main demands was better government services, especially education, in these small towns. You visit these towns today and ask, "Has anything improved since 2016? Have you received the promised better schools, transportation subsidies, or textbooks?" And the answer is always no.

Is that one of the key challenges – ensuring that things actually happen, rather than just being promised?

It's incredibly easy to make a promise, and it's even easier to cut a ribbon in a capital city and declare, "This is the solution." Over the last quarter century, $78 billion has been spent on conflict education. In Gaza alone, $3 billion went toward peace education. But if you look closely, even when the funds reach their intended destination, what's actually being taught? There's something called the "negative face of education," where, if the wrong curriculum is taught or it's applied inconsistently, it can actually make things worse.

In my work in Gaza, I interviewed students who went through these peace-focused programs, which, ironically, never mentioned anyone being killed. For instance, Palestinian textbooks make no reference to any Israeli ever killing a Palestinian. What ends up happening? Support for violence doubles among the students who read these textbooks, because they see it as all lies. They think, why should we trust anything coming out of the peace process if this is the kind of education you're giving us?

A lot of decisions are made in government ministries and donor offices that, on the surface, sound good and safe. But in reality, they often prove to be either ineffective or outright counterproductive. That's been my experience, and it's incredibly frustrating.

How has this problem evolved with the development of technology? Today, access to information – and sometimes misinformation – is much easier than it was 30 years ago.

This is a question that's very close to my heart. There are three main types of education: formal education, which you find in textbooks; the hidden curriculum, which involves going to school, submitting to authority, and understanding the teacher-student hierarchy; and then there's the outside curriculum, or public pedagogy – everything you experience outside the classroom, especially in a conflict zone. These external influences are often much more significant.

Not many people have fully analyzed this, but about 15 years ago, two academics from San Diego looked at the numbers. In a developed country, outside of conflict, where students can actually attend school, they found that only one-tenth of one percent of the information students experience daily comes from formal education. In a conflict zone, where access to education is inconsistent, enrolment is lower, and there are many other pressing concerns, this issue becomes even more pronounced.

People learn from their families, their friends, technology – pretty much everything. It's less about misinformation and more about how education can sometimes be almost irrelevant. In a perfect world, we'd teach critical thinking and empower students to sift through all that information, figuring out what's important and what's not. But, unfortunately, rote learning remains the norm. Countries like the UK and the US continue to fund education projects where actual critical thinking and skill-building are extremely rare.

How do you navigate education in this imperfect world?

How do I do it? I yell at a lot of people. I get very frustrated.

I remember being in this town called Lopez, in the middle of nowhere on the Colombian Pacific coast. There were no roads. We were interviewing the rector in charge of the school. He was all smiles, saying, "Everything's great. We follow the rules. It's wonderful."

But then we cut to an interview with a 16-year-old girl who said, "It's crap. I can't wait to get out of here. We don't learn anything. My hope is that when I get to university, they'll actually teach me something. But here it's garbage."

How do we navigate situations like that? We recognize that the

16-year-old is probably being more honest with us than the rector, but we also cut some slack for the rector. Often, they have about $7 allocated per student per year. It's not that the administrators are the bad guys – they're just trying to save face.

We take a philosophical approach to these situations. We understand that the answers aren't simple. We try not to get bogged down in official responses and focus on having faith that some of these young people will find their own way forward. We do whatever we can to help them along the way.

How do you reach out to young people?

It really depends on the issue. There are certain topics we have to tread carefully around. In the Middle East, for example, there's something called "falaga," a form of corporal punishment that students are reluctant to talk about. They often say, "We can't tell you the truth because as soon as you leave, we'll face the consequences."

It's the same thing in Colombia with discussions about gold mining. I won't claim that everything is perfect – building rapport and respect is crucial to understanding what's going on. It's about trust, and it's not something that can be established in a quick 30-minute meeting. It requires a deeper, long-term investment.

The bigger issue is that no one ever seems to want to talk to these young people. When I'd visit local bars in these areas, I'd find 14-year-olds getting drunk with the money they made the night before. I'd ask them about why they dropped out of school, what went wrong, and if there's anything we can do to help future generations. Many of them open up because no one ever asks them anything.

In my experience, there are people who are willing to talk but haven't had the chance to be heard. The reason they might seem intimidating is simply because they've never been given that opportunity.

I read that you've worked with institutions like the National Council for Afro-Colombian Peace, the Norwegian Refugee Council, and the Regional Indigenous Council of Cauca. How do you navigate working with such a diverse range of stakeholders from different cultures and backgrounds?

It's been wonderful. The Norwegians are a bit of an outlier, but as development stakeholders, they're fundamentally great. These groups, while very different, work really well together because they all understand what it's like to be marginalized. The Indigenous communities in Colombia and the Afro-Colombian communities are distinct, but they share that common experience, which makes cooperation incredibly rewarding.

Let me give you an example. From the Afro-Colombian side, we interviewed Francia Márquez, who is now Colombia's vice president. She came with her secret service because she's been targeted for assassination so many times. But it was amazing to sit down with her – she listened to what we had to say, and we listened to her. We immediately started collaborating.

There's one challenge, though, that we haven't been able to follow up on yet: the sicarios – young people who are trained as assassins at 15, and by the time they're 18 or 19, have no other future options.

Márquez said, "We desperately need vocational training to teach them skills for something else, but no one will touch this problem. Can you help us solve it?"

We haven't been able to pursue this yet, but I think it could be a game changer. It's a tricky situation, though, because many traditional stakeholders say, "We can't work with murderers." And here I am, a white guy from Minnesota talking to the Black vice president of Colombia about how we can help these people – legitimate murderers – turn their lives around before they're 18. On paper, that seems impossible. But if you come with good intentions and have honest conversations, I think unexpected and wonderful things can still happen.

What work would you like to do with those young people?

We've brainstormed ideas, and one possibility was starting a garage or something similar. In these communities, many international NGOs teach sewing or similar skills. But when you're dealing with people who've been involved in violence, that might not be enough. I thought about buying beat-up cars, repairing them, and selling them for a profit. It's something people could invest themselves in, and there'd be a financial incentive as well. It could be a metaphor for their lives – something that's broken, but with effort, can be fixed.

When opportunities like this come up, you can't let them slip away. We hope to resurrect this project. I know it's a long shot, but even if it only helps a few people, sometimes you have to take the risk. Not every project is guaranteed to succeed, but you'll never know unless you try.

Just going back a little, how did you get involved in the Colombian Peace Accords?

I've followed conflicts around the world – Nigeria, Gaza, and others – and I've seen how poor the track record is. Colombia's civil war, like the Israel-Palestine conflict, has lasted for over half a century, so when a peace deal was finally on the table in 2016, it was a huge deal. I'd been to Colombia before and knew how wonderful the people are, so when COVID hit, I didn't want to sit around in London for two years. I wanted to contribute in some way, especially with the peace agreement, and see if it would lead to real change.

We're at the halfway point of the 15-year implementation period, so we're trying to contribute whatever we can to the stakeholders involved. We're saying, "We're halfway through, and things aren't working. Let's try to course-correct." In my heart, I hope Colombia can turn things around, but unfortunately, violence continues to rise. The economic divide keeps widening, and things continue to move in the wrong direction. It's tough, so while I'm not optimistic, I'm still hopeful.

What's the biggest issue facing Colombia right now? What's perpetuating tensions?

At its core, it's the longstanding hierarchy where people of Spanish descent own all the best land, while Indigenous and Afro-Colombian communities are marginalized, lacking access to services or economically viable land. This is why so many turn to gold mining in swamps – because there's simply nothing else to do. It's a really tough situation.

It's not just a matter of racism, though. It's what happens 50 or 100 years after the fact when these communities are still segregated. If you grow up in the valley, in a central part of the country, it's easy to raise cattle, log, and access education. But if you're on the margins, hours away from a road or commercial centre, the system is stacked against you. That's the fundamental challenge, and it's something everyone recognizes.

Then there's corruption. There's a lot of it – some legal, some illegal – but all of it is insidious. Tying it back to education, the money just doesn't make it to the schools. What I find amazing and inspiring, though, is how well different ethnic groups integrate in Colombia. It's one of the things I love most about the country. But systemically, there are a lot of challenges that make life difficult. Now, you've got criminal enterprises stepping in to fill the gaps left by older political movements that used to drive the conflict. It's a tough situation.

I don't want to speak for the entire country, but from what I've seen, the drug trade plays a huge role in the economy and has an enormous influence on government and business sectors. It metaphorically sucks all the oxygen out of the room. There are other industries – like cattle production – that also have a significant impact, creating environmental degradation.

I'm not opposed to these industries; many Colombians see them as a positive path forward. But they all come with negative consequences. I just wish various governments were more proactive in attempting to balance out the trade-offs.

I read that the mitigation initiatives are usually compromised by problems like the ongoing violence and corruption. What happens usually and how do you navigate those challenges?

This brings us back to the gap between theory and practice, where many people make all kinds of promises. First of all, are they truly serious about it? How do we navigate this? I think adopting a philosophical perspective is key. Take the Israel-Palestine peace deal signed between 1992 and 1994, for example. If you go back and review the documents, it's clear that there was never an actual goal of achieving peace. The declassified US government documents also indicate that military solutions were always seen as ineffective. The real focus was on developing a process for peace, not the pursuit of peace itself.

I lived in Gaza for four years, and I never let myself get overly stressed about the situation or the American involvement, because I understood from the start that it was all a loaded proposition. There was never a real goal to change things; it was about running out the clock. To approach this with the right mindset, you have to maintain a philosophical perspective, not get too attached to any one outcome, and recognize that there are many difficult people involved at various levels.

I often get into trouble for saying this, but I've had more interactions with Hamas than most people in the West, and if I had to choose between dealing with Hamas or the American government, I would trust Hamas more. For instance, I met with the Palestinian Authority Prime Minister in Ramallah, just outside Jerusalem. To get to him, I had to go past armed Palestinian Authority security. But when I entered his office, it was protected by private American security.

The Prime Minister was eager to work on education projects in Gaza but had no real influence or power. He could take a photo or sign something, but it didn't carry any weight. On the other hand, when I met with the Hamas Prime Minister, there was no security, no sandbags – he was part of the community. That allowed for a much more open and honest conversation.

As an American in Gaza, I think the best approach is to stay open-minded. If you come in with preconceived ideas, you're likely to be wrong. The situation is not black and white – it's full of grey areas. Giving people room to explain themselves is a great way to learn and avoid burnout. If you go into these conflicts with all your idealism, hope, and energy, you'll likely burn out fast and end up heartbroken. But if you focus on listening and understanding, you'll not only learn more but also be able to pace yourself through the emotional highs and lows.

You said you meet people in Gaza with an openness and wanting to listen. Is that the attitude of the people you meet with as well?

It's a bit of a mixed answer. Politicians in Gaza, for sure, but Gaza as a whole has a rich history when it comes to education. When you're working with higher-level figures from any political faction, they tend to be incredibly intelligent and savvy, fully aware of how everything fits together. They appreciate that you're taking the time to understand different issues. However, when you're interacting with regular people on the street, it can be frustrating at times, as they may not have the same level of context.

There's also a lot of trauma involved. I've had confrontations with some people who would demand religious tolerance for Islam, yet when another religion came up – anything other than Judaism or Christianity, which are both respected in Gaza – there would be aggression. I'm not sure if it's a matter of perspective or cumulative trauma, but it's definitely a challenge. I'm not going to pretend that everyone in Gaza is perfect. I've faced dangerous situations, and I've had to deal with some unscrupulous people during my time there. So, by no means would I claim that everyone is without fault. But, more often than not, and to answer your question directly, people in Gaza do treat you with a great deal of respect.

If you have some patience and stamina, you can build truly meaningful relationships. Out of the 25 people closest to me, about a dozen of them are from Gaza. This wasn't something that came naturally – I'm not Muslim, I'm not Palestinian, and I'm not associated with left-leaning political movements. I just really connected with the people.

What are your thoughts on what's happening in Gaza and also the war between Russia and Ukraine?

I won't pretend to fully understand what's going on with Ukraine. There are all sorts of rumours about what the Americans and Brits promised the Ukrainians regarding protection after they gave up their nuclear weapons 25 years ago. Then, there's the pressure we've put on them to reject peace deals. Honestly, I have no idea. What I will say is that it's incredibly painful to witness the death toll and the amount of money that's been spent. So, who knows?

As for Gaza, I'll say this: I can't think of a better way to weaken Israel than what's happening right now. If I had a malicious plan for under-mining Israel's long-term security, this is exactly what I'd do. I'm not sure if everyone is caught up in this idea of being tough, but there's a lot of tough talk coming out of Israel. It's like the law of the jungle, where being hard is the answer. This is actually the focus of my PhD research – how Gazans are absorbing these messages.

Israelis often say they want to teach Palestinians a painful, kinetic lesson. I think they've massively overplayed their hand. They're losing a lot of support. I'm not sure what it's like in the UK right now, but in the United States, there's unprecedented criticism. The credibility of Hasbara and the Israeli security establishment is hitting new lows. It's heartbreaking what's happening. In the short term, the big losers are the Palestinians. But in the medium to long term, the real losers will be Israel and the United States, which honestly doesn't surprise me.

What advice would you give to those working in conflict resolution, especially when navigating the complexities and challenges of such sensitive situations?

If anyone is sincerely interested in working within conflict resolution, I'd simply suggest judging stakeholders by their actions, and only working with people you have learned to trust – no matter what flag they fly. For example, in 2010 the World Cup was held in South Africa, and the motto was "the world comes together in South Africa." The world united in South Africa – except for Gaza, which was under siege. So, we decided to do our own project there. When United Nations Development Programme (UNDP) found out, they wanted to fund everything we were doing, saying it was great. But as soon as the project gained momentum and Al Jazeera expressed interest in live coverage, they came in saying, "We're taking over your project, and there's nothing you can do about it."

Things got really messy after that. For instance, we had reserved half of the stadium for women to watch the game. But UNDP took all those seats, banned the women from attending, and gave them to Hamas political officials. I had to argue with UN security at the stadium, who were dragging young girls with hijabs out, insisting they were part of my team.

If that wasn't enough, the UN High Commissioner for Refugees and the UN High Commissioner for Human Rights hired a colleague and me to research youth violence after the Arab Spring when all the jails were blown up. Our contract was run through UNDP, which handled all the administrative work for UN agencies in Gaza.

When I returned to the US, I received a call from someone asking where I was, because "someone from UNDP leaked that you're spying for Israel and that they don't want to share any of their funds with your contract."

I have a lot of choice words about this, but I've worked with three or four different UN agencies, and if I never work with them again, I won't lose any sleep over it. That said, I have good things to say about some other agencies.

Looking at what is beginning to happen now and towards the near future, do you believe leaders will use AI or robotics to achieve territory expansion and even to grab resources like oil or gas?

I'm definitely no expert in this – I won't pretend to be – but it's clear that Israel has a $1.1 billion contract with Amazon and Google to use AI for targeting. What's being discussed is the significant gas reserves off the coast of northern Gaza. Many conspiracy theorists in Gaza are suggesting that the reason Israel is focusing on northern Gaza instead of the south has to do with these energy reserves. Hamas is traditionally based in the south, but Israel is forcing people out of the north, which is where access to these reserves lies.

If Israel occupies or controls northern Gaza, they could gain access to those energy reserves. Here's an example where cloud computing is being used for targeting, displacing people, and taking control of over a billion dollars' worth of natural gas just offshore. I'm no expert, but it's hard to ignore the signs that this is already unfolding.

Speaking of Gaza, you said you are working on a new project between Colombia and Gaza. Can you talk about that?

It was early November of 2023 and I was talking with some of my Colombian colleagues as the Israeli counter-attack was ramping up after October 7th. Many of these guys being former FARC fighters are deeply ideological and were outraged by the violence being unleashed on Gaza. When I asked why don't they do something to help, they replied, "What can we do? We're 7,000 miles away and we don't have weapons anymore." I asked, "You guys grow coffee now, right? And you know Palestinians love coffee, right?" I then went on to explain that coffee – along with almost anything else – was not being allowed into Gaza as the Israelis (and their American and Egyptian partners) blockaded Gaza. Things were so bad, I explained, many friends in Gaza were grinding up date seeds to mix with hot water to at least pretend to have coffee. That conversation sparked an idea: we created "Café Para La Lucha" (Coffee for the Struggle). The basic idea was that we would smuggle coffee grown by former FARC rebels in rural Colombia to various humanitarian destinations in Gaza with the dual goals of both providing coffee to those who could no longer find it in Gaza, as well as reinforcing the deeper message that the Gazans were not alone (and that we could all be doing more to connect with Gaza during the war).

To get started, we first worked with Colombian designers to create highly visual packaging that connected the mountains of southern Colombia and the beaches of Gaza, as well as embracing a phoenix – the symbol of Gaza City – to ensure the coffee was infused with as much symbolism and meaning as possible. And from there we began packing up the FARC-grown coffee and sending it to Palestine – through very circuitous and often informal routes – that began arriving in Gaza a month later. But because many people in the Palestinian diaspora outside Gaza were also suffering during the war, we also sent coffee to Palestinians around the world – with our coffee currently having been received in 35 countries. And as is commonplace anywhere around the world, when sharing coffee, conversations naturally followed. And this included Gaza, where people started writing to thank us for the coffee. And what was most valuable to me was the dialogue that was developing, independent of the political filters in Washington or Brussels or any other western capital, whereby Gaza and Colombia could share experiences and perspectives, be they empathy or strategy. Tomorrow, I'm heading back to Colombia to meet with the FARC and share more of those letters. In the end, it's more than just sharing coffee. As is described on the back of the coffee packaging, it's about warming hearts and sharpening wits as the various struggles continue. We're reaching out to other groups, including some colleagues in Nigeria who are interested in joining this approach.

The idea is that many of these communities, despite their different contexts, can lean on and learn from each other. I personally don't think the best way forward is to filter everything through political or institutional lenses, saying, "We can't talk about that." Instead, we should be asking, "What advice do people in Gaza have for people in Colombia? Colombia is in the middle of a peace deal that's falling apart. What can they share with others considering peace deals?"

I'm not against peace, and I'm not trying to stir trouble, but I do believe it's important to be honest about what's happening. In my experience, people in these situations are pragmatic and wonderful – if you're honest with them, they'll be honest with you.

That's when we can cut through the façade, where we pretend to be making progress, but the data shows little is actually getting done. Our track record in resolving conflicts on a large scale isn't great. We need to explore more diverse conversations, even if they bring up uncomfortable truths. So, the coffee is going from Colombia to Gaza to start these conversations.

Take the United States, for example. We're apparently so ineffective that we can't even use our political influence to get the Egyptians and Israelis to allow anything into South Gaza from Cyprus. For the one boat that might manage to get through, it will take 60 days just to build a dock in North Gaza. Meanwhile, The United Nations Relief and Works Agency for Palestine Refugees in the Near East (UNRWA) had 17 truckloads of food stopped at Wadi, and the Israelis wouldn't let them through.

That's the reality. This is something that we all need to be talking more openly about. In response, I mention the taboo topic of smuggling. I'm not getting into details, but two months ago, we were able to get coffee into Shifa Hospital in Gaza City when nothing else was getting into north Gaza. It's not a perfect situation – and we're not talking about huge quantities – but let's just say there's space under people's seats. We're definitely finding ways around the system that push the limits of good judgment and logistics. Of course, we're not trying to save the day – coffee isn't going to solve the conflict.

But what we are trying to do is send a message that both questions the larger geopolitical status quo, as well as a further message of solidarity. I can tell you that the people who've received the coffee (when the American government couldn't use its muscle to similarly deliver foodstuffs) – it absolutely thrilled people. Of course you're never going to please everyone. One shipment of coffee went to Al-Mawasi, a new camp in the South, and a few people said it wasn't smooth enough compared to the normal coffee they're used to, which amidst genocide is curious. Who knows? We'll see what happens. It could all fall apart, but for now, we have a choice: we could sit back and be frustrated by the situation, or we could spend £10,000 to smuggle some coffee into Gaza and to Palestinians around the world.

I've received tearful messages in return, with people simply crying in gratitude. For me, that's a good metric to keep trying.

For over 20 years Patrick has prioritized living amidst conflict to better appreciate both the challenges facing marginalized communities as well as their local insights that, while habitually overlooked, are essential to forging longer-term peace. This experience has included leading programming in Colombia, Gaza, Jordan, Nigeria, Somalia, and many other contested contexts for various multilateral agencies and international humanitarian organizations. Yet, while his professional roles are extensive, he is most proud of never turning down an opportunity to share a casual chat with those routinely labeled as dangerous adversaries. Patrick holds a Ph.D. in International Relations from the University of London, an M.S. in Policy and Economics from the University of Minnesota, and a BA in Economics from Trinity College.

SANDRA MELONE

What was your high school experience like in Rwanda, and how did it shape your path into peacebuilding?

I now realize, in hindsight, that growing up in Rwanda, especially with a father who was in the diplomatic service, deeply influenced my professional trajectory. At the time, I didn't recognize the weight of the experiences I was accumulating. It was just life, a normal one. I only understood the significance of my background later, when I found myself working at Amnesty International and later still, I became involved in peacebuilding at Search for Common Ground, particularly after the genocide in Rwanda.

In 1994, when the genocide occurred, my prior time spent in Rwanda led to my involvement in human rights work centred on Rwanda. As I became more involved, my focus expanded to include Burundi as well, where I worked on conflict transformation. In retrospect, I can see how my upbringing set the foundation for the peacebuilding work I would go on to pursue. It wasn't a conscious choice at the time, but life has a way of unfolding in unexpected and profound ways.

What inspired you to create Zancora, and what role do you play as its CEO?

A couple of years after turning 50, I realized that there are only so many more years left to seize new opportunities. I feel like I still have a lot of energy and valuable experience to offer, but there's a limited window before I reach a point where, hopefully, I'll be a trusted advisor. After working for over 25 years in the same organization, it felt natural to seek new challenges and perspectives.

I now have a chance to start a new chapter, and I'm eager to see how different organizations, governments and companies operate. I'm curious to find out if the skills I've gained through peacebuilding and my work with Search for Common Ground can be applied in other sectors.

That's why I decided to create a platform for consultancy work called

Zancora. For each project, I work with a small group – sometimes one-person, other times a few – tailoring the approach to meet the specific needs of that partnership. The work I do focuses on what I'm passionate about: conflict mediation, conflict-transformation training, gender issues in conflict, and addressing gender-based violence, particularly in areas of active conflict.

More specifically, where have you been working?

My professional experience has been truly global. As you rightly pointed out, my upbringing has played a pivotal role in shaping my career trajectory, and I have had the privilege of working across several countries in Africa. I have a love and proclivity for Africa and since I speak both French and English, it has facilitated my work in many regions. Additionally, my career has taken me to the Middle East and Asia. Given the widespread nature of issues such as conflict transformation and gender-based violence, which persist across the globe, I can pretty much apply my expertise in virtually any part of the world.

Tell me also a bit about the work you do with Search for Common Ground. How did you get to work with Search for Common Ground and what has it been like?

My journey with Search for Common Ground began after I had spent some time as a young professional working in human rights at Amnesty International. Through an introduction made by someone I met during my childhood in Africa, I was introduced to John Marks in 1995, the founder of Search for Common Ground.

I became captivated by the approaches of conflict transformation. Unlike human rights advocacy, which often focuses on protection, peace-building and conflict transformation aim to take into consideration the whole of society and the whole of the borders of a conflict, and consider who are all the actors, the good guys, the bad guys, and what are all the entry points that one can leverage in order to have the possibility for resolution of nonviolent conflicts?

In the world of human rights advocacy, the focus is often on protecting specific groups, individuals, or communities. It's a vital and fascinating field, but sometimes it can get very granular. However, what doesn't always get as much attention is the broader question: How do you bring all the actors together so that the conflict doesn't even arise in the first place?

That's what really piqued my interest. I had the privilege of working at Search for Common Ground in various roles, including managing the organization for nearly a decade. It was an incredible journey. When I first joined, we were a small team of maybe 10 or 12 people. Fast forward a few years, and we grew to about 850 or 900 staff across 35 countries. It was truly a remarkable experience.

At a certain point, I decided it was time to branch out and step back and not work around the clock, seven days a week, which had been my reality for a couple of decades. I was getting tired, and honestly, a bit older, and I didn't want to keep going at that pace. So, I transitioned to the board of directors, and now I'm the chair. This keeps me involved in peacebuilding at Search for Common Ground which I'm passionate about, but I can finally get some rest. I no longer have the daily demands, and that's been a good change.

Can you tell me a bit about the conflict you worked on with Search for Common Ground and the most challenging situations?

I was hired, as I mentioned, to help build our first program in Africa, which was in Burundi in the wake of the Rwandan genocide to help prevent the further escalation of Hutu-Tutsi conflict in neighbouring Burundi. That was a very intense civil war; I spent a couple of years there. I worked, in particular, with women's groups and on how women could be part of conflict transformation, considering that the men and the politicians were making their deals in boardrooms.

Part of my job after Burundi was to open the European headquarters in Brussels. I had the opportunity to help build and develop projects for Search for Common Ground and the country offices across Africa, across the Middle East, and in Asia. Not to forget, of course, former Yugoslavia and a little bit in post-Soviet Ukraine many years ago.

We had projects in eastern Congo, Palestine, Nepal, Indonesia, Pakistan, Syria, Lebanon, Iraq, Jordan, and more. I mean, it's been a lot of different pieces. I wasn't always brokering peace in all of those places, but I was always either leading or being part of a team working on those issues locally.

Was there a particularly challenging country among all of those? I'm sure all of them were challenging in their own way…

Well, I think you said it right: they're all very challenging. Some dynamics are similar. For example, we could talk about the extraction of natural resources, not only through local entities and people, but through regional and international bodies. That conversation has another layer about consumer demand for products of the extraction – products such as smartphones. Guess how those smartphones are made? And guess how the minerals are extracted from eastern Congo? – With child labour.

And then you add to that in certain parts of the world like Nigeria, some of the more traditional Islamisms have other forms of "isms" at the end. The more you add those things on top of poverty and natural disasters, the more the conflict is horribly difficult. I would put up there places like Sudan, Yemen, and eastern Congo for sure, as some of the hairiest ones. There are places I've worked like Chad – I loved Chad – where you're not a man unless you're armed. Literally, you have to be armed to be considered to be a man. I'm being simplistic, but it's the way it is. There's always huge potential for everything to escalate; the smallest car accidents, the smallest argument of any kind and arms of all sorts are just drawn out.

Since every country is different, you have to be quite adaptable in terms of the strategies you put in place to resolve the conflicts? Is that a challenge as well?

Indeed, it's a considerable challenge, but also arguably the greatest opportunity. In peacebuilding mediation, no approach can succeed if you assume from the outset that your team or the process itself is already well-defined or inflexible.

The key lies in having your ear to the ground, maintaining a keen awareness of the ever-evolving dynamics. This requires the ability to identify shifting circumstances, pinpointing windows of opportunity, and understanding who your allies are. It's equally vital to pair this local insight with perspectives from those who may not be directly embedded in the community or conflict, as their detachment allows them to view the situation from a higher vantage point as they are not as wrapped into the conflict dynamics that exist in that area.

This delicate balance demands a combination of both active listening and a constant inquiry into several critical questions: What needs to remain constant? What requires a shift? Who should we engage, and which parties have experienced shifts in their positions? If so, in what ways?

Ultimately, the most effective strategy combines local expertise – individuals who are deeply knowledgeable about and representative of the community's diversity – with external voices capable of bringing fresh, objective air into the conversation. It's not just about confirming one side's righteousness, but rather about creating a space that is neither Hutu nor Tutsi, where you can open the possibility of crafting a shared reality for the different parties in the conflict.

How did you go about finding those people that could inform you of what was in the community's mind and what the community was feeling?

It's a matter of investing time and, above all, a genuine commitment to the process. First, you have to recognise the necessity of this. If you're working in a place like Nigeria, for instance, you must have a team that truly reflects the country's diversity – north and south, Muslim and Christian, young and old, educated and uneducated, male and female, traditional and non-traditional. The divides and differences that exist within a community or conflict must be represented in your team's perspectives, or else you risk missing critical insights.

One of the most significant factors that can drive a conflict further off course is when those who are supposed to facilitate peace fail to engage with all relevant parties. It's easy to fall into the trap of excluding certain groups, be it the government, a company, or even a particular side of the conflict, simply because they're seen as "the bad guys." Whether it's side A or side B, everyone can find someone they deem the antagonist.

However, the beauty of peacebuilding – though challenging – lies in recognising that if someone is part of the problem, they are also part of the solution. Failing to acknowledge this means you risk deepening divisions and stalling the potential for meaningful change. By sidelining certain parties, you may unintentionally solidify them as enemies, preventing them from being part of the dialogue and, ultimately, the solution. Engaging everyone, even those you might consider as enemies, is essential for fostering genuine, lasting peace.

When you were in Burundi, you founded the Women's Peace Centre. Could you share a bit about that experience?

John Marks, Susan Marks, and I understood early on that any effort to foster peace must take a holistic view of society, identifying key entry points and stakeholders. In Burundi, our assessment revealed that meaningful change was required on multiple levels.

At the political level, an official peace process was happening in South Africa, with meetings in South Africa and Switzerland and Tanzania. But then it became evident that these discussions often lost their impact the moment the participants returned home. It's a very human tendency: agreements forged in conference rooms abroad would be forgotten or disregarded, as individuals reverted to old patterns of engaging with each other. So, we knew that something needed to happen in between those meetings in the big boardrooms abroad, for sustained dialogue and shuttle diplomacy to bridge the gaps.

We also observed the role of media, particularly radio, which in places like Rwanda and the former Yugoslavia had been weaponized to foment one party against the other, spreading fear and inciting violence. Something needed to change with the way the media operated. While I wouldn't go so far as to suggest the media act as mediators, they should at least consider the multiple facets of the issues, interview and collaborate with people from all sides, and strive for impartiality. They should play a role in shaping the conversation, regardless of the direction. We recognized that this approach could create significant influence – not necessarily deep, but certainly far-reaching.

And then what we observed in Burundi was a deeply patriarchal society in which the traditional right to own land, for example, even though they were under Napoleonic code after Belgian colonialism, was never given to women. In a place where husbands, fathers, and brothers were killed during the conflict, women were left to care for five, six, or seven children without the legal ability to inherit their husband's land, their father's property, or their brother's house. It became clear to us that not only were women the majority of the population, particularly during the conflict, but that if they couldn't access the resources needed to care for the children of the country, then the whole society was in jeopardy.

We realised we had to focus on women. But addressing this issue wasn't just about making decisions ourselves. It required understanding the political landscape, working with the media, and, most importantly, listening to the women themselves. This ties back to what you asked me earlier: we had to spend time understanding what needed to be done, what Burundians wanted to do, and what actions wouldn't put them in greater danger from the authorities or rebel groups. That meant listening to people from all walks of life and hiring a diverse group to help identify the key issues and figure out how to provide meaningful support. And that's what we did. It was difficult, but it was also deeply rewarding. Of course, there were criticisms. People would say, "They're pro-Hutu" or "They're pro-Tutsi." But isn't that a miracle?

There's one thing I would add, which is your credibility as a peacebuilder, as somebody who cares deeply and who wants to be part of helping people live in violence-free societies: it's what you do when the situation gets worse.

During a coup d'état, which became known as Les Événements, the US government, a major donor and investor in development and peacebuilding efforts in Burundi, ordered that all organizations receiving its funding leave the country. The US government said that "Everybody leaves. Anybody who gets our money leaves."

This included many nonprofits, but Search for Common Ground refused to abandon Burundi. We fought all the way to the White House, saying, "No, you cannot leave the people in a conflict just because there is something you don't like happening." Ultimately, we received an exception and stayed. That decision mattered. We stayed, and that meant that when things got a bit calmer and others started coming back, Burundians of all parties only trusted us.

Tell me a little bit more about the scope of action of the Women's Center for Peace, what they do exactly?

We began by identifying the wives of politicians from all parties, sides, and ethnic groups as a promising entry point for fostering dialogue. This became our track of work for quite some time. We explored what these women, as a group, thought about the possibilities for peace. Could they become advocates for peacebuilding? Could they work across ethnic divides? It was an extraordinary process.

Over time, we were able to expand our efforts to include women in actual political leadership roles. We created platforms for these women to engage directly with the challenges at hand and take part in the fight for change. This became a significant women's political initiative.

Then, we realized that there was a big piece of work that had to be done at the legal level. Even though modern law dictated that women could have access to property, very few people knew about these rights and even fewer acted on them. Women began telling us that what was needed was sensibilization or vulgarisation of the laws. In other words, there had to be a clear explanation of how women could access their legal rights, how they could request property ownership, or how they could claim a deceased family member's property. That became another major strand of our work.

Lastly, we launched a project focused on "Women and the Media." At the time, it was incredibly rare for women to have a voice or access to media platforms. This initiative aimed to change that dynamic and ensure women's perspectives were represented.

What did you do with the media?

We conducted training on what it means to be a journalist, focusing on how to be as impartial as possible and how to bring together different parties for civilized discussions. We also encouraged interviewing people who don't usually have a voice. Many of our programs revolved around using media and culture as tools to engage with people. In contexts like Burundi, it's incredibly dangerous to openly discuss issues like violence, political parties, ethnic groups, religion, and gender. These are deeply taboo topics that can put people at serious risk – both physically and otherwise. So, the question was: how do you help people at all levels understand these dynamics and empathize with how others are experiencing their lives?

For example, if you've been raped, it's often impossible to talk about that openly in many cultures. But if you stage a play about a woman experiencing rape, you can create space for dialogue. If done thoughtfully, you can even engage security forces in discussions about the themes of the play. The same applies to songs, games, and other forms of art. We invested heavily in arts and culture as tools for engagement. One of the most impactful projects we worked on involved creating a radio soap opera.

We received funding from International Alert, a peer organization, to produce Burundi's first-ever radio soap opera, which we, at Search for Common Ground, developed. It was called Our Neighbors Ourselves and portrayed real life through radio theatre – a hugely popular medium at the time. This opened up an entirely new way to discuss sensitive issues in a safe and engaging manner.

You're also a founding member of the Child Soldiers Initiative. Where is this problem most prevalent? What are the challenges to ending the recruitment of child soldiers?

There are quite a lot of countries where children are used as soldiers and as weapons. To address this, we invited General Roméo Dallaire, the Canadian general who commanded the UN forces during the Rwandan genocide. One of the great tragedies of modern history is how the international community, through the Security Council, refused to give the UN troops in Rwanda the mandate to shoot back once the genocide began. General Dallaire pleaded with the Security Council, day after day, for authorization to intervene and stop the killing. His request was repeatedly denied. As a result, he and his troops were forced to stand by and witness the genocide.

Since then, General Dallaire has dedicated decades of his life to preventing the recruitment and use of child soldiers. He has also worked tirelessly to address the challenges of reintegrating these children back into their communities or into other communities when their own reject them. The reintegration process is incredibly complex and painful. Often, these children have been drugged, raped, or forced to commit atrocities. Even though no child should ever be held responsible for such actions, communities often fear or shun them. It's an unimaginably difficult situation.

We had an incredible partnership with General Dallaire when he housed the Child Soldiers Initiative at Dalhousie University in Canada. They continue to do outstanding work to this day. Building on that foundation, Search for Common Ground has also undertaken efforts in multiple countries to prevent the recruitment and re-recruitment of child soldiers, while supporting their reintegration into society.

Where is that problem more prevalent? Which countries?

Well, historically, it's been Eastern Congo, but you can see it in Uganda and several of the conflicts in the Middle East like Yemen. You see it in several Asian conflicts as well. On a human rights level, in the US there's voluntary conscription of minors in the US Army. Being 16 years old does not make you an adult. So, how are you allowed to be a soldier? It's a different dynamic, but it ranges from that to more extreme forms.

In terms of recruitment communication is so easy with social media and the internet. Does it make the situation more difficult?

Yes. You might remember the infamous Joseph Kony campaign, which was extraordinary in how it leveraged Uganda's social media. But the problem goes much deeper than that. It's not just about warlords like Kony – it's also about gangs in major cities around the world. In some cases, these groups even provide basic services. In settings where a child doesn't have food in front of them, joining a gang or armed group might feel like survival. And in other places, children are simply abducted. What can you do if you're taken at eight years old?

There are also many intermediate scenarios. In Nigeria, for instance, recruitment often centres around money. Someone might offer, "I'll give you $1 a day," which could be far more than the child or their family would otherwise have. They promise food – rice and beans – and maybe even fish on Saturdays. These promises can be life-changing in desperate situations.

When you look at some of the jihadist movements, the issue becomes even more complex. These groups sometimes provide schools, clothes, and other benefits for the child's entire family. Recruitment methods vary widely, but they often exploit extreme poverty and lack of opportunity.

The real tragedy is what happens to these children (male or female) if they ever manage to leave. What becomes of them afterward? Communities don't want them, and they're often deeply traumatized. It's a heartbreaking and profoundly complex issue.

Your work also revolves so much around women, namely, with Elles du Sahel. Can you tell me more about that? What kind of work you do with them?

We came together about two years ago, thanks to the incredible work of an NGO called Oasis Sahel. They had been focusing on sexual and reproductive health rights, as well as advocating for girls' and women's equal access to education and healthcare across the Sahel.

Oasis Sahel brought together an amazing group of powerhouse leaders, community leaders, network leaders, and feminist women from across the five Sahel countries to discuss what was needed. They asked: What's missing? How can we translate the commitments made by national, regional, and international authorities on girls' and women's rights into tangible actions on the ground? Because there's a huge gap between what governments claim they are doing and what actually happens.

The women were very clear: they needed to amplify each other's voices across borders. While there are strong, deeply-rooted networks within each country – Niger, Mauritania, Mali, Burkina Faso, and Chad – the connections between countries weren't functioning effectively. Yet, the challenges they face are transnational, while the political bodies they need to influence are regional. So, they needed a way to advocate to these authorities from the ground up.

That's exactly what we're doing at Elles du Sahel. We focus on advocacy in Europe, the US, and across the Sahel region, working to support girls and women throughout the region and ensure their voices are heard.

What kind of support do they need? What is most urgent?

I don't know how to say it better than, "Put your money where your mouth is." When a government claims that girls and women have the right to health and education, I would say, show us where the health services and education actually are. What we see instead are little girls working at home, not attending school, women unable to access obstetrician or gynecologist care, and girls who are raped, forced to carry the children of their rapists, and denied an education.

So, put your money where your mouth is. When a government says it has signed conventions and agreements – like the Istanbul Convention, or commitments to gender equality – then show us the results. The most effective solutions are those that begin with solid, long-term education. But in the meantime, there's a lot that can be done, from providing health-care services to running hygiene and gender-based violence campaigns.

When you talk about education, are you referring to educating the women themselves?

I'm pretty sure the men need it just as much, if not more, than the women. It's not just about educating girls and women – it's about educating boys and men as well. However, we're dealing with highly patriarchal societies, and how you go about this work depends on where you are. The approach is very different in places like Nouakchott or rural Mali compared to other regions. We take our lead entirely from the women we work with in the Sahel, listening to them about what's feasible and culturally appropriate. If we don't do that, we risk creating more problems rather than solving them. The same principle applies to peacebuilding and advocacy – understanding what is possible and sensitive to the context is key.

You've worked to set up the European Peacebuilding Liaison Office?

The European Peacebuilding Liaison Office (EPLO) is a super cool initiative, and it was very fun to be there at its inception. I often think back to John Marks, the founder of Search for Common Ground, who was my boss for many years. He was incredibly visionary. In 1996, he recognized that if we wanted to establish real credibility as an international organization and gain access to additional resources for conflict prevention, we needed to set up a base in Brussels. It was the obvious choice, being the hub of the European Commission, NATO, and other key institutions.

I came from Burundi to help with the opening, and it was a remarkable experience. At that time, some European governments were starting to allocate budget lines within their Ministries of Foreign Affairs and development cooperation for conflict transformation, peacebuilding, and civil society engagement – things that hadn't existed before. They began directing funding and political attention to these areas of international development, rather than just focusing on humanitarian aid, education, and the other types of development they had been doing for decades.

We were among the first peacebuilding NGOs to establish a presence in Brussels, and over time, others started following suit. Many came to explore the idea of being based in Brussels instead of cities like Bonn, Paris, Geneva, or London. I gave advice to everyone, and it was a win-win situation for everyone involved.

Eventually, there were 10 peacebuilding organizations based in Brussels, and we realized that not every European organization working in peacebuilding needed to be based in Europe. But we could support them by being there, creating a secretariat – the European Peacebuilding Liaison Office. EPLO could help all these non-profits connect with European Union institutions, sharing our advice and field experience with them, and vice versa. It also gave us the opportunity to access resources and funding.

EPLO has had a series of great directors over the years, with Sonya Reines-Djivanides leading it for quite a while now. It's grown into a highly credible voice in peacebuilding policy, bringing peacebuilders from around the world to Brussels and raising awareness about the real needs on the ground. It's been a fantastic journey.

Do you believe that climate change and the increasing desertification of Africa could lead to more refugees and migration from certain countries or areas?

Absolutely – 1,000%. It's not just that it can happen, it already *is* happening. You can see it around the world. And it's not just climate change; environmental issues like this have always been a driver of migration.

If you look at the Sahel in particular, it's one of the most obvious examples in the world. You don't need any scientific instruments to notice the change from one year to the next. The desert is advancing, and the population is growing.

Take a country like Niger, which has the world's lowest gross domestic product but also the highest – and growing – birth rates. The average woman in Niger has seven children. Along with that comes a high number of deaths, miscarriages, and so on. Meanwhile, the desert is rapidly encroaching on the land.

As the population grows, there are increasing conflicts across the Sahel, particularly between traditionally nomadic peoples who move their animals to greener areas twice a year in a practice called "transhumance." These people now have to travel farther to find green land, often into areas that are more populated, less fertile, and undergoing more modernization. This leads to inevitable clashes because there's no alternative. They have to feed their animals, but the people living in the South need to preserve their land and resources to feed their families. It's a dire situation.

Add to this the rise of jihadist and Islamist movements crossing from the Gulf, moving through the Sahel to the western side of Africa. Combined with the deeply patriarchal nature of many of these societies, it's creating a perfect storm. Climate change is certainly a major factor. There's scarcity of resources, a lack of economic opportunities, and increasing insecurity. People are concerned about feeding their children while also fearing for their safety. It's all interconnected.

SANDRA MELONE

Sandra Djuvara Melone is the CEO and founder of Zancora Consulting, established in 2021. Zancora offers expert services in peacebuilding, conflict resolution, human rights, gender, and more, supporting institutions, organizations, and individuals with advisory, mediation, training, and project management. Sandra is also the Co-Founder of Elles du Sahel, a network advocating for improved funding for girls' education and sexual and reproductive health. She serves as the Chairwoman of the Board for Search for Common Ground, Europe, a global leader in peacebuilding, and previously held the role of Executive Vice President for 10 years, expanding the organization to over 700 staff across 36 countries. Sandra's early work at Search for Common Ground involved founding the Women's Peace Centre in Burundi and establishing the European headquarters. She is a founding member of the European Peacebuilding Liaison Office and the European Platform for Conflict Prevention and Transformation. Sandra has served on the boards of several influential peacebuilding organizations and is the President of the Neagu Djuvara Cultural Association, which she founded in 2018 to honour her grandfather's legacy as a renowned Romanian historian and diplomat.

JULIE NORMAN

You've worked extensively with many organizations and in many areas of the world. Can you tell me a bit about your experiences?

I've been working in international conflict for almost 20 years. I started pretty soon after my undergraduate studies, working with an NGO in Cairo, Egypt, during the Iraq war. Soon after that, I also started working in Israel-Palestine, again with local NGOs and community-based groups. Israel-Palestine is really where I ended up situating a lot of my work for quite a while and where I still do most of my work. Much of that started with NGOs and then working with community-based groups through friends and contacts there as well as doing work in refugee camps. Especially at that time, I was doing a lot with participatory media and youth media, working with young people to create videos, photos, and podcasts to tell their stories locally. I would take those back to the US or Canada or the UK (where I was living) and share them as a way of starting conversations about Israel-Palestine.

I did that for a while, then started doing some work in Lebanon. It was a bit of a shift, but people who had been involved in the Lebanese civil war as fighters were now peacemakers and were trying to prevent other young people from going down the route of violence. I worked with that group for a while and then did some consulting work with larger NGOs and groups, in addition to some work with young people in Iraq through the British Council.

I also conducted a multi-year project with the NGO Christian Aid where we looked at how to address conflicts in fragile contexts where there's also a humanitarian crisis. That was more South Sudan, Burundi, Congo, and a little bit in Myanmar. In a nutshell, those are the places and types of things I've been doing.

What made you go into international conflict?

I had always been very interested, for whatever reason, in conflict, but also peacebuilding. To date myself, I was in high school in the late 1990s when it was peace time – the Oslo Accords, the Belfast Agreement, the Good Friday Agreement, Northern Ireland and Israel-Palestine. It seemed that there was a lot of hope surrounding these long-term conflicts. And then while I was an undergrad, 9/11 happened. Especially for me as an American, it changed everything in terms of how we thought about the world. I was very uncomfortable with a lot of the narratives I was hearing in the US at the time and felt that I don't just want to read about this stuff. I want to go and actually be in places and hear what people have to say and think, instead of taking someone else's word for it. So that's what pushed me to start working more overseas. I wanted to work in the Middle East largely for that reason, but I have also been very interested in Israel-Palestine since I was younger. That kind of work led to working in other conflict areas after that.

What would you say is the most difficult challenge you've had to overcome?

If you don't mind me being totally honest, at the end of my first year in Egypt, I was traveling around some other parts of the region, and I had a very bad incident with violence. I was kidnapped and raped. That did happen. I had otherwise a very good year working there. It was hard in many ways obviously, but I also felt that one of the reasons I had gone and wanted to work in that part of the world was to challenge stereotypes and things like that. And so, to come back to the US and be able to speak openly about what happened to me, but not confirm a lot of stereotypes that people had about the region regarding violence and how women are treated was a big challenge. Even for myself, I needed to make a very conscious decision that I wasn't going to stop because that happened. I wanted to keep working in conflict areas and in other parts of the world, even knowing that things happen. I wanted to keep working to be able to prevent things like that from happening. It was the first time I had personally experienced violence in that direct way. And it changed the way I thought and still think about violence and conflict and what kind of justice options are open.

Would you be willing to tell me a bit more about that experience?

I can say a little bit. It was in Syria, but this was before the Syrian Civil War. It was a random person. It wasn't part of a hostage-taking thing or something like that. It was a bus driver. I won't say much more beyond that it was an awful experience, but I would also say a lot of people helped me afterwards, which was what I try to remember. I was hesitant for a while even to say where it happened because I didn't want to smear a whole country with this episode that happened to me. And there were so many people who were kind and good to help me after that. That's what I try to look back on from that time.

I'm so sorry that happened to you.

Thank you. Randomly, I was doing my sexual violence lecture today, so I was talking to students about it in class. It's not a big deal to say it now. I'm pretty public about it. But to anyone that might be reading this book, I think it's important to know that things like that can happen, and it will affect you, but it doesn't have to define or destroy you in any kind of way. You can keep doing meaningful work.

This unfortunately can and will affect many, many women and men now too – people that we know and love. The idea is that it is traumatic – and you don't minimize it – but you don't need to be defined as being a victim. And it's not your fault.

What do you think about the work that organizations and national governments are doing to prevent that? Do you think it's effective?

I think there's a lot more attention to it now than there used to be. International law recognizes wartime rape in a different way than it did even 20 years ago when I first started working. I think there's a lot more public awareness that this happens not only in conflict zones, but in regular life as well. And in all places, it's a very hard crime to prosecute and to punish. I think there have been more efforts to try and prevent it in many places, and there are a lot of very good community groups providing strong support and really trying to help people. But this is a crime that will probably exist as long as there are human beings, and that's unfortunately a fact.

I think there's been a lot of good work to advocate, to support survivors, to try and break taboos, to create spaces for them to talk. Even though the #MeToo movement is criticized for different reasons, it has opened a space for these kinds of stories and for people to know that they aren't alone, which I will be honest, I did not feel, but I was surprised at how many other people did feel.

Why do you say that it's so difficult to prosecute?

Because it's very hard to prove sexual violence cases. In many cases, it's hard to find the perpetrator, and it's also very hard to prove that it wasn't consensual. So even if there is physical evidence, being able to prove that it was coerced is very difficult. Beyond that, in many places, like when I was raped in Syria, you could get in trouble for having extramarital sex. It was this very strange thing that I was told, don't go to the police because you might get in trouble if you go and report this.

In some places, even in Western countries like in the UK and the US, there are certain kinds of barriers. In some other places, there are even higher barriers. In a lot of countries, it's still the law that if a rapist marries their victim, that absolves all kinds of charges. And that was true where that happened to me. So yes, there are lots of barriers to justice, but I would say even in the US and the UK, it's one of the lowest prosecuted crimes because it's very hard to prove. And moreover, it's very difficult for victims to come forward and talk about things like that and be confident that it's going to lead anywhere and that they'll be believed.

Obviously it affects predominantly women. In that vein, what do you think the role of women specifically in peacebuilding is?

It's a good question. I will be honest that I don't lean in too much to the narrative that women are natural peacebuilders and men are naturally more violent. I've met a lot of women who I wouldn't describe as peace-makers, and more importantly, I've met so many men who have devoted their lives to peacebuilding, conflict resolution, and human rights. I try not to be too binary about that. But I would say that globally, and especially in many international contexts, women have not always been included in negotiations and peacebuilding processes, both in terms of governing and even NGO leadership. A lot of things that are changing rapidly and for the better, in say the UK or the US, are still not the case in much of the world. That needs to be changed, to have women in these spaces, but not to the exclusion of men who I think also can be very, very positive peacemakers.

Organizations such as the UN and their agencies are increasingly criticized for not being able to stop global conflicts. Having had direct experience with them, do you have anything to say on that matter?

I feel that the United Nations gets a lot of criticism, and some rightly deserved. But the United Nations is only as good as the community of countries that make it up, who all have their own interests. The United Nations was and is intentionally a weak organization so that countries can't set up a world government. There are a lot of inherent contradictions in the UN, but the things that the UN can do well, I think it does do well. It's very good at raising awareness and getting food to places that otherwise would not have access. There are a lot of international baseline services that trace back to the UN. It's very helpful that we have the UN doing those things. Where the UN struggles more is in peacekeeping and conflict prevention. It would be great if it were different. But at the same time, that's more because of countries' political will, rather than the UN.

I appreciate calls to reform the Security Council, but I think the UN is always going to be limited in what it can do. For NGOs, it's a bit different. One reason that I dabble in NGOs but haven't left academia to go and work for them is this tension where you can see a lot of the good that's done, but there's also a lot of bureaucracy, a lot of red tape. 90% of your work is often the fundraising and trying to work with donors or filling out reports and grids, where the time and resources could be used for helping people. You see the inefficiency in a lot of these things, but the alternative to not have them, I always think is worse.

Do you think the nature of NATO and the UN might change in the foreseeable future, especially with the US election coming up?

NATO will be more affected than the UN, but even NATO is an alliance that goes up and down with its level of strength as conflicts demand it. We've seen a much more robust NATO in the last few years because of Ukraine. I do think if there's a Trump presidency, the US's role will subside, but I don't see the alliance falling apart. The UN also goes up and down with US involvement and funding and support, but I don't see the organization as going anywhere.

Can you tell me a bit about the project you worked on: "Conflict Sensitivity and Community Resilience in Conflict Zones"?

This was a multi-year project that I did with Christian Aid. We were funded by Irish Aid and then by the EU. It's a funding chain that's not atypical in these kinds of spaces. We often think about conflict aid in one big lump, but people who work in the sector see it as three pillars. The first is direct humanitarian aid when there's a crisis – so that's food relief, sanitation, those kinds of basic needs. The second is development, and longer-term elements. The third is peacebuilding, conflict prevention, and trying to stop violence. These three pillars usually work independently, and that's been intentional historically so that you don't mix politics with getting aid to people. However, in a lot of conflicts we're seeing now, they're very intertwined, and there's been a recognition that you can't address one without the other.

I was part of a project trying to look at community-led approaches to weaving these strands together and seeing communities in places that were facing all these challenges. What were they prioritizing, and how were community members leading on it? That was in South Sudan, in Burundi, in the Congo, and in Myanmar. We did multiple field visits, mostly going out to very remote areas or to displaced person refugee camps. We talked directly to people who were experiencing the worst of these conflicts and humanitarian disasters, to see what was working, and what wasn't working for them. We then presented the research back to the NGO to inform their programming moving forward.

It was super informative, and it was a huge learning experience for me. My take is that it is necessary and hopeful to integrate those pieces, but it also asks a lot of local partners to be able to do all those things effectively. But I do believe in locally-led processes. And so, I think the academic, international sense that we should weave all these things together is true, but it's also true that local partners often are really strong and have capacity in one area only. That needs to be a starting point, rather than introducing this burden that assumes expertise in, for example, conflict prevention as well as food delivery.

How do you see that playing out in Israel–Palestine right now?

I would say Gaza is going to be one of these contexts where this is the case. Gaza has a strong background of being a highly educated society, so that has a lot going for it. But Gaza's going to face massive dual challenges of reconstruction alongside an ongoing conflict situation that probably is not going away anytime soon. It is going to be a big challenge for Gazans first and foremost as well as for NGOs and internationals trying to assist with that, with working out how you start rebuilding and get the aid in without entrenching a conflict situation or dynamic that you don't want to be feeding into. It's an ongoing question right now, and all of us who care about that part of the world are trying to figure out how to do that.

How has your academic career influenced your work in policy and practice, and vice versa?

They definitely go back and forth for me. I'm a teaching professor rather than what most professors are, which is more research oriented. It works for me because I can bring a lot of stuff into the classroom from places where I've worked. In my Political Violence class, I can draw on this a lot, or in my Middle East class. And having the privilege to read, learn, and see some of the theories, background, and history is helpful when I go to do aid work. I'm not just showing up and being handed something. I've had the chance to learn about a context, to try to understand a place at least as much as I can from an academic perspective. And I would say I've learned a lot from my students too, which is great. They'll often push me to think about things differently, or students from certain parts of the world will help me to appreciate a different perspective before going to do work there.

What are the challenges that you see to peacebuilding today?

I would say, as always, the lack of political will. I think people often think about it as a finance/resources thing – and that's part of it – but not really in a lot of the conflicts that we see. It's more a question of certain states and certain leaders within certain states seeing conflict as more advantageous and more lucrative to them.

We're at a weird moment right now with conflicts. States are very belligerent, as well as non-state actors. In a lot of history, we've had one or the other: interstate war in the 20th century and before, whereas post-Cold War, there was more intrastate conflict like civil war. But now we're seeing all kinds of conflict, overlapping with each other, and a lot of our frameworks, tools, theories, and resources have not caught up with that kind of complexity.

When you say that there are so many different actors, can you speak a bit about the arms industry in the UK?

I'm not an expert on it, but in the UK as well as the US, where I'm from, the arms industry is a major industry. It's where we have a lot of links with countries, some that are friends and allies and some that we have a lot of reservations about with their human rights record. We use these things for either business or for maintaining stability. I would say that's obviously come up the most with Israel-Palestine and the aid that goes to

Israel in terms of military arms sales. The UK government, as you probably know, has suspended some transfers, and the US I think will be pressed to consider that at some point as well. But that's a major feedback loop.

Outside of that, small arms trafficking is a major issue around the world. That's extremely lucrative on illicit markets. So, we have the big arms trades which are challenging in their own way, but also these illicit arms markets as well.

Do you think social media disinformation and AI are changing the landscape of conflict resolution in any way?

They're definitely changing how people are seeing conflict. Social media has completely changed how people are viewing Israel-Palestine. I would say that's always been the case, but with this war more than ever before, when I talk to journalists, they say they have never seen this much misinformation flying back and forth as there is with the Gaza war. Anything you see, you need to double check and fact check. AI obviously contributes very much to that with the different kinds of images that can be created and circulated very easily.

Why do you think it's so high for the Gaza war in particular?

I think, as I said earlier, because Gazans are a society where people were and are very connected, very highly educated. Even though journalists can't get in, Gazans were very good about getting images and stories out, and a lot of those did not go through traditional media but through TikTok and socials. Young people around the world were seeing these images on a scale that was unprecedented in war imagery consumption. It went up gradually with TV, people were seeing more, and with the internet people were seeing more. But with things like TikTok and Instagram – and with as many citizen journalists as are now active, with anyone with a phone being able to record and upload images – it has completely changed the landscape.

Do you think that AI and social media are two things that NGOs and multinational organizations should be harnessing?

I would say social media for sure, and NGOs have started to do that. With AI, I don't know enough about how to utilize those tools, but I imagine there are ways to use the tools for positive impact and not for manipulation or disinformation – more for reaching people in an efficient way. I'm curious to see what NGOs will do in that space.

Do you think it's made peacebuilding efforts more difficult at all?

Yes, I would say so, because of the levels of misinformation that are there, and people will think they have proof of something that they don't really have. There is a gap between what policymakers and negotiators are seeing and what people are consuming on their phones, a disconnect in how the conflicts are being seen.

Can you tell me a bit about your recent trip to the Middle East?

I was in Israel-Palestine for about a month this summer, and it was a really difficult time to be there. I spoke with people across the board – West Bank, Israelis, a lot of remote interviews with the Gazans. It was striking almost in the mirror images of comments. I would need to look at my notes and see who said what because so many of the comments could have been said by people from either community, in terms of the level of pain that people were feeling, the level of personal as well as collective loss and trauma and the feeling of existential threat that came from that, the extent to which both communities felt unheard, the way they both felt that the international community did not understand what they were going through and had abandoned them. There was a real disillusionment with the international organizations and institutions you were asking about before as well as the media. They both felt the media was very biased against them. The immensity of the kind of trauma right there now is indescribable. And the actions that both communities are willing to take and/or support was much more extreme than I've heard it in the past.

At the same time, there are a lot of amazing peacemakers too, people conducting dialogue and cross-community work at this time. It was a difficult time to be there, but I think an important time to hear from people, to make sure people did feel heard and try to get their stories out, whether it's in the book that I'm writing, in short pieces that I wrote right after I came back, or even just in my classes, to try to get those voices out.

Is there an effort that the international community can take to make people feel more heard and less disillusioned?

A lot of people, a lot of Palestinians, spoke about the student protests that they were seeing on the news. Those were widely seen and appreciated, even though governments weren't making any moves beyond that. But they did see the solidarity from campus groups around the world, which meant a lot.

I think Israelis did not feel that and wanted, even within some of those more Palestine-leaning circles, at least an acknowledgement of the 7th of October, an acknowledgement of sexual violence, an acknowledgement of the hostages. They felt all the elements that were still part of their pain had been completely erased from the narrative. And I think even small nods of acknowledgement would go a long way for some that I spoke to.

You're designing a new course, 'Disagreeing Well.' Can you tell me about that?

I'm designing this with my friend and colleague, Thomas Gift. He works in the US, and I work in the Middle East. In both places we see students and people in general who are either at each other's throats when they try and engage, or more often, don't talk about it because they're afraid of saying the wrong thing. We felt that universities should be a space where students can come and discuss controversial and difficult topics and learn the skills of how to disagree with someone but do so in a respectful way. How do you have conversations about difficult things, not only in the classroom, but also with family members? So, we are designing this course that we hope will help students as students, but also as people to go forward in life and be open and more confident expressing their opinions, and have a bit more grace in hearing from others who they disagree with.

Dr. Julie M. Norman is an Assoc. Professor (Teaching) in Politics and International Relations at University College London (UCL), specializing in conflict, political violence, Middle East politics, and foreign policy. She also serves as a Senior Assoc. Fellow at the Royal United Services Institute (RUSI) and coordinates UCL's Israel-Palestine Initiative. Dr. Norman holds a PhD in International Relations from American University, with focuses in Human Rights and Conflict Resolution, and a BA from Duke University. Before UCL, she was a Research Fellow at Queen's University Belfast and a Lecturer at McGill and Concordia Universities in Canada. She has also held fellowships at institutions like MIT and Dartmouth College. Her research covers conflict, political violence, and resistance in protracted conflicts, particularly in the Middle East. Dr. Norman is the author of several books, including *The Palestinian Prisoners Movement* (2021) and *Sounding Conflict* (2023). She is a regular media commentator and has published widely in academic journals.

JEHAN PERERA

What does the National Peace Council in Sri Lanka do and what do you do as Executive Director?

The National Peace Council is an organization that was established in 1995 during a time of ceasefire, when the Civil War in Sri Lanka was taking place. The ceasefire coincided with the election of a new government led by a prime minister who had campaigned on the basis that what was taking place in Sri Lanka was an ethnic conflict rather than a terrorism problem. She agreed to find a solution to the war through negotiations and political reform. That's what motivated those of us who were working in different walks of life at that time to come together to form the National Peace Council. I'm one of the founding members.

We saw our basic mission as being one of explaining to the people of the country and creating awareness among them of the need for a political solution rather than a military solution to end the war. We felt this task required civil society support to the government, and the government was embarking on this new course of conflict resolution. At the same time, we also were aware that there had been previous attempts in prior decades, going back to the 1950s when efforts had been made by leaders to resolve the conflict, which was not violent at that time. It had taken the form of civil disobedience, for example, and it was thought that political settlement would resolve it. But they had failed, and part of the reason was that the majority of the major ethnic group, the Sinhalese, thought that the solutions that were being offered were injurious to the interests of the Sinhalese and of the unity of the country.

In a sense, the solution that was and continues to be necessary is a solution based on sharing power between the ethnic majority – Sinhalese – and the ethnic minorities, Tamils and Muslims. The Sinhalese are 75% of the population and the non-Sinhalese are 25%. So, whenever it comes to a question where the interests of the Sinhalese diverge from those of the Tamils and Muslims, it's inevitable that the decision will go in favour of the Sinhalese because they are 75% of Parliament. We have a system in which the Sinhalese are a permanent majority when it comes to decision-making on the big issues, and will always make decisions they think are fair to them, but which the minorities might not see as fair.

The solution that has been advocated in Sri Lanka for the past 70 years is devolution of power on a variant of federalism, specifically devolving power in the northern and eastern provinces, where the Tamil-speaking people are a majority. They will form the government of those areas and have some power; they can decide on their own without having to get approval from the Sinhalese. But that solution is very controversial in our country. It's viewed by the Sinhalese as a step to separation of the country. They point out that many countries that had federal systems have divided, like Czechoslovakia, former Yugoslavia, or the former Soviet Union. Federalism is seen as a first step to separation, and they are very apprehensive about it.

Our work, from the time we started in 1995 to now, has been to advocate to people that federalism is not about the division of the country, even though it has happened in some countries. It is about keeping the country together and ensuring justice for the ethnic minorities. It's the best way to keep the country united, ensuring the minorities also have a stake in the country and can achieve justice within the framework of a united Sri Lanka.

That is the work we do, taking that message, in various forms: workshops, training, conferences, common platforms for people to meet and interact with each other, lobbying with decision makers to ensure that people are treated equally, and using the legal system to ensure that abuses will be corrected. In the National Peace Council, that is the work we do and I, as executive director, give leadership to that. I am responsible for being the spokesperson for the organization and assisting in fundraising and setting out the vision and political analysis.

You've said before that the government and the majority of the population doesn't seem to see the ethnic conflict as a problem that still requires urgent attention. Why do you think that is?

Yes and no. After the war ended, the ethnic majority who live outside the areas where the ethnic minorities are living in or where they are a majority – they don't realize there's a problem. Life is normal for them.

When the war was on, they felt apprehension insofar as they were never sure when a bomb might go off, even in the capital city or in the Sinhalese majority areas. In those times, they were aware, and they could see on the media and newspapers that people had died, had been fighting, that there was destruction, killings, movement of people from one part of the country to another. Now, that has all ended. For the ethnic majority there's no sense of a real problem. The war is over, problem over. That is how the ethnic majority tends to see things.

We have then to tell them that yes, the war has ended, but the ethnic conflict continues. The problems that led to the war still remain unaddressed. After the end of the war, there are new problems that have to be dealt with, and one of those new problems is that of post-war justice.

During the war, there were a lot of human rights violations, and a lot of people went missing. When people go missing, there is always the hope in the minds of their families that their loved ones will come back. They are still hoping they will come back, even though 15 or 20 years have passed since they have been missing.

That issue needs to be addressed as well as the issue of justice and punishment. People also want to restart their lives. They may have lost everything they had during the war and become very poor. They need assistance to rebuild their lives. That whole set of problems remains in addition to the original problem of a political solution to the ethnic conflict that is based on sharing power.

Overall, we have more problems than we did before the war started, but they are less acute than during the war. Then, everyone was living in a lot of fear and suspicion. People of different ethnicities suspected each other of being on the other side, of being a security threat. That's all gone. During that period, even people like myself who stand for peace, non-violence and a negotiated settlement, when we spoke in those terms, there was suspicion that we were supporting the other side. In my case, since I'm Sinhalese, I was supporting the Tamil Tigers because I was trying to reduce the strength of the military response, and, therefore, I was helping them by talking about peaceful negotiations settlements. I was potentially a threat. That problem isn't there anymore, I'm able to be more outspoken than I was at the time because I'm confident now that I won't be seen in the same light. If someone starts being seen as a security threat, then that person becomes very vulnerable.

The flip side of that is that people don't think there's such a great problem at all and wonder why am I talking about it. I suppose this is a problem in any part of the world: the majority doesn't see that there's a problem; it's the minority who does.

But you are part of the majority Sinhalese and see that there is a problem?

True, but there is another factor that helped me be part of the majority and still see the problem, that relates to the multiple identities we have in our country. It includes gender, class, and caste as well as race, ethnicity and religion.

My ethnicity is Sinhalese, my mother tongue is Sinhala, but my religion is a minority. I am a Christian. The religion of the majority of the Sinhalese is Buddhism. So, although I am part of the Sinhalese ethnic majority, I am also part of a religious minority, a small minority. There have been problems in the past and even in the present between the communities.

For instance, when I was growing up in the 1960s, the state began to take over the Christian schools because it said the Christian schools were excellent schools that had benefited during the period of colonialism and were giving an unfair advantage to the Christian children or children of other religions. So the government, to equalize the situation, decided to take over the Christian schools by force.

Of course, the Christians didn't like it. They wanted to keep their schools, but the government, through law, insisted the schools be turned over to the state. I grew up in that period. My own parents were going to sit-down protests in the schools. Even at a young age, I felt my parents were doing something they might not come back from or where something might happen to them. I saw the powerlessness of a minority when faced with the intransigence of a majority. I am able to see both sides. I am part of the majority and part of the minority, and it helps me understand and empathize with the feelings of the minority.

What about the other people working in the National Peace Council? Are there people from both ethnicities and different religions?

The leadership of the National Peace Council comes from the minority side. I am a Sinhalese Christian, our chairman is a Christian Tamil, our Treasurer is a Hindu Tamil, and our general secretary is a Buddhist

Sinhalese. In our board and governing council, we have those who are from ethnic and religious minorities. In our staff, the clear majority is Sinhalese and Buddhist. They are the ones who go and work in the field, meet people, interact with them.

That goes into my next question: what's the contact with the population like?

The way we have designed our system is that we work through partner organizations. Outside Colombo, there are other civil society organizations, smaller ones, working at the district level. We have 25 districts in our country, and they might work for that particular district. We partner with them, and we want to do activities throughout the country rather than send one person from our staff to organise activities. We find a district partner organization, and then we go and resource people with the funding that we have obtained from our donors. It's a shared effort. Those who organise the programs will be close to the people because they already work in that area.

Our strength is that we are able to identify these district partners and work with them. We have consciously decided not to set up branch offices of our own but rather to work through district-level partners. Two reasons for that: one, it reduces the administrative burden on us to raise funds and to sustain a countrywide network of our own staff and offices; and two, we are strengthening civil society because we support groups that have organically developed in their own areas.

What are the challenges of contact with the population?

There's no problem in contacting the population. There's a lot of interest in our work, much greater than we can provide with our resources, so we consciously select what we call community leaders and influencers rather than working with the general population. The beneficiaries of our work are often religious clergy from all the religions. We have set up interfaith communities at a district-level and at a subdistrict-level.

We feel that those who are clergy are trusted messengers to the people. We try to influence them, and then they go to the people directly. In addition, we work with other NGOs, community leaders, local government officials, and community police, as well as school teachers and local business people. Basically, civil society leaders in those areas. They can also be considered part of the general population, but they are at a slightly higher level, have certain means, and hold leadership positions. We work with them rather than going and working with farmers or workers because we feel our limited resources are better put to use if we work with those who are community leaders.

What kind of challenges do you still face in the work you do?

The work we do is very small scale. Even though we are considered a large organization – we have close to 40 members of staff – it's still a drop in the bucket compared to the government. The government has 1.5 million staff. There's no comparison.

The government is also much more powerful than us in terms of reaching people and giving them messages that are, perhaps, the opposite of what we give them. Same with political parties. They are much larger than us, have more resources, are more exciting to people than us, because political parties offer people the hope of getting power. If they support a political party and go for a political meeting, their side might win one day, and then they are in power. If they work with us, they don't get much.

One of the problems we face is that we reach a limited number of people, and we can't reach them all the time because we have to go from one place to another with limited staff. In a way, it's like the work we do can be blown away the next day. If there's a crisis, a politician will go and say something completely different to what we say. It's hard for us to succeed if the mainstream politics of the country is giving a different message. We can't cause the large scale change of attitude that's needed for real change to take place. That's one major problem that we've experienced. We are small in relation to the population. The work we do is very hard to sustain. Our groups are sustained, but they can't change the country by themselves.

Our philosophy is that the best we can do is try to show those in positions of power what is possible, that it's possible to change the thinking of people. If we can do it on a small scale, it can also be done on a larger scale if there is political will. We are working and trying to create larger groups. We are now working with state officials, who are more powerful than the community leaders, and now we have enough credit to go and work with the state.

In the past, they didn't want to work with us. They thought we were traitors or that our thinking was not acceptable. Now, our thinking is considered more acceptable, so the government is willing to work with us and talk to us about the issues. It's a gradual process and not one that is sufficient at the moment to cause a change in the laws in parliament itself. We have not been able to influence the thinking of those who really have power because it's hard to reach them. They're not interested in attending our training programs and workshops. They think they know what the problem is and are less receptive to working with us. And they have their own agenda. In the end, it's about getting political power. They do what it takes to win the next election.

Regarding the information the population gets, what's the impact of social media? How does it affect what you do?

We don't use it as much as we could. There are other groups who use it much more. Our stand is face-to-face interaction with people. We go to them and discuss things with them. Social media is very ephemeral, it comes and goes, and there's a lot of it. It's not just us putting our ideas up there; there are political parties, activists, so, in the end, there has been more negative social media than positive.

On a larger scale, it doesn't mean the people who use social media are more enlightened than the people who don't. They're basically the same. Social media offers us a tool, but others use the same tool. We think social media is doing a good job insofar as it counteracts a government that is not so democratic, not doing the right things, and very corrupt.

At the moment, they're coming up with new laws to regulate the media. It is easy for the government to control mainstream media, which wants to make profits and can have their arms twisted. Social media is harder to control. Anyone can go and put up a post. It has become harder for the government to control the news flow, and now people are getting alternative media sources, most of which are really critical of the government. That doesn't mean there are messages that are constructive or healing in terms of bridging the ethnic and religious divides. That doesn't necessarily happen.

Because social media takes a critical attitude against the government, it has an impact on the government's popularity. It's because of social media that we hear about a lot of the negative things that are happening inside the government. The mainstream media doesn't report those things because they self-censor out of fear. Social media is not afraid. A TV Station can be shut down. A case can be filed against a journalist. Social media is more anonymous. But that doesn't mean they're putting statements out that are conducive to bringing ethnic communities together or in terms of peacebuilding.

You wrote about the impact the diaspora in India, the United States, Japan, and EU countries can have in the resolution of the conflict in Sri Lanka. What can they do?

People who are in the diaspora don't have to suffer the consequences of what they say. Sometimes, they stand for absolute principles in the sense of saying that we need to have self-determination or that we need a separate country. But when the government reacts to that, they don't have to face the consequences. They can take harder stances because they're very far away. Those who are in the country often are more willing to make the compromises because they can face consequences. They don't want to be in conflict; they want to, somehow, be in a midpoint. Whereas those in the diaspora can stay where they are and ask for 400% of what they want, those in the country will probably give up 50% of what they want to try to find a middle way.

They can also stand up for justice that the state does not provide. They can stand up and demand it in a way that people who are inside the country can't. I would say, however, that the diaspora should visit the country more, spend more time in the country, come and see, talk and engage with people here. Of course, when they do come here, they probably get even more angry, but if they come here and spend more time, they will be more willing to try to find win-win solutions which benefit both sides.

Do you believe the conflicts happening now – between Russia and Ukraine and in the Gaza Strip – can impact the way the international community looks at what has been happening in Sri Lanka for decades?

The international community isn't so interested in Sri Lanka anymore, not that they were ever very interested aside from some groups linked to the diaspora. Now, the interest is probably even less because the attention is focused on what is going on in those other countries where the stakes are much higher for the world, for Europe and America, than what happened in Sri Lanka. But in a way, what's happening in those countries is also not good for those who are working for peace in Sri Lanka because we can see that the western powers are permitting certain atrocities to happen – the same atrocities that they were criticizing in our country and that now they're keeping quiet about in other countries.

With that comes the issue of the double standard, which encourages people to take a harder stance in our country, especially with regard to issues of justice for what happened in the past. As a result, many other countries are becoming more cynical about human rights, justice, war crimes, and punishment for war crimes, and they will be less likely to urge Sri Lanka to deal with its own past because they can see what's being allowed to happen in Gaza and Ukraine. They will be less likely to demand accountability on the part of the Sri Lankan government because that same accountability is not being demanded of the fighting forces in those countries. It's negative for justice and what we stood for.

Jehan Perera is a founder member and presently Executive Director of the National Peace Council of Sri Lanka (NPC) which was established in 1995. NPC focuses on building public support for a political solution to the ethnic conflict and on supporting inter-ethnic and inter-religious conflict mitigation through community cohesion. He is also on the board of the People's Action for Free and Fair Elections and the Centre for Communication Training. In 2017 he was invited by the government of Sri Lanka to join its delegation to the UN Human Rights Commission in Geneva as a civil society representative. He is a political analyst and columnist for national newspapers and websites focusing on inter-ethnic reconciliation and peace building. He writes a regular weekly political column for the national media. He is also a visiting lecturer in conflict and peace studies programmes at universities. He holds a Bachelor of Arts degree from Harvard College and a Juris Doctor from Harvard Law School.

TONY SCHIENA

Can you tell us about your organization and what it offers?

MOSAIC stands for Multi-Operational Security Agency Intelligence Company – though not necessarily in that order. Our primary focus is intelligence. While some assume we're a Private Military Company (PMC), our core function revolves around intelligence operations. Of course, there are times when our work overlaps with security, but intelligence remains our main area of expertise.

Our clients typically include nation-states – more specifically, their intelligence agencies – or high-net-worth individuals who own major corporations. For example, earlier today, while I was at NASDAQ, I had to step away for two critical calls. One was with a prominent Wall Street client dealing with a cyber defamation issue, and the other concerned an African nation facing political instability.

Our work often involves due diligence, market entry strategies, and mergers and acquisitions, where clients need to assess risks associated with potential deals. Take one of our past assignments, for instance: a major Wall Street firm was acquiring a data-rich company in a multi-billion-dollar transaction. At the last minute, they realized they hadn't fully vetted the cyber infrastructure. The concern was: "Are we buying something that already has leaks?" We conducted a thorough assessment to ensure the security of their investment.

That same day, I was also involved in discussions regarding the potential overthrow of a government in an African nation. Our work spans a broad spectrum – from corporate concerns like fraud, extortion, and cyber threats to geopolitical risks, physical security, and crisis management. We handle the full scope of security challenges that come with immense financial power and influence.

How did you get into the world of security and intelligence?

It wasn't something I planned. I was studying international trade and law in college, aiming to become a maritime attorney. But my law professor saw potential in me and recruited me for a completely different path–one I never expected.

My entry into this field was rapid and intense. South Africa was undergoing a massive transition at the time, dismantling the Apartheid system. The country was on the brink of civil war, and the environment was highly volatile. I was thrown into the deep end, navigating security and intelligence issues in real time.

It was a fast-paced introduction and an equally quick transition out of that phase. Looking back, I'd say I'm truly a product of the private security and intelligence industry. My career has been shaped by the dynamic and unpredictable nature of this work, and that experience continues to guide what we do at MOSAIC today.

Can you share a specific instance in which your tools or strategies led to a meaningful resolution of a conflict?

At the heart of any resolution is a strong moral compass. I won't pursue a course of action I don't believe in because, ultimately, it won't lead to a good outcome. Integrity guides every decision I make.

There have been times when we've had to operate in the gray areas to secure justice for a client who was genuinely wronged. When I believe in a case, I go the extra mile to make things right.

What tools or strategies did you use to achieve a successful outcome?

Let me share an example, one that isn't strictly military or private sector but a blend of both. A powerful family helped fund and support a political leader's rise to power. However, as is often the case, once in office, that leader turned against them. The family was forced to flee their home country and live in asylum abroad.

The situation escalated when the leader of that nation sought to forcibly repatriate them – essentially abducting them and sending them back to face persecution. All the family wanted was to be left alone and live in peace, but they were trapped, unable to travel freely.

We were brought in through legal channels to assess the situation and find a resolution. In cases like these, no one is ever completely clean, but the question isn't about absolute right or wrong, it's about finding the best possible outcome in a corrupt system. The government in question was highly corrupt, whereas our clients, while not without their own complexities, were the clear victims in this case.

The key was leverage. In intelligence, leverage is everything. How do we gain enough influence to bring the other side to the negotiation table? The answer wasn't military force or direct confrontation but strategic backdoor diplomacy. We gathered intelligence – critical information about the leader's actions and vulnerabilities – and used it to apply pressure.

The conversation shifted from, "You're doing this to my client," to, "We know what you've been doing how do we resolve this?" It was through this delicate negotiation process that we reached an agreement. As a result, the family regained freedoms and the leader of that country agreed to back off – not because of goodwill, but because of the leverage we held.

This was a case where resolution didn't require boots on the ground or aggressive action. It was about understanding the power dynamics at play, using intelligence strategically, and finding a middle ground that both parties could accept.

Is it a case of building trust between the two parties?

Not really. There's no real trust between the parties – just a carefully orchestrated dance. But even a song and dance is a better outcome than where things started. The fact that the family was left in a position of power rather than that of wanted persons hiding in a country that gave them asylum, speaks volumes.

A similar example happens in corporate fraud cases. When a company is defrauded and wants to recover its money, my firm – through our law practice – steps in to resolve the matter. Whether it's through legal proceedings or intelligence work, I've never seen a case where the full amount is recovered. There's always a settlement, a compromise, a meeting of minds. And in these cases, no one ever recoups interest. That's the reality of resolution – it's about finding a workable middle ground rather than a perfect outcome.

Can you share an experience where the wrong strategy was employed, worsening a conflict? What would you have done differently?

Afghanistan as a whole is a prime example of a failed strategy. I personally spent time in and out of the country, particularly in Mazar-i-Sharif, in Northern Afghanistan, where I was involved in training the Afghan National Army (ANA). One specific unit I worked with later became the Criminal Investigation Division (CID) of the ANA. Their mission was to investigate Taliban-related murders in small villages.

The first team that was sent in faced a disastrous outcome. Due to some bureaucratic failure – perhaps an assumption that criminal investigators wouldn't need weapons – they were deployed unarmed. The result? They were captured, and many were executed – some even beheaded.

After that, I was tasked with training the next group. My focus shifted to survival tactics: how to escape if captured, how to manoeuvre without a weapon, and how to increase their chances of making it out alive. I would pretend to be a Taliban operative and then show them how I could trick them and disarm their weapons etc. That experience reinforced a fundamental lesson – never send people into a hostile environment unprepared. The bigger lesson was, however, watching new recruits marching by while standing next to a full-bird US army colonel and have him nudge me and say, "How does it feel that you're training a group where the majority very well may try and kill you?" We have seen this scenario numerous times where the US government and CIA have armed and trained groups, as their proxy, to fight an enemy and then that same group turns against them. In this case the Afghan soldiers he was referring to were already on their way to becoming Taliban.

Another critical lesson I learned was about the risks of using contractors. Initially, I built what was essentially a boutique private intelligence agency – everything under one roof: legal analysis, special forces operators, and intelligence specialists. It was efficient, controlled, and highly specialized.

But when an organization grows too large, you start relying on outside contractors. That's where problems arise. Contractors hired for surveillance, for instance, might not follow the same ethical or operational standards as trained in-house personnel. If they overstep – cross legal lines or act too aggressively – it creates serious blowback for the client.

A prime historical example of this issue was Blackwater in Iraq, particularly in Fallujah. Their rapid expansion meant they were no longer just hiring top-tier special forces operators. At a certain point, they were down to recruiting regular police officers and former soldiers and PMC contractors that lacked the ethics and skills of their predecessors. That lack of quality control led to major consequences.

For me, maintaining a tight, elite team is crucial. My business model is built on working only with the crème de la crème. When high-level clients need us, we deliver. But I won't expand beyond what I can personally oversee. Any larger, and it would require a completely different business model – one I have no interest in pursuing.

Because your risk goes up if you have people doing things that are out of control?

Absolutely. I want to be able to sleep at night.

You could start a war rather than help things?

Yes, absolutely and I want to be able to look at myself in the mirror.

Can you describe a particularly challenging moment? What obstacles did you face, and how did you overcome them?

From the moment I was recruited into this world until today, trust has always been a rare commodity. In a business like mine, you don't fully trust anyone because, at the end of the day, people can be compromised. That's why, as a private company, I choose carefully who I work for.

One of the most challenging moments of my career was during the fight against ISIS in Kurdistan. It was a time that I almost lost my life, Kurdish soldiers dived me to the ground as we received incoming sniper fire from ISIS snipers targeting me. ISIS weaponry consisted of the rudimentary, improvised devices to sophisticated sniper rifles, mustard gas and radioactive material. At the time, the Kurdish forces were the only organized group actively fighting ISIS, while Russian and American forces were holding back in Mosul, observing but not engaging. This was also during the Obama administration's so-called "red line" stance against weapons of mass destruction (WMDs) and chemical weapons.

While training Kurdish soldiers on a base, I discovered that ISIS was using mustard gas – and not just that, but also radioactive material. Kurdish fighters were describing a strange, glowing, sticky substance. When they brought their cell phones near it, the devices would malfunction.

I asked, "What did you do with it?" They told me that Western advisors had instructed them to dig a hole and cover it with sand. That was shocking. Western military advisors were telling frontline fighters to bury radioactive material on their bases, instead of properly handling it.

To make things worse, the Kurds were fighting on the front lines without gas masks. I went up into the mountains to see the badly wounded – no medical support had reached them, no doctors, nothing, I was the first and I think the only. All they wanted was to recover so they could fight again. I examined their injuries, inspected a weapon that had deployed mustard gas, interviewed the deputy head of intelligence and base commander and immediately knew this had to be escalated.

I called a close friend, a SEAL Team commander working on the ISIS desk at the Pentagon, and told him exactly what was happening. But the response from US advisors was complete denial. Instead of acting, they questioned me: "What are you doing there again, Tony?"

At that point, I was beyond frustrated. It was clear they didn't want to acknowledge the reality on the ground. I hung up and focused on getting gas masks to the Kurds immediately.

I reached out to Prince Ali of Jordan, then to King Abdullah, and arranged for the delivery of gas masks. Ironically, these were American-made masks, as Jordan's military supply comes from the US

Then it went to the press. I told them that ISIS was using WMDs – chemical and radioactive weapons. The next day, an article was published exposing the situation, which ruffled a lot of feathers. But within 24 hours, German intelligence confirmed the same findings: ISIS *was* using these weapons. People started suspecting me of being BND[1] as the article mentioning German intelligence confirming ISIS using chemical weapons has a photo of me photographing a Kurdish soldier with mustard gas burns. It didn't help that I speak conversational German either.

This created a major challenge for the Obama administration. The so-called red line against WMDs had been crossed, and they had been ignoring evidence of it. This time it wasn't Assad and the usage of sarin in Syria, this was chemical and radioactive weapons used by the most ruthless and evil terror group of our time.

That experience made me question a lot. I even had a representative from the Canadian foreign office reach out, asking me to report directly to them because they were starting to doubt the accuracy of their own special forces' reports. That's when you realize the level of fragmentation within military and government operations.

It's like law enforcement (and one of the reasons 9/11 happened), the police don't always cooperate with the sheriffs, the sheriffs and police have issues with the FBI, and so on. In the military and intelligence world, it's the same thing. Everyone is operating within their own agenda, following their own instructions, and keeping information siloed. It's not about the mission – it's about internal politics and control.

---

1   BND is the German Intelligence Service

Presumably, they had some mandate not to escalate things?

I was embedded with a deputy director of intelligence, and his approach was always cautious. He'd say, "Show me what's happening." So, he'd observe ISIS moving weapons in ambulances, digging trenches, and covering them with oil to create smoke barriers for concealment. He saw it was all happening in real-time, but the Americans or Russians or anyone else wouldn't react.

He explained, "If we report an incident happening over there, they won't act. But if we report something in a specific area, maybe, in a few hours, they'll do something." It was like there was an invisible line, the selective engagement was frustrating.

I might have pushed the needle more than was good for my business, at least when it comes to dealing with the US government. I lit a fire by exposing Obama's failure to act on his own red line against WMDs.

Do you think the use of AI and robots will lead to greater conflict between nations?

I've seen some military AI demonstrations, and while they're impressive, they're also terrifying. If a weapon can think for itself, where does that lead? It's like we watched *Blade Runner* or *Terminator* years ago, and now we're seeing parts of that come to life. Does life dictate art or art dictate life?

Again, it all comes down to *who* is in control of the technology. Who is giving the orders? If the wrong people are running an AI-powered military program, it could lead to the same kind of reckless decisions we saw in Iraq. Of course, the main chatter and concern is about the advancement of AI to a point where AI makes its own decisions, autonomously.

What if a rogue nation or a group like ISIS gets hold of this technology?

Then we're all in trouble. ISIS was already using a mix of crude and sophisticated technology in terrifying ways. I saw them attach what looked like a badminton shuttlecock to an explosive and drop it from a drone – primitive but effective. They also took standard gas canisters, welded makeshift wings onto them for greater travel distance, and packed them with metal bolts and screws. When those exploded, the molten metal tore through everything in its path. If terrorist groups were to get their hands on advanced AI weaponry, the consequences would be catastrophic.

Years ago, I participated in a *Vice* documentary called *Superpower for Hire*. It featured Eric Prince from Blackwater, my friend Simon Mann, and others in the private military world. At the end, I was asked, "How powerful will private military companies (PMCs) become?"

I said, "PMCs will reach a point where they could turn against the nations that hire them."

We saw this happen with the Wagner Group in Russia – they turned on Putin. Now, imagine a Wagner-like force equipped with AI-controlled weaponry. If a private military company – or worse, a rogue faction – gets access to highly advanced, autonomous military systems, what's to stop them from deciding they no longer need to follow orders?

What happens when AI weaponry or other advanced military technology ends up on the black market?

It's inevitable. Weapons always end up where they shouldn't.

Take the current situation with Ukraine, for example. A lot of the US weapons sent there aren't staying in the right hands. Many have already made their way to the Ukrainian mafia. People assume the Russian mob is bad, but the Ukrainian mob is just as ruthless. I've dealt with them firsthand – I was getting death threats from Ukraine after running a very successful mission of which SBU, Ukrainian intelligence was aware of but made enemies of a formidable Ukrainian organized crime organization. It escalated to a point where both the FBI and CIA were informed.

The same thing has happened before. The anthrax that was sent to the White House? That was a South African strain, traced back to their old Chemical and Biological Weapons (CBW) program. A former South African intelligence agent warned about this strain of anthrax becoming available on the black market. When governments change, the people who worked on these programs don't just disappear – they take their expertise with them, and some are willing to sell it.

If an AI-powered weapon system gets into the wrong hands, it won't just be one nation's problem – it'll be a global crisis.

Do you think chemical and biological weapons (CBWs) are properly controlled?

Absolutely not. There's an international agreement banning CBWs, signed by almost every country except North Korea, Iran, Syria, and maybe one or two others. But that doesn't mean the major powers aren't still developing them.

The US still works on these weapons. The UK does. France does. Why? Because CBWs are just as effective – if not *more* effective – than nuclear weapons, and they cost far less to develop.

These weapons are supposed to be highly secured, but history has proven otherwise.

For example, what if a foreign intelligence agency wants to obtain a particular strain of a deadly virus? They don't need to break into a high-security lab. They just need to find someone inside – someone willing to be compromised. Maybe they bribe a technician, who walks out with a vial. But if the transport conditions aren't right, the material degrades, or worse – it leaks.

Or imagine a natural disaster, an earthquake that damages a lab where CBWs are stored. Suddenly, something lethal is released into the environment.

Look at what happened with COVID. The entire world was shut down by a virus. Now, imagine if that had been a *weaponized* virus.

The reality is, CBWs and advanced AI military systems need to be tightly controlled. But if history has taught us anything, it's that they won't be.

Some people believe COVID escaped from a lab, don't they?

I do. A few months after it happened, while it was still an epidemic, I released a book that I co-authored with a former British agent who lives under the pseudonym John Kingsley, called *Surviving Epidemics and Bioterrorism.* The difference is that it wasn't weaponized. If it had been, hundreds of millions more would be dead.

Do you think cyber warfare will become more prevalent between nations?

Absolutely. Cyber AI is where the battlefield is now. We are deeply connected to the internet, and for years, people have understood that we'd reach a point where entire governments, corporations, and infrastructure could be compromised through cyberattacks. Now, that moment has arrived.

The dark web only adds another layer of danger. There's an entire underground economy thriving on cybercrime, human trafficking, fraud, and extortion.

For about 15 years, I've run an organization dedicated to fighting human trafficking in both the US and the UK. My work in this area started with being deputized by Sheriff Mike Brown in Virginia and a DOJ, Department of Justice task force called ICAC – *Internet Crimes Against Children* – which was designed to combat online solicitation and trafficking.

The internet is a powerful tool for intelligence collection. You can spy on others, be spied on, and very easily, you can be compromised. Information is leverage, and cyber warfare is all about controlling that leverage.

The problem is, we're always playing catch-up. Criminals, fraudsters, and state-sponsored hackers are evolving faster than law enforcement or security agencies can respond. There aren't enough resources, funding, or manpower to fully combat these threats.

AI will likely become a key player in this war – on *both* sides. The digital landscape is shifting rapidly, and anyone who isn't keeping up is already behind.

How do you decide which clients to help and which to turn down?

It's always a judgement call. Take this morning's call about an African country – this isn't my first time dealing with these situations.

A couple of years ago, I was in Uganda when a general and his entourage flew in from a country further south just to meet me. From the moment I shook his hand, I knew I wanted to wash mine afterward.

The conversation didn't last long. What he wanted was *not* something I do. I left that meeting, ignored all their follow-up calls, and told myself, "That was a complete waste of time. They could have been clearer upfront."

They wanted you to stage a coup or something?

Along those lines but not exactly. But they were *not* the kind of people I do business with. Since I had already made the trip, I decided to make something of it. Instead of heading straight back, I drove six hours overland, hired a guide, and went deep into the jungles of Uganda near the Rwandan border to track silverback gorillas. I spent time with them, it was now, well-worth the trip.

At the end of the day, you have to make the right decisions – not just for your safety, but for your conscience. You have to be able to look yourself in the mirror. At the end of the day, on this planet, all others will be left with is your name and what you stood for.

If you want to stay intact – not just physically, but spiritually – you have to know where to draw the line.

And presumably, there are clients who just want land and resources and are willing to kill for it?

Some are overt about it, but most are covert. A lot of the nations we think of as *clean* simply carry out these actions in a more sophisticated and strategic manner. Unfortunately, that's the reality.

Do you think increasing desertification and climate change, particularly in Africa, will lead to more conflict as land becomes more valuable?

Absolutely. Large-scale displacement always leads to instability, and when people are forced to move, human trafficking spikes.

We've seen it firsthand. During natural disasters in Trinidad, for example, when families were displaced, children were kidnapped. Traffickers would drive around in vans, offering food and water, only to abduct them.

The same thing happened in Ukraine. We were there at the very beginning of the war, receiving calls from foreign governments asking us to help evacuate their people. After doing work inside Ukraine, I deployed some of my guys to the Polish border to monitor the situation, and we immediately saw how organized crime was capitalizing on the chaos.

Whenever there's a refugee crisis, multiple things happen at once. Refugees are trying to escape for a better life, but in the process, they become targets. The mafia, cartels, and criminal networks seize the opportunity. On the other hand, countries that don't *want* an influx of refugees see tensions rise between locals and new arrivals.

I've seen it all over the world. I was in Greece when refugees started landing on the islands, and I was in southern Italy during the migration waves. Both of those countries actually handled the situation relatively well – it could have been far worse.

But look at South Africa. Over the years, people from other African nations have flooded into Johannesburg looking for work, and the locals reacted violently, believing they were losing job opportunities. That fear and resentment fuelled xenophobic murders and attacks.

Then there are the drug cartels, which are now deeply involved in human trafficking. A human being is more valuable than drugs – drugs are sold once, but a trafficked person can be exploited repeatedly. This is why human trafficking has become one of the most lucrative criminal enterprises. On borders like the US-Mexico border, the cartel-controlled trafficking industry is a whole different beast. It's organized crime at its most ruthless – these are networks that don't just operate in the shadows; they influence governments.

Border conflicts often intertwine with issues of religion, culture, and national identity. How do these factors complicate conflict resolution?

It makes it exponentially more complicated. Look at the Sunni-Shia divide – it's a centuries-old conflict that still plays out today. We've seen it across the Middle East.

One of my former clients was a middle eastern country's first head of intelligence. He was trained by the British because this country didn't have an intelligence agency at the time. MI6, the Americans, and others helped set up their security apparatus, and he became the first leader of it.

Years later, I met with him after he had fled the country. He wanted to hire us to recover "assets" that had been "stolen" from him. Of course, the reality was that *he* had stolen a lot of money from the government, fled, and then made reckless investments.

We managed to track down one of his *assets* – a private island he had bought off the coast of Panama. I called him and said, "Good news and bad news. We found your island. The bad news? It only exists for two hours a day. When the tide comes in, it disappears."

He had been scammed. Deservedly so. But beyond the corruption, the country has a deeper issue with the sectarian divide. He had been responsible for torture and repression. So when an uprising happened, people went straight to his house. His guards were armed, and they fought back.

When you're dealing with conflicts fuelled by generations of animosity and religious division, you're just plugging holes. There's never a true resolution – it's only ever temporary.

Now, look at Palestine. If Palestinians were forcibly removed from their land, what message does that send? It would create a whole new wave of extremism.

When religion is the primary motivator, you don't just create resistance fighters – you create suicide bombers.

If the perception is that the US is fully backing the Israeli agenda, that anger will be directed back at the West. History has shown us this time and time again. It's an incredibly delicate and dangerous situation.

Ceasefires have been a common mechanism for de-escalation. What are the key challenges in making such agreements durable rather than just temporary pauses?

Trust is the key factor, isn't it? But the real question is, how do you establish trust? Even if trust exists on paper, enforcement is another challenge. From an operational standpoint, a ceasefire needs oversight – constant mediation by a neutral third party to ensure all sides uphold the agreement. Without that, a ceasefire is just a fragile truce waiting to collapse.

The real complexity arises when multiple groups exist within one side of a conflict. Not all factions will agree to the ceasefire, and even if a deal is struck, a single rogue faction can break it in an instant.

South Africa, for example, managed to dismantle apartheid without descending into full-scale civil war. There was violence, no doubt, but it could have spiralled into absolute chaos. I was there – it's remarkable what was achieved.

Was that due to Nelson Mandela's leadership?

Absolutely, central and pivotal but people often forget about F.W. de Klerk. He played a critical role. He was the one who stepped down and said, "This is the end of this." He and Mandela even received a joint Nobel Peace Prize.

The geopolitical landscape at the time also played a role – the Soviet system was crumbling, the Berlin Wall had just fallen. Communism wasn't the enemy anymore. People forget that it was the CIA that initially provided intelligence leading to Mandela's arrest because he was viewed as a terrorist back then and the US Department of Defense included the ANC in a 1988 report billed as profiles of "key regional terrorist groups" from around the world. Shockingly he was on the US government's Terrorist Watch List until 2008 but clearly in the early 90s, de Klerk recognized that it was time for change, and he acted on it. Nelson Mandela became the first democratically elected President of South Africa in 1994.

The fact that the country avoided a full-scale civil war, largely because of a leader who decided to step down and do what's necessary for equality and another leader to take his place that led from his heart and not his pocket, remains one of the most extraordinary transitions in modern history. Reflecting on the various conflicts around the world today, it's a truly remarkable feat and should serve as an example to the world.

Do you credit the Truth and Reconciliation Commission for that?

Yes, the TRC played a crucial role in South Africa's transition. It helped facilitate integration, including within intelligence agencies, and provided a structured way for people to move forward.

It's remarkable. One day, people were enemies; the next day, they were working together in the same offices. And despite all the economic and social challenges that followed, the country legally became an integrated society. That alone is a major achievement and Archbishop Desmond Tutu, who I spent time with at the United Nations in New York many years later, did an exemplary job as Chair of the Commission and of course credit to, then, President Nelson Mandela by appointing a bishop and theologian to chair a commission that's objective was to help heal a nation.

How would a similar process work in Israel and Palestine?

The reality is, Israel isn't just about providing a homeland for the Jewish people after the Holocaust. It's a strategic foothold for the US in the Middle East.

So it's about having a military base in the region?

Exactly. Among the Arab nations, Israel serves as an extension of US power. The massive U.S. Defense budget that funds Israel isn't just about protecting a democratic ally – it's about maintaining influence in the region. Right now, that agenda is more apparent than ever. But anyone who looks at the situation logically can see what's really at play.

Do we need more women at the table when it comes to negotiating peace? Have you observed a change in conflict resolution dynamics when more women are involved?

Absolutely. Under the last U.S. administration, most department heads at the CIA were women and in the current US administration, Tulsi Gabbard is the Director of National Intelligence overseeing US intelligence agencies. What does that tell you? In intelligence work – especially when it comes to emotional intelligence – women bring a different and critical perspective.

Men tend to be very outcome-driven: "We need to achieve this goal. How do we get there?" Women, on the other hand, are more likely to consider the human cost: "What is happening to civilians? To children?"

Are women more likely to think about the consequences, the collateral damage, the effect on the community?

Yes. Women are mothers, and that perspective matters. They see life and the loss of life in a more holistic way. They recognize collateral damage for what it is, not just as an unfortunate byproduct of a military strategy.

The ends don't always justify the means, and I think women are more likely to factor human life into decision-making. That perspective is critical when negotiating peace because it balances the cold strategic approach with a deeper understanding of long-term consequences.

Do you think that, for example, in the Middle East, they need to have more women involved in negotiations?

Absolutely. But the real question is: What's the barrier to that?

The biggest obstacle is deeply ingrained cultural systems that won't change overnight. Change takes time, and often, it requires a catalyst.

Saudi Arabia, for example, is evolving. I spend a lot of time there, and while they've made progress – like finally allowing women to drive – there's still a long way to go. In Iran, after the protests, many women have stopped wearing the hijab, and when the religious police try to intervene, they're often ignored. These shifts signal change, but it's a slow process.

That's why integrating more women into conflict resolution is critical. Their perspectives bring a necessary balance, and smarter intelligence agencies have already recognized this.

In my own company, my lead analyst is a woman. The female analysts bring a different level of insight and attention to detail. They see things from angles that men often miss. If we want more effective conflict resolution, we need to incorporate those perspectives much more.

What advice would you offer to aspiring conflict resolution practitioners? How should they train? Can they learn it at university?

The best way to learn conflict resolution is to get out there and experience it firsthand. Conflict resolution is about people. You need to learn how to read people, how to understand different cultures, and how to navigate human behaviour. That's not something you can fully grasp in a classroom – it comes from real-world experience and interpersonal skills.

If you're serious about this field, join an organization that operates on the ground. Groups like Amnesty International, Hope for Justice, or Anti-Slavery International work in conflict zones and tackle major humanitarian issues like human trafficking. These are incredible places to start, even on a part-time basis.

If your interest leans more toward defence and security, then consider working with a company like mine, even temporarily, to gain field experience. There are many organizations actively trying to resolve conflicts in challenging environments. Their intentions are in the right place, and you can learn a lot from being part of those efforts.

Above all, stay true to what you believe in. Know what you're willing to be part of and, just as importantly, what you won't be part of.

If you do things according to your values, whether you're working against a corrupt government or mediating between conflicting parties, things will align the way they should. But the moment you compromise on that, that's when things start to go wrong.

Tony Schiena is a counterterrorism expert and former intelligence operative, having served in various capacities in the private security sector as well as aiding government and various law enforcement agencies. He is the founder and chairman of MOSAIC. Tony's career started during a pivotal part of world history in which South Africa averted an imminent civil war, abolishment of the oppressive system of apartheid and smooth transition of government.

Tony is currently Senior Advisor to NW3C (National White Collar Crime Center) and is on the Board of Governors of Global Society of Homeland and National Security Professionals and also an Honorary Member of Homeland Security Philanthropy Council.

The Mosaic Federation was formed by Tony and the current Assistant Deputy Commissioner of the Metropolitan Police Force. Tony has spoken at the United Nations, G20 women's conference in Paris, the Vatican and various other prestigious platforms on human trafficking. His organization also collaborates yearly with CNN International on a successful, global, strategic communication initiative on modern-day slavery.

SIMON SMITH

Can you describe the role of an ambassador and what they do?

Top of my list of what an ambassador is all about is building bridges and making contacts; it's about bringing people and institutions together. It's about bridging divides. While this can sometimes involve managing conflicts, more often, divisions exist simply because people do not know one another or realize how much they have in common. The ambassador's job is to recognize those opportunities for cooperation and facilitate relationships that might not have formed otherwise.

It is useful when explaining the role of ambassador to think about its translation in German. 'Ambassador' is a word that does not explain itself very well. The German word for ambassador, Botschafter, meaning "messenger," captures an important aspect of the role. An ambassador delivers and receives messages, but this should never be a passive process. At its worst, diplomacy can feel like little more than relaying information, but that is not what the job is truly about. A skilled ambassador does not simply pass on messages – they interpret, mediate, and shape them to ensure clarity and understanding. If an ambassador finds themselves acting only as a messenger for too long, it may be a sign either that they are not using their position effectively or that those they represent are not making the most of their role.

There is a lot that can go wrong when countries don't understand each other. There's a lot that can go wrong when international organizations are not delivering what the membership of the organization wants, or the membership does not understand what the role of the international organization is. There's a lot to be done to make sure that the understanding is in as good a place as it can be. In these moments, it is often the ambassador, as the most senior and authoritative representative of their country, who must step in to ensure that communication is not just exchanged but truly understood.

Is there a trade element to it? Because I know the chamber of commerce in countries is always about promoting trade, but would a diplomat get involved in something like that?

Absolutely. While I've spoken in general terms, the role often involves facilitating connections, especially in the context of trade. Throughout my diplomatic career, I've worked on trade and investment, and a key part of that was connecting companies with experts who understood specific markets. Often, these companies were new to the country or market in question. My job, or that of my team as ambassadors, was to link them with the right people who could offer valuable insights. Sometimes, we could share our own knowledge and say, "We have a lot of experience here, so come sit down with us, and we'll answer many of your questions." But if a company is serious about doing business, they'll need to speak with the true experts in the sector they're interested in. And again, we could help make those connections.

Ambassadors also get involved in larger-scale projects, particularly when substantial investments are at stake. This often means representing a company's interests. I have significant experience in this area, particularly in challenging business environments like Russia and Ukraine.

The host government might intervene by saying, "We understand the challenges a company might face when making a large investment here. Here are some reasons why it's in everyone's best interest to support the company, not make it harder for them."

In such conversations, the goal is to create mutual understanding and reach an agreement that both parties want the investment to succeed. This leads to better communication between the authorities and investors, helping them to understand each other's objectives. It also fosters cooperation and reduces the risk of unnecessary confrontation, which can arise when investors are caught off-guard or face changing conditions that affect their investments.

So there's a lot of smoothing the waters and trying to clear the obstacles out of the way for people?

Yes, and I think "smoothing" is a good term. However, in some situations, it can be pretty uncouth. I've had instances where I needed to be quite direct without crossing into disrespectful language. There have been times when I've had to bluntly point out that the actions of a host government were putting broader issues at risk, beyond just a specific investment. In those cases, I'd shift the conversation to focus on the reputation of the country as a favorable environment for investment. I would tell them, "In my humble opinion, if your actions or lack of action cause this investment to fail, that will ripple much, much wider beyond just the company involved. This could damage the reputation of your entire investment environment in your country, and that's something you need to seriously consider."

Could affect the whole landscape for doing business bilaterally?

Absolutely. I mean you don't want to go into that conversation using that argument all the time. I think there is a risk of losing credibility in crying wolf if you use it too often. But if there are times when you genuinely believe that an investment going wrong could stand a pretty good chance of sending a sort of deterrent and discouraging signal to other potential investors, then that's certainly something which, as an ambassador, I felt I needed to be prepared to say.

Do you think the approach to conflict resolution has evolved over time, or has it largely remained the same?

I haven't personally been involved in formal, large-scale conflict resolution negotiations. However, from my perspective, the formal methods of negotiation haven't changed significantly. I think there is a well-constructed theory to it and, as a practitioner, I do sometimes look a little bit skeptically at the application of 'one size fits all' theories and processes to the conduct of negotiations. But on the other hand, it is probably no surprise that principles and a lot of the processes in negotiation may not have changed hugely because, fundamentally, they're about the same thing. They're about bridging a divide. They're about building shared understanding. They're about persuading two sides that the benefits of an agreement will outweigh the other benefits that they may perceive, or the sacrifices that they may perceive that they're required to give, or the compromises that they're required to make.

Perhaps what has changed over the last 30 years or so – though I'm speaking somewhat informally here – is a greater reluctance to formally call for negotiations. In the past, it was more common to say, "This situation is ready for formal talks, so let's bring the parties together and work it out." One of the examples that is often on people's minds is the data and negotiations revolving around the status of Bosnia and Herzegovina's heads governor and a settlement to the wider conflict in the former Yugoslavia that happened during the mid-1990s. My sense is that there's now less eagerness and urgency to dive into that kind of negotiation, where the goal was to separate the parties and essentially confine them to a room, limiting their tea and biscuits until they could focus on their differences and reach an agreement.

I sense there's more skepticism about whether it will actually work. As a result, there seems to be a greater focus on the processes that encourage conflicting parties to be ready to negotiate, rather than just saying, "We've had enough, this has gone on too long, we're going to force you into a room and make you sit there until you reach an agreement." I think that's probably a thing of the past.

So, there are a lot more pre-negotiations than there used to be?

I'm thinking back to Cyprus, but it's not an example to shout about or to write home about. And Cyprus is, in a sense, a frozen conflict. It is a conflict that has, thank goodness, not caused the loss of that many lives in the last decades or so, but it is also a conflict in which there are two parties who remain in disagreement and remain unprepared to reach agreement. Thinking back to that, there were numerous phases where the effort to reach a solution went into formal phase and where there were formal preparatory talks set up that both sides were present at. In fact, there might have been a sort of preparatory phase where you have what's called proximity talks, where the parties don't actually talk directly to each other, but they will talk through a mediator and the mediator will pass the message on.

And that can be one way of building the expectation, building the understanding of the sort of demands that will be made on the two sides in the negotiation. So, you have those formal and pre-formal elements, but you also often have efforts, over the course of several years, that explore the issues with each side separately, rather than at the same time. You'll have slow motions for a shuttle diplomacy, where you will have potential negotiators who are talking on a regular basis to both sides. They are not only deepening their own understanding of where the obstacles might lie but also trying to chip away at the mentality of the people of the parties to the conflict of both sides and to say: "Well, look, you say that this is going to be a big problem, but let's think that through".

"How much of a problem is not solving this going to be for you?" You can inject one or two very direct questions into that process and say: "What is it you are prepared to give up in order to get some other objective?" During the periods between formal negotiations, many countries appoint a special envoy to focus on a specific issue. These envoys don't have an official mandate, meaning they aren't endorsed by organizations like the United Nations. They work solely as fact-finders and facilitators on behalf of their own governments. When I was working on the Cyprus issue, for example, the British government appointed a special representative for Cyprus, but he represented only the British government, not anyone else.

He didn't pretend that he had a mandate from anybody else. And so the jobs that I used to do alongside him were exploratory. They were making sure we hadn't overlooked anything, ensuring we didn't make the mistake of viewing a position from one side as unreasonable without considering if there were valid reasons for that inflexibility that we might have missed. And it was very valuable to us in a sense to dig deeply into those positions and make sure that we understood them properly.

Can I ask why the British government got involved? Is it because of the number of British residents there or because of the colonial history of Britain being involved in that island?

The main reason is always tied to colonial history, and it's probably the top reason why the British government wanted to make a special effort. The fact is, there are still two sovereign British military bases on the island of Cyprus, which are important military and operational assets for the UK. We could have an entire conversation about the rights and wrongs of that, but it remains a fact. There's also the feeling that if we could help settle a potential conflict and had the capacity to do so, that should be reason enough. But the starting point really was the sovereign bases and the so-called sovereign base areas.

It's about protecting military and broader security interests. The second factor, which is even more significant than the number of British residents in Cyprus, is the large Cypriot communities in the UK. These include both Greek and Turkish Cypriot communities, many of whom moved to the UK in the 1950s and 1960s. As a result, there are now third-generation descendants who might not speak Greek or Turkish, but still identify as Turkish or Greek Cypriot. They vote in British elections, and their votes are important to any party seeking to form the next UK government. In my experience, whether the government is Conservative or Labour, both have seen it as useful to be perceived as constructive and engaged in seeking a solution to the Cyprus issue.

Coming on to North and South Korea, which is kind of a similar division of a territory, what were the British interests that were involved there that led to you becoming involved in the negotiations?

There's a long history of formal negotiations with North Korea, but I'll focus here on the British perspective. Before I begin, I'd like to clarify that, to my knowledge, there has never been a serious internationally-led negotiation addressing the direct issue of the reunification of the Korean Peninsula or a definitive end to the Korean War. As is widely known, the Korean War has never formally ended. An armistice was agreed in 1953, but it was not a peace treaty and did not resolve the war. Since then, there has been no real prospect of a negotiation to address this central issue.

Against this backdrop, there have been numerous attempts to engage in more informal processes aimed at understanding both sides' positions. These efforts involved exploring how they viewed potential opportunities, what would be required for a satisfactory settlement of the war and looking ahead to assess the feasibility of reunification in some form. Over the 70 years since the armistice, I don't think we've come anywhere near a situation where it seems at all realistic to bring both sides together and say, "The goal of this process is to reach an agreement that results in a united Korean Peninsula."

But have they not had negotiations about living side by side more peacefully with each other?

They've certainly done that, absolutely. However, this often involves very specific and partial agreements, which can be a sensible alternative. If the prospects for an overall settlement seem slim, it may make sense to accept that reality. Sometimes, this happens because the parties involved are unwilling to agree, but it can also be due to other parties, who have a significant stake in the outcome, being opposed to a solution being reached.

Given North Korea's isolationism, presumably opening up would create a lot of instability for them?

Well, that's one of the reservations that you find among the parties themselves. If you talk about North Korean visions of reunification and

South Korean visions, it is very, very rare that those visions have come anywhere near to being close to each other. So that's your first obstacle. The second obstacle is that, to put it very bluntly, there might be a very different vision of acceptable unification to a policymaker in Washington compared to a policymaker in Beijing. The disparity of vision about how this might happen is an obstacle to bringing together. And again, one could look at this through the eyes of the decision makers in Beijing, and they may be telling themselves to say (I'm going to simplify this quite a lot) that a reunified peninsula on South Korea's terms is not something that we in Beijing are going to put up with.

Is that because of the American bases in South Korea and the fact that missiles could easily reach China from there?

That's certainly a factor. The range of missiles isn't the main issue, as China would likely know where other missiles could come from. The concern for China, however, is that they're not enthusiastic about the idea of a unified Korea on their border, especially if it's suddenly 1.5 times larger in population and almost twice the size in landmass. If reunification were to happen on South Korea's terms, China might find themselves facing a unified Korea deeply aligned with the United States. As for the reasons other countries might oppose reunification on North Korea's terms, those are probably even more obvious. The idea of sacrificing South Koreans for the Kim Dynasty is disturbing to many, and it's easy to see why that prospect has little appeal. As a result, formal negotiations haven't gone much beyond discussions of ending the Korean War or reunification.

Instead, much of the focus has been on finding ways to bring North Korea into compliance with international norms on nuclear non-proliferation and the development of nuclear weapons. There have been phases of negotiation, especially through the Six Party Talks, which included the United States, Russia, North and South Korea, China, and Japan. This kind of negotiation involved six parties, but other countries could still play a useful role by developing their own dialogue with North and South Korea, softening their positions. The goal was to show North Korea the benefits of a cooperative approach, particularly in terms of economic cooperation and global trade, which could help their economy grow.

You can present these opportunities to them, but you can't force them to accept. In 2000, the UK opened diplomatic relations with North Korea.

At that time, the British government believed that engaging with the North Koreans and establishing a communication channel was far better than learning about them from afar. The early years of this diplomatic relationship led to a small-scale negotiation of its own, as establishing a diplomatic relationship always involves negotiating terms.

This agreement included provisions designed to de-risk the situation and reduce the likelihood of confrontation. Although it was a small part of the larger picture, it aimed to contribute by improving communication and helping North Korea understand the benefits of engaging with the global trading system. The clear message was that to access these opportunities, they needed to align with the Nuclear Non-Proliferation Treaty and halt their nuclear weapons development.

The Six Party Talks were intensely focused on this issue – how North Korea could be transparent about its nuclear activities. The effort was to persuade North Korea that engaging with the international community would be more beneficial than continuing a confrontational stance. Over the past few years, this has been the main focus of negotiations with North Korea. While it's not a final goal like reunification or a peace treaty, it aims for more limited objectives. However, even this process ultimately failed to convince North Korea to drop their hard-line position and engage constructively with the international community.

Can you foresee any kind of resolution to the Korean conflict in the next 50 years?

I think it's become even less likely in the foreseeable future. It's a bit early to tell quite where this extraordinary new relationship between Russia and North Korea will go. But we saw Kim Jong visiting Russia a while back, and it may still turn out that there is a bit less to that relationship than meets the eye. Neither side has a great history of making a success of these kind of new relationships.

In the current situation, both sides may feel they need each other more than they have in recent decades. This could lead to that relationship developing further. However, if it does, I can see it making the prospects for reunification, meaningful reconciliation between North and South Korea, and a peace treaty even more distant. The new Russia-North Korea relationship has likely already made those prospects less likely.

These countries have massive arsenals of outdated weapons. Do you think Russia is using up its stockpile because it knows it will have to invest in next-generation weapons, and so it's trying to use what it has to expand its territory?

I'm not sure that's what's happening right now. It seems more like the Russians are becoming concerned about the declining stockpiles of conventional weapons they have. Certainly, one outcome of their agreement with North Korea was a degree of resupply of conventional weapons for the war in Ukraine. However, from what I understand about the numbers and stocks involved, this isn't a long-term solution to Russia's problem. For the foreseeable future, the arms supply situation for Russia will likely remain similar. There's little evidence to suggest that Russia is planning a radical shift in the type of warfare it's using in Ukraine. The focus will likely be on increasing the production of conventional weapons, but this will be done against the backdrop of efforts from countries that want to prevent a Russian victory in Ukraine, looking for ways to limit Russia's ability to produce more conventional weapons.

Given this situation, it would make sense for Russia to explore other methods of warfare that don't rely on heavy industrial production. In theory, if deploying conventional weapons in the quantities needed becomes much more difficult, Russia might consider using nuclear weapons. Personally, I think that's unrealistic. I'm confident in the deterrent capabilities of countries outside of Russia, and I don't think it's a realistic option. I believe even Putin understands the deterrent positions around him, and that using nuclear weapons is not something he's likely to pursue.

When you were involved in negotiations after Russia took over Crimea, what were the discussions about?

Well, there were no negotiations, to be blunt. At that time, Crimea was indefensible for Ukraine. The Ukrainian armed forces had no capacity to resist Russia's surprise attack. Many Western governments concluded that there was little they could do in the short term. NATO wasn't about to send forces into Crimea to reclaim it for Ukraine. So, the response focused more on imposing economic sanctions on Russia in response to the invasion and annexation of Crimea. Technically, you could call that a negotiation of sorts, but it was really more of an argument or debate within institutions like the European Union.

Do you think the lack of any sort of fight back on the question of Crimea led Putin to believe that it would be okay to take more land, and that Ukraine would just capitulate again and give in?

Yeah, I don't think that happened immediately. The process went through a few more stages after the annexation of Crimea, which led to the second invasion of Ukraine. It didn't go from "we've gotten away with taking Crimea" to "let's take the rest of the country" right away. I think the next stage for Putin was realizing, "Wow, that worked, and that's pretty good. So, what's next?" But his answer to that was recognizing the risk of launching another large-scale invasion of Ukraine. He asked himself, "Do I really need to take that risk right now?"

Almost certainly not. I think he calculated that he could achieve his goals with Ukraine by gradually weakening its ability to govern itself. After Crimea, his next objective was likely to turn Ukraine into a failed state by undermining its institutions. He probably had a timeline of three to four years, during which he believed Ukraine would weaken to the point where it couldn't defend itself. Then, without needing to send in an invading force, he could destabilize the country from within.

A puppet government or something?

Yeah, exactly. The first stage was actually to do something quite similar to that, but confined to these two regions of Luhansk and Donetsk in the east of Ukraine. And there is quite a lot of evidence that there were implants from Russia in those two regions. Even before Crimea was annexed, there was already a plan for infiltration in place. After Crimea's annexation, this plan led to the emergence of these so-called separatist militias. These separatist movements could not have existed on their own without the crucial support they received from Russia.

He funded governors to take control of regions and then invested in promoting a pro-Russian stance in those areas. Is that what you're saying? Then he relied on those governors to support him when he launched the offensive, ensuring he had people in place within Ukraine who were on his side. Is that a simplified version?

Yes, that's pretty much the case.

However, I don't think the initial plan was to view this as stage one leading inevitably to a full-scale invasion of Ukraine. I think he genuinely believed this approach would be enough. When I was in Ukraine, many Ukrainians mentioned that Putin wasn't aiming for some massive, decisive blow against Ukraine. Instead, his goal was to "amputate a few of Ukraine's toes" and let the country slowly bleed out without proper treatment. There's some logic in that. His original plan seemed to be that he wouldn't need a full invasion because those local figures would do the job – they would sow division, distract people, and apply tremendous pressure on the government in Kyiv. Over time, he assumed Ukrainians would become fed up and would prefer to return to what he believed was the stability they had under Russian influence.

The key miscalculation was that Putin underestimated how many Ukrainians, even in the east, had stronger ties to Ukraine than to Russia. There was, even then, a significant number of people who, when looking at the situation simply, would ask: "Do we want to end up effectively enslaved to Russia for the next 50 years? Or do we want to be like Poland, which since joining the European Union, has seen its economy grow five times faster than ours, has access to the single market, the freedom to move across the continent, and all kinds of benefits?" Many more Ukrainians thought this way than Putin likely realized. He misjudged the situation, assuming that the people in eastern Ukraine would prefer Russia's protection, while those in the west were just interested in a relationship with the European Union. He thought the division would be simple and that by sowing discord in eastern Ukraine, the job would be easier.

He believed that approach would be enough to bring Ukraine back under Russian control. However, it was only when he realized that strategy had failed – when Ukraine was firmly on the path to eventual EU membership – that he began to reassess. By then, things weren't going as badly for Ukraine as he had hoped. The economy was growing modestly, and there had been significant strides in reforming systems to tackle corruption. There's still a long way to go, but from Putin's cynical perspective, he saw Ukraine as just as corrupt as Russia. A corrupt country, in his view, is a vulnerable country, and he knew exactly where to target its weaknesses.

That said, I don't want to overstate the progress Ukraine made between 2014 and 2021, but by 2021, Putin was facing a much stronger Ukraine than he had anticipated seven years after annexing Crimea. It's at this point that he started to realize, "We haven't succeeded. Maybe we need to do something drastic to prevent this from continuing."

Why does he want Ukraine? Is it the reserves, the resources? Is it to be a kind of heroic leader getting parts of the Soviet Union back? What is his motive?

There are several reasons for this. Fundamentally, it's a clash of systems. When Ukraine chose to sign the association agreement with the European Union in 2014, they were making a choice of systems. They were moving away from the Russian system, where the judiciary is far from what a democratic country would recognize, and where business thrives through manipulating the courts with bribery. In Russia, both political and corporate governance are highly manipulable and exploitable, compared to systems that adhere more firmly to the rule of law. So, the first reason is business-related: Putin and his Kremlin run a business.

This business generates massive sums of money for Putin and his allies in the Kremlin. The money generated is also a means of controlling and incentivizing economic governance across much of the country. In this system, if you're a business person, regardless of your business size, you ultimately have no protection if the Kremlin decides to take over your business. Interestingly, until the end of the Yanukovych regime in Ukraine, the Ukrainian presidential administration operated similarly. I spoke to major business people who told me they realized that one day they could wake up to an order from the presidential office to transfer their business assets to the president's son because their business was needed to grow the president's son's business.

One statistic circulating during the Maidan protests was striking: it claimed that the average growth of Ukrainian businesses in the past three years had been around minus 10%. In contrast, the growth of businesses connected to Alexander Yanukovych had been about plus 750%. It may sound like oversimplified data, but the figures spoke for themselves. This highlighted the perception that from 2010 to 2014, Ukraine had an administration that had adopted the Russian way of doing business. Yanukovych's great dilemma was when he realized that to win the presidential election a second time, he couldn't simply cheat his way to victory.

So, he started to appear more enthusiastic about joining the European Union than he really was. In fact, I think many in his administration were convincing him that this deal could be far better for Ukraine than he originally thought. Eventually, he was persuaded to seriously consider the association with the EU. But when Putin summoned him to Moscow and made it clear he needed to stop this, Yanukovych made a sharp U-turn on the EU agreement, triggering mass protests in Ukraine. While this digresses a bit from the topic of negotiations, it's essential background for understanding the situation.

So, what does Putin want? He wants Ukraine to adhere to his business model. The second issue, which is almost as important, is that Putin does not want Ukraine to become an example to the Russian people that there's a different, more successful way forward. He does not want Ukraine to show that embracing the rule of law, transparency, accountability, and functioning democratic institutions can lead to success, as Poland demonstrated after the collapse of the Soviet bloc and the Warsaw Pact. Putin wants to keep deceiving the Russian people into thinking that this is not how things should be done, and that Russia is different.

Obviously, there's a security aspect that he doesn't want NATO on his doorstep, does he?

Well, I think he's made all that up, to be honest. I mean NATO is a threat to him. He has amplified the threat and made it seem real, but he voluntarily withdrew from the cooperative structures that NATO had set up for him during his first term as president. I suspect he found it easier to do this around 2005–2006, when the price of oil had risen dramatically from about $15 per barrel when he first became president, to around $170 per barrel by the end of his first term. This oil boom gave him the leverage to say he no longer cared about cooperating with the transatlantic community because the revenue from oil was flowing in.

He didn't worry much about the rest of the Russian economy because oil and gas revenues were pouring in, and those short-sighted Europeans had locked themselves into long-term gas contracts that made them dependent on Russian supplies for the foreseeable future. With this newfound strength, he turned away from the cooperative structures, such as the NATO-Russia Council and NATO-Russia partnership. Instead, he started creating a narrative that NATO was a threat to Russia, a narrative entirely constructed by the Kremlin. This went hand-in-hand with another myth he built around "Russophobia" – the idea that Russia was being excluded from the Olympic Games because of an alleged state-sponsored doping program. Putin has been very successful in convincing many Russians that all of this is happening because the world hates Russia, not because Russia has actually committed any serious or villainous actions.

What do you foresee being the probable outcome of the Russian and Ukraine war?

I don't expect an early resolution. I don't think Putin will achieve his goal of subjugating Ukraine; he won't be able to destroy it, which I believe was his objective with the invasion. However, the Ukrainian resistance and the ongoing support from its international allies will be sufficient to thwart Putin's attempts to crush Ukraine. The restraint shown by Ukraine's supporters so far will likely continue. That said, I do see a potential risk we need to monitor: the possibility that the populations in countries supporting Ukraine may grow weary and frustrated. The dreaded "Ukraine fatigue" could set in.

Right now, I don't see strong evidence of Ukraine fatigue at an alarming rate, but Putin is clearly hoping for that outcome. There are valid concerns that it might happen. For instance, if the recent conflict in Gaza escalates into a broader war, Putin would likely see that as a diversion and distraction from his own actions, and he could exploit it. Moreover, Putin is likely watching the potential for a more cooperative Republican president, such as Donald Trump, to take office in the US closely.

At the moment, none of these factors indicate an imminent end to the conflict. Though I wouldn't personally advocate for it, if the situation continues to stagnate, there might eventually be pressure on both sides to find a way to end the war. This would bring us back to formal negotiations. But you can't start formal talks unless there's a reasonable expectation of bridging the existing gaps. As it stands, those gaps are completely unbridgeable. In such a scenario, I'm sure there will be voices urging a ceasefire, armistice, or some form of resolution. Interestingly, people are beginning to point to the armistice in 1953 that ended the Korean War as a possible example of how to stop a long-standing conflict – but that's another conversation altogether.

It could turn out to be something like the North and South Korea situation, where both sides decide to stop fighting, and Russia keeps Crimea. But they will need to negotiate over the Donbas region. I don't think the Ukrainians are going to accept Russian control there, so the negotiation might be something like: "We'll

let you keep Crimea if you leave the Donbas."

Many people are suggesting that exact scenario. However, I would encourage them to consider Crimea's strategic importance. If Putin retains control of Crimea, with its communication and supply routes, what do you think he's going to do next? Do you really believe that after taking Crimea, he'll just go back to Moscow and think, "Great, the international community gave me Crimea, I'm done"? No, he'll look for his next move – likely targeting Europe and further destabilizing democratic systems globally. I personally think this would be a huge mistake. Any reward Putin gets from this invasion would only motivate him to do more.

You mentioned the Israel–Palestine conflict as a distraction from the war in Ukraine, helping Putin. Do you think Iran is siding with Putin? Has there been collaboration between them to fund the Hamas attack, creating a diversion from the bombing of Kyiv?

Yes, there is a connection, but not in the way you're suggesting. From what I've gathered through discussions with people who likely have better intelligence access, there's no serious belief that Putin directly orchestrated the attack in Gaza. While it's not out of the question, no one believes it's that straightforward. However, Putin would likely see the situation as beneficial. His forces have been performing poorly for the past couple of years, and any diversion that shifts attention away from Ukraine could be seen as good news for him. If people focus on the situation in the Middle East, it might ease the pressure on Russia.

As for Iran, it's clear that they've been supplying drones for the Russian assault on Ukraine. This has turned out exactly as Putin intended. I remember 10 to 11 years ago when the Russians were somewhat cooperating with the West during the Joint Comprehensive Plan of Action (JCPA) negotiations with Iran. But there were times when they'd appear helpful one week, then unhelpful the next, sending signals to Iran that they understood their position better than the West. This has evolved into a more formal alliance. And now, with North Korea also on board, it's clear that Putin has realized he won't be able to rebuild relationships with the Euro-Atlantic community. So, he's looking for support elsewhere – even from countries he would have once avoided.

There's a lot of Russian and Chinese investment in Africa as well. Do you think that climate change and the desertification of Africa

is going to lead to more war refugees and migrants from those areas coming to Europe?

Yeah, I think it's a big risk. Absolutely.

Do you think NGOs and British companies should be trying to help solve those problems so that people don't have to leave the land or go to war?

Absolutely. I also regret that it is all the while difficult for companies to take a leading role in that when they have a government, as we regrettably now do in the United Kingdom, which is basically backtracking on its objectives. It turns out that COP 26 in 2021 was only for Christmas and it wasn't real. The British government, in my opinion, is shamefully backtracking on the commitments. By November 2021, at COP 26, they had played a significant role in shifting the momentum toward where investments needed to go. They had helped make it clear that investing in renewable energy was not only sensible but also profitable. And now, in a strange turn of events, we're being told that fossil fuels are essential after all, and that you're foolish if you believe we can move away from them.

It's such a remarkable U-turn, especially considering the argument was already being won. Five or six years ago, we were still facing objections that renewable energy was good in theory but too expensive and not economically viable. That battle had nearly been won, with the understanding that this simply wasn't true. But it's deeply concerning that the UK is now one of the countries where the government seems to think, "We can't be bothered with this anymore."

Do you think Britain has a moral obligation to help countries suffering from climate change, especially since we were the first nation to industrialize? We've had the longest benefit from using fossil fuels, and we've caused some of the greatest impacts.

I'm being a bit cynical about this, and of course, I agree with you. There is a powerful moral case for saying it's our responsibility to help. But I also take a realist view and understand that this moral argument alone won't necessarily be the critical factor.

Well, that's what it comes down to, isn't it? Winning votes in the next election?

I can't really picture any genuinely democratic country where a party would centre its environmental policy on the idea that we need to pay for this because it's our moral obligation. You'd need more than that to persuade voters. It would likely turn them off.

I'm not suggesting that this would win votes, but that's just my personal view.

But that's the key point. If you frame it by saying, even if you don't buy into the moral argument, there's an economic case – it's profitable, saves money, and helps you build new industries – it makes more sense. That's why I'm so appalled that we've backtracked on this.

What do you do at Chatham House now? What's your role?

A lot of what we do is focused on influencing policy. We've been talking about the possibility that the war might continue without showing quick results. More and more people will propose ways to end it, and we're addressing those ideas.

That's just one example of what we do. We produce written analysis on Ukraine to inform these discussions. The main goal of this particular report wasn't to say, "Please don't make efforts to end the war," because no one wants to frustrate those efforts. But we want to make sure that if people do propose solutions, they're fully aware of the potential consequences. They need to think carefully about the possible outcomes of their ideas and whether they could end up making things worse.

We've also emphasized the reconstruction of Ukraine. It's clear from many past conflicts that reconstruction should not only start after the war ends. You need to start planning for it while the war is ongoing, as the risk of Ukraine collapsing increases if its infrastructure isn't repaired in real time.

Reconstruction isn't something you begin only after the war ends. There is an ongoing international conference on Ukraine's reconstruction, aiming to mobilize the necessary investment for Ukraine's recovery. At Chatham House, we organized a precursor conference to emphasize the importance of involving communities across Ukraine in this process. The idea is that local communities should have a say in the reconstruction of their country – whether it's their schools, hospitals, businesses, or other vital institutions.

I believe reconstruction won't be effective if it's imposed from the top down, with the government simply receiving money and spending it. The concept of inclusivity in reconstruction is, though it might sound like a cliché, absolutely vital. While international conferences are essential to mobilize the large funds needed, they alone won't answer all the questions. They must involve communities from across Ukraine to ensure a truly effective reconstruction.

In your paper, it says there's no chance of peace because there's no way to negotiate with Putin – especially on issues like Crimea.

That's correct. We outlined the consequences of rewarding Putin with Crimea, or any other territory, or letting him off the hook for the war crimes committed by his armed forces in Ukraine.

Do you think he'll be let off the hook for those crimes? Won't he be arrested if he tries to travel abroad?

If he tries to travel abroad, yes, that could happen. But it's a big challenge. I fully agree that the solution to this conflict should ensure Ukraine remains a sovereign, independent country with the freedoms its people deserve. But I think there is a strong argument that says it needs to be a just settlement as well. You will find people who are saying that's one of the things that you have to just sort of grit your teeth and say for the sake of, if we reached a position where a settlement on other issues was in sight, but it fell down because there was an insistence that all these people needed to be brought to justice.

But that could be used as a bargaining chip to let him off the hook, couldn't it?

Well, I mean it shouldn't be in my view, but I think that it's certainly one of the things. You would need to envisage that question is going to need to be, the other thing is purely and simply that you said it yourself, that if Putin stays at home and if he survives this war and he then stays at home and out of sight and out of the clutches of the international criminal court, well he gets away with it. There are no mechanisms that I'm aware of that will allow him to be sort of arrested in his bed at some point.

SIMON SMITH

Simon Smith is a retired British diplomat who served as Ambassador to South Korea from 2018 to 2022. Born in Bristol in 1958, Smith studied German and French at Oxford University. He began his career in the Diplomatic Service in 1986, focusing on economic, trade, and investment roles in Tokyo and Moscow. Smith served as Ambassador to Austria (2007–2012), where he was also the UK's Permanent Representative to the UN in Vienna and Governor on the Board of the International Atomic Energy Agency. He then became Ambassador to Ukraine (2012–2015) before his posting to South Korea. Smith first visited North and South Korea in 2002–2004 as Head of the Foreign, Commonwealth & Development Office's NE Asia & Pacific Department. He speaks multiple languages, including Korean, Russian, Ukrainian, and Japanese. Smith is married to Sian Stickings, who was awarded an MBE for her contributions to British and local communities in Russia.

ANJAN SUNDARAM

Can you tell me about your career in journalism?

I've been a journalist for about 20 years, mostly in conflict zones and reporting on dictatorships. I began in the Congo, then reported on the Central African Republic, and now I've shifted to environmental conflict in Latin America and Mexico, reporting on the environment frontlines and indigenous communities. In terms of dictatorships, I've reported on Rwanda and Cambodia. I also presented a couple of TV series. So, I've been engaged with conflict and violence, reporting on it over the last 20 years.

You started off as an incredibly successful physicist, didn't you? You won the Indian Physics Olympiad in 2000 and then earned a master's degree in mathematics from Yale. But you later left Goldman Sachs to go into journalism. Can you tell me a little about why?

Yes, I was a gold medal winner in India's cohort for the Indian National Physics Olympiad and then studied mathematics. I thought I was going to be a mathematics professor and maybe work in mathematics in some form, either in academia or an investment bank eventually. I had a job at Goldman Sachs working between the quants and clients, explaining the mathematics to major institutional investors.

The reason I left mathematics was because while mathematics is incredibly beautiful, it's incredibly abstract. I wanted work that was more rooted in the physical world, in the material world in terms of people's actual concerns. As much as I enjoyed mathematics whenever I was doing it, I was asking myself 'Why am I doing this? What difference does it make to anyone's lives?'

At that point I read in the *New York Times,* middle of the newspaper bottom of the page, this little article saying that four million people had been killed in the war in Congo, and it struck me that that article wasn't on the front page. One thing led to the next, and it drove me to buy a one-way ticket to Congo and to report from there, in an attempt to understand for myself what was happening, but also to understand why certain topics don't make the front pages of the news while others do. I wanted to understand the structure of international news. That eventually became the subject of my PhD, which I completed at the University of East Anglia in Norwich.

So, what did you find about why certain stories make the front page and others don't?

In my PhD, I proposed a new model for international news, a post-colonial model for the first time, that illuminated how international news is still characterised by colonial structures. I drew a parallel between the old colonial officers who were sent out from major colonial capitals, like London or Paris, to the peripheries of the world. There, they would extract natural resources and other valuable commodities and send those back to the colonial capitals to be transformed into wealth.

Foreign correspondence and international news still work in a similar way; foreign correspondents are sent out from global capitals like New York and London to the so-called 'peripheries' of the world. They often extract the labour, work, and information from local reporters who are given disproportionately less pay, less credit, and fewer prizes. This information is then transformed by the foreign correspondent, published back in their home countries where they receive, you know, Pulitzer Prizes and so on. The colonial nature of this structure can be seen in how the work and contributions of the local journalist are often obscured, and so this colonial structure has led to different lives and different parts of the world being valued in different ways.

So, four million Congolese can die, and it may not make the front page. But a handful of Western people might be killed, and that absolutely would. That was very evident to me when I was reporting. If a UN peacekeeper or a foreign national was endangered or killed, my editors would be on my case trying to get me to speak to everybody first – their family, their cell mate if they were in prison, anybody – whereas it was a struggle to get news published about even dozens of Congolese being killed. There was a sense that their lives didn't really matter as much, sometimes not at all.

This came to a head when, to give you a little example, I was in the Central African Republic in 2013 in a church ground where 3,000 people were taking shelter. I was with an American colleague, and the government showed up and threatened to kill all these people the following morning if they had not disappeared. The nun who was running the church decided to stay and to continue to offer shelter to those people all night. So we waited. My colleague and I called all the foreign embassies, and they said "We can't do anything. People are being killed every day in the Central African Republic. It's a war. We can't really save them; we can't really protect them."

In the middle of the night, my colleague called his office, the New York City Human Rights Watch, and informed them that we were in this church and that soldiers might attack in the morning. Immediately, his office called the White House and the Élysée in Paris and said that an American citizen was in danger. The White House located the faction of the army that was in control of our town and warned them, not about the 3,000 people, but that if anything happened to a US citizen, "You're in trouble." The attack was called off. It shows how 3,000 African lives are worth so little compared to one American life. That plays out all across our news, across our perceptions of which wars are important, whose lives are important, where we should intervene. It plays out, and I think the media is partly to blame for that.

Do you think that the media can fix that? Do you think that there's a solution to it, and also to the fatigue that everyone has in reading these stories?

We live in a time when many Global South countries like Nigeria, Kenya, India, China are rising economically. And it's time to stop complaining about Western journalism because Western news is going to have the lens that it has given the history of Western nations. It's going to be hard for the Western news to break away from that easily. I think the counterbalance has to come from Global South international reporting, which doesn't really exist right now. If Indian citizens, such as myself, want to see Indian lives valued, or Nigerian lives valued, instead of complaining about Western news, I think the time has come for Indian and African and Asian news organizations to start reporting in the way that they would like to see those lives valued, and thereby give those lives the importance that they deserve. I really believe that that will happen, eventually. It's just taking time. I'm an advocate for it happening sooner rather than later because I don't see any excuses for not doing so.

So tying a lot of those different threads together, what do you think the role of the journalist in conflict reporting is?

The reason I find conflict reporting interesting is because of the danger. There are very few reporters out there, so information is scarce. It feels like by obtaining information, verifying it, by telling stories within that conflict, I'm shining a light on a situation that exists. Often these conflicts exist in obscurity, and we all know that when there are no eyes, no witnesses, perpetrators of violence feel emboldened. You see this in wars: when there are few reporters, like in the Congo or even in more immediate domestic violence situations, perpetrators feel like no one's watching and they can do what they want. I believe that the journalist, merely by being present and by bearing witness, sends a signal to those perpetrators that they *are* being watched, they can be held accountable, and that alone can have an effect of mitigating the violence and the levels of violence and the kinds and forms of violence that are perpetrated on the victims.

Moreover, it's often said that journalists write the first chapters of history. We shine a light on situations that then investigators can follow up on and hopefully hold the perpetrators of violence accountable in international human rights courts.

So these are the main functions. Conflict violence often comes about as a breakdown in communication and in institutions, and I've found that violence often correlates with a sense of helplessness. Perpetrators of violence often feel like they are helpless, and they have no other avenues in order to make themselves feel heard. Journalism can offer the possibility of being heard.

Often when I speak and try to interview warlords or perpetrators of war crimes or crimes against humanity, it's surprising to me that so few people have tried to speak to them. They're often very eager to receive me. Yes of course it's dangerous, and I'm putting my safety in their hands, but often they're eager. They go out of their way to guarantee my safety because at the bottom of it all, they want to be heard and I'm offering them a chance.

Journalism in that deep and fundamental way offers a path for violence to be mitigated and for the core reasons of the conflict to be heard, illuminated, then eventually addressed rather than for parties to continue to feel helpless, like there are no institutional pathways for them to enact the changes or advocate for the changes they want to see. So, I find it's often speech and speaking that can be immensely powerful.

In that vein, can you tell me about Rwanda and being in an area where journalists were persecuted?

I think what's remarkable about Rwanda is that President Paul Kagame has, at the same time, destroyed the country's free press, perpetrated crimes against humanity – the UN has called some of those crimes possible acts of genocide – and despite all of that, he's been able to continue to be invited to speak at institutions such as Harvard University, Yale University, and multiple governments – and to speak on topics such as human rights and conflict resolution. I believe that this achievement, if you can call it that, is due to many reasons: he is very astute and politically calculated, and, since you asked, it's a function of his destruction of the Rwandan press.

As I said earlier, international journalism still, because of its colonial structure, relies on the local press to extract the information and publish it. The veracity, the truth, the value of international journalism is often deeply linked to the quality of the local journalism that exists in a country. In Rwanda, with the local press being destroyed, foreign journalists come in and speak with propagandists from the government. Naturally, they know far less than their local counterparts, so they end up publishing that information.

Anywhere, journalists are dependent on their local counterparts, and when those local counterparts are propagandists, that's what gets published. So, you'll find in the international press and eminent institutions – publications such as *Times* Magazine and so on – remarkably pro-Kagame, pro-dictatorship articles, making a case for Kagame's dictatorship, making a case excusing his crimes in much the same way his government would do. He's managed to achieve that, to have these narratives published in international journalistic institutions because he's destroyed the local press.

I think it's a very dangerous template, that other dictators and authoritarian leaders can copy. But essentially Kagame is exploiting the colonial nature of the international news system so as to cover up his crimes and cast himself in a way that has attracted great respect from world leaders and universities.

So when you were in Rwanda fighting against this, did you fear for your safety?

Oh absolutely, all the time. It's part of my work. Over the last 20 years I've learned how to train myself, how to keep myself safe. I've obviously made some mistakes early on – and I've learnt from those – but because the nature of my work is inherently to put myself at risk, that's also the value that I find off my work. I go to places where, because of that risk, there are few eyes, few witnesses, and therefore, I feel that I can contribute a valuable perspective. There are two sides of that coin.

I've had to understand how to mitigate the risk to myself and how to continue to operate because the goal is to stay alive and tell the stories I see. Not everyone is in that position. The people who I'm writing about are more directly engaged in conflict or in activism, and they're directly putting their lives on the line for their cause. My goal is to tell their stories and try to piece together the truth in order to understand why these conflicts are occurring and continuing.

I'd like to talk about your most recent book, your third memoir, and how you explore the effects of your profession on your personal life. Can you tell me a bit about that?

My most recent memoir explores my marriage and divorce as well as my reporting on the ethnic cleansing of Muslims in the Central African Republic, to where I travelled seeking to investigate the genocide against the minority Muslim population, which had just taken power there. The book is the third in my series of memoirs that describe major conflicts and dictatorships that affect the lives of millions of people and yet rarely make it to the front pages of our media, or into the global public consciousness.

But the memoir also illuminates a second, more personal under-reported dimension of international reporting. I think international journalism and conflict journalism as well as front-line humanitarian work have, for a long time, taken a heavy toll on people's personal lives. There is a perception of the bravery of the protagonist, people such as me, so there's been an aversion to speaking about the personal cost. In this memoir, I wanted to both describe how my marriage enabled me to do my work (it gave me a solid foundation from which I could set out from home and go and report on these conflicts happening around the world) and how reporting on these conflicts damaged and destroyed the marriage. This is a narrative that many front-line human rights workers – humanitarian workers and front-line journalists – have experienced. Yet, we haven't spoken about it as much. It's only recently that front-line war correspondents have begun to receive the emotional and mental support that they really need in order to continue this kind of work.

For readers, what's the name of your book?

It's called *Breakup: A Marriage in Wartime*, and it came out in April 2023.

Pivoting back to reporting in conflict, does a reporter have moral obligations in your opinion? And how might that be balanced against the interests of a paper?

Because I'm a freelance reporter, I don't have a paper to balance my interests against. I go in, and I try to report as truthfully and honestly as I can. I tell the stories that immerse readers in conflicts and the situations I'm experiencing as a way of building empathy, building bridges between those conflicts and readerships around the world.

The hard part for me is then to find a publication willing to publish the stories that I write from my own perspective, which is not always easy because, as you indicate, publications and papers do have their positions and do want stories reported in a certain way. I freed myself of that by being independent, writing what I want, and then finding an editor wherever they might be to publish my work.

Does a reporter have moral obligations? Absolutely, yes. How do I answer this? All war reporting in a sense does have this moral position where we are trying to hold power accountable. Our job as the fourth estate is to make sure that those in power don't abuse their power. If they do, we shine a light on it so that people know and hopefully those abuses can stop. That's, for me, the fundamental role of the journalist in society. Of course, the journalist can play other roles like informing the population or entertaining the population, but I feel like those latter two only have meaning if we're performing the first role, which is to hold power accountable. Without that, I wouldn't call it journalism.

In war, that abuse of power, takes a very specific form. It's the use of violence against often vulnerable populations. So when a war corr-espondent goes in, I believe that their moral responsibility and moral perspective is very clearly to speak and advocate on behalf of the populations that are suffering violence, to make sure that as much as possible, the effects and abuse and perpetrations of violence occur in as broad daylight as possible. That's very difficult, of course, because in a war zone, infrastructure is destroyed, roads are destroyed, it's very difficult to gain access informationally or physically. Often the perpetrators of crimes and violence don't want you to get to a place or they feel threatened if you are a witness to some of their violence. All this is exactly what the war correspondent is trained to negotiate, understand, and navigate in as safe a way and as intelligent a way as possible. But this is the kind of terrain in which the war reporter operates, and the ultimate goal is to hold power accountable. To do that, you have to sometimes be very clever in how you navigate and negotiate with that power, so as to be able to go in, come out safely, and publish the stories that you have witnessed.

How do you balance having to maintain your position with the government – if you need the permission of the government to get into a country for example – and the narrative that you want to tell?

My solution often is to only go into a conflict zone once. I prepare myself, I make all the contacts, and I go in. I go in once, I go in as deep as I can, and I extract as much information, knowledge, and stories as I can. I leave, and I don't come back, usually. If I come back, it might be years later.

Often it's exactly that: if I'm going in with the permission of the government, with the implicit support of the government in a way and if they don't know who I am, which they often don't, they're willing to just let me be. Once I publish my stories, they might have a different opinion. Then, it's far more dangerous for me to go back, which is why I don't. I think continuing to work in a war zone, to publish from that war zone in defiance of authorities, is incredibly dangerous. That's why often in a single war zone you'll need a whole team of reporters. In Ukraine, the *New York Times* has a rotating cast of journalists going in. It's just incredibly dangerous to have one person looking in and reporting on these stories. They become a target.

In that way, I see conflict reporting as a collective work. I'm building on the work of conflict reporters who have gone in before me and published reports that now make it dangerous for them to go back. So, I go, I build on their work, I publish what I can, and then I can't go in for some time at least. Somebody else will go in instead.

But you're right that it becomes incredibly dangerous when you publish stories. Often the conflicting parties have deep and large interests, and they feel threatened just by words.

When you're in the field speaking to people, how receptive are they, experiencing conflict in the moment, to you as a journalist?

Often, they're very open. I think that many people are aware of that. An example is that after the Holocaust, when US soldiers liberated the concentration camps, the first questions that the survivors of the concentration camps asked was not for food, medicine, water, or anything like that. They asked the American soldiers, "Do people know? Do people know what happened to us?"

I think that's a universal, deep need that we have, especially if violence is being perpetrated on us. I believe that one of the deepest sources of hope is the knowledge that other people might know what is happening and that the goodwill, the spirit, the humanity in them might compel them to intervene. That's what journalists are there for and what people honestly often feel.

When I show up in a remote conflict zone, people will tell me, "Nobody's come here in 20 years." They'll put their own lives at risk in order to show me what's been perpetrated upon them – the violence, the mass graves – and I believe that's a sign of how valuable they feel my presence and my work are.

Do you feel that reporting conflicts – and the global perceptions of conflicts that happen as a result of reporting – do they influence the actual conflicts themselves?

Certainly. As I mentioned before, the presence of the journalists bearing witness shifts the kinds and levels of violence that are being perpetrated. Then there's the actual publication – other powers such as governments and international criminal courts – finding out about the crimes. Legal and political pressures can be exerted. All those mechanisms do offer the possibility and have affected the ways in which conflicts have been perpetrated or have evolved around the world. They impose limits upon the warring parties. While the conflict may not end as long as the core issues remain unresolved, in many ways the violence might be limited or constrained in certain ways.

That infrastructure, those constraints, have been tested most recently in the Middle East. There's a sense of impotence among many journalists that conflict has continued for so long and on such a scale despite the reporting, which also calls into question the effectiveness of some of those international structures in limiting the scale of violence.

Can you speak about what's going on in Israel-Palestine and/or the Russia-Ukraine conflicts. How do you perceive them in light of everything that you've been talking about?

I perceive those two conflicts as some of the most visible conflicts in the world. Both of them have graced the front pages or the headlines in many countries around the world, but personally, my own work focuses on conflicts that are of similar scale that don't make it to the front pages: the war in Congo, the war in Central African Republic, indigenous communities fighting environmental wars in Latin America. All these conflicts are deeply important to the world and our future, and yet they don't get publicised in the same way because of a history of racism, colonialism, and classism in international news.

I see an opportunity in these places to do meaningful work to raise the profile of these conflicts as much as I can, to bring to bear in these places the power of journalism. And so yes, my position, my work – it focuses on remedying and restoring some of the balance that should exist in the world. Lives should be valued equally; conflicts in Africa and conflicts in indigenous communities should be reported on as fully as conflicts in Ukraine or the Middle East, yet they aren't. That's kind of been a core focus of my work over the last 20 years, and probably will continue to be over the rest of my writing career.

Can you tell me about this fairly recent surge of right-wing movements in Latin America in light of what's going on with extraction and the environmental conflicts?

It's interesting; extraction is not just a feature of the right-wing in Latin America. Latin America – all the Americas – are highly colonial societies. They're countries that were built upon, in many cases, genocide or mass killings of indigenous populations. In some countries like in the US, Canada, Argentina, Chile, and Uruguay, there was a near total wiping out of those populations. The political culture that governs all the countries in the Americas are rooted in extraction, have been for a long time, and it doesn't matter if you're right-wing or left-wing; both sides of the political spectrum promote and make mining projects. They use the funds in different ways – right-wing is more for private gains, and left-wing extracts resources to create a social redistribution project – but the extraction is still a feature across the continent.

I don't really have a good answer for why the right-wing has risen, except that this is a pendulum that continues to swing from left to right according to seasons. My hypothesis would be that some populations feel that the left-wing governments haven't been left enough, haven't gone as far in transforming their countries and getting rid of poverty and making good on their promises. That can be seen everywhere, though, most recently with Trump. In the US, there's a collective frustration and as a result, a desire to give right-wing policies a chance to produce the economic and social benefits that people are looking for.

Can you tell me what you're seeing in terms of lithium mining being such a big thing? We live in a technological age that is highly reliant on lithium and it's causing many issues in indigenous communities.

The lithium triangle is made of Chile, Bolivia, and Argentina. It's a valuable resource now especially with the production of electric vehicles. But many of these lithium resources unfortunately exist on remote territories that are safeguarded and protected by indigenous communities. Now, a consortium of global corporations, governments, and in many cases, organised crime are seeking to try to exploit those resources, creating conflict with the indigenous communities. It's a global phenomenon.

You've done a lot of work on the way AI is changing humans. How do you think social media, disinformation and AI are changing the landscape of conflict and conflict resolution?

I think access to these resources is empowering a population with information. Unfortunately, it's also polarising the population because the way that social media works often creates bubbles due to economic incentives: they show you what you want to see, a phenomenon that's been widely documented. As a result, it's led to a decrease in the perceived authority of traditional news sources, which has created a situation where people rely on their peers in order to obtain their news and perspectives on the world. I think that's made it harder to change people's perceptions and their predispositions.

It's also interesting because the future of journalism in this regard has to offer greater transparency, to offer readers a way to connect with the stories, the people, the characters, the organizations being reported on. People are no longer content to rely on intermediate third parties like the journalists to tell them the truth. Greater subjectivity, greater transparency on the part of the journalists for their own biases and offering readers and audiences ways to directly connect with populations and stories are really key. That's what's going to sell to this population and make them feel like they are actually getting the truth.

That's certainly a big challenge that journalism is facing right now. What do you think are the other challenges that specifically conflict journalism is facing?

Journalism is under threat around the world. Julian Assange was released, but there was a huge movement to prosecute him for publishing information. That was the first time the US was criminalising the publication of information, not just the leaking. That and the tax on journalists around the world has indicated that journalism is under threat.

What I've seen on the positive side is where journalism used to be about the lone-wolf foreign correspondent providing their heroic perspective on the world, now it's become a form of collaborative endeavour. You can see that with the Panama Papers and other leaks. Newspapers are working together, pooling their resources, to hold the rich and powerful accountable. It shows that journalism is adapting, is evolving. However, I do overall think that with billionaires buying newspapers and the publication fees going down, freelance journalists are under immense pressure, which puts the field of independent journalism in crisis.

Can you tell me about what you're doing now in Latin America?

I do some reporting on indigenous communities. Indigenous communities around the world represent about five percent of the global population, but they protect around about – by some estimates by the World Wildlife Fund and UN – 80 percent of the world's biodiversity.

There's no question they protect a huge chunk of the world's bio-diversity, so with biodiversity being destroyed around the world, many companies, governments, and organised crime are coming for these remote indigenous lands and trying to extract resources. Unfortunately, this leads to conflict that often isn't reported because of failures in international news.

My goal here has been to raise the profile of some of these brave indigenous environmental defenders so that their battles cannot be ignored – so that we as a global community can begin to decide whether we want to treat them as human beings and report on the violence being perpetrated on them, at least out of a desire for our own survival and to protect these ecosystems for the next generations that come after us.

The global environmental war is a key opportunity for the world to transcend historical legacies of racism, classism, and colonialism and to realise that we are all in this together. We all rely on the climate, on ecosystems, on nature, for our survival, and we'll need to start working together even with the people we've historically seen as lesser, the people we haven't devoted as many resources to supporting. All of that will need to change if we're going to protect this global good that is the environment.

Anjan Sundaram is an acclaimed Indian author, journalist, and academic known for his award-winning memoirs *Stringer, Bad News,* and *Breakup.* Regarded as "one of the great reporters of our age" by BBC's Feargal Keane, his books have garnered attention from figures such as Christiane Amanpour and Jon Stewart. He contributes regularly to *The New York Review of Books* and Granta Magazine. Sundaram graduated from Yale University with a degree in mathematics and earned a PhD in journalism from the University of East Anglia. He began his journalism career reporting from Congo and Rwanda for The *New York Times* and The Associated Press. His debut memoir, *Stringer,* about his time as a reporter in Congo, was widely praised, as was his follow-up, *Bad News,* which examines the rise of dictatorship in Rwanda. His third book, *Breakup,* explores the personal effects of war reporting. He has hosted TV series *Coded World* and *Deciphering India.*

EMILY WINTERBOTHAM

Can you tell me what you do at the moment as director of the Terrorism and Conflict group?

My role at the Royal United Services Institute as director involves managing a team of 13 people based in London, Brussels, and Nairobi. We work on a variety of projects and programs addressing all forms of extremism and developments, with a particular focus on countering terrorism and preventing violent extremism.

What are the challenges to peacebuilding today?

Having worked in Afghanistan, I've encountered specific challenges related to peacebuilding in that context, which have become more complex in 2024 due to the evolving nature of the threats we're facing.

There's always been a struggle to determine the most effective form of peacebuilding. The wars in Iraq and Afghanistan led us to adopt a more stabilisation and counterinsurgency approach, which, though flawed, had its rationale. This approach was built on traditional conflict and peacebuilding models from the 1990s.

However, the situation today is different. We're now dealing with hybrid warfare. The rapid development of technology, the role of globalisation, and the variety of hybrid tactics make confronting conflicts much more challenging. This stretches the limits of traditional peacebuilding models and complicates the efforts of communities involved in peacebuilding under the framework of liberal internationalism. There's less consensus on how to address conflicts, and the international response is increasingly fragmented. The conflicts themselves are growing more complex.

What do you think the impact of AI and technological development will have on the way conflicts happen?

Firstly, AI isn't fully understood yet, and it's often easy for people to say, "It's going to have an impact; it's a threat," without truly grasping its potential. But what is clear is that technological advances shift the dynamics of conflicts. I'm particularly interested in how AI is being used in misinformation and disinformation during warfare. While AI can amplify these issues, it's not required to successfully carry them out – it's just one part of the equation.

The real challenge arises when there's no universally accepted truth, but instead, multiple versions of the truth. We saw this with the Russian invasion of Ukraine. That said, it's important not to get too carried away with the idea that AI alone is distorting reality, because in many recent events in the Middle East, you don't need AI to actually distort what's happening; the real footage is evident in and of itself.

Overall, AI could be a threat, but there are plenty of very real grievances and narratives that exist independent of AI's influence.

What are the dangers of manipulation, misinformation, and disinformation?

I'm concerned that we're seeing a clash with Western democratic values, and hostile states seem to be more adept than the West at using misinformation and disinformation. That's not to say the West hasn't employed strategic communication for centuries, but when thinking about the fight against ISIS, for example, we had campaigns focused on portraying certain pieces of information. From our perspective, those were truthful narratives designed to undermine the falsehoods of the enemy.

However, when popular opinion can't distinguish where to find reliable information, that's a significant concern. The backlash against Western democracies, while concerning, is not surprising. There's always a double standard at play. For example, you see influencers on platforms like TikTok idolizing figures like Osama Bin Laden as the original anti-Western hero. This narrative is terrifying and inaccurate, but it's also understandable when you consider how interventions in Afghanistan were framed under the guise of human rights and women's rights, when, in reality, they were motivated by distinct security objectives.

I remember that in 2009 and 2010, I conducted research in Afghanistan. Many Afghans, with no access to social media or a global news perspective, would frame the war in the sense of "The Americans must want to be here. They are so powerful, and yet they haven't managed to defeat the Taliban, which is so small. So, they must want something else. They must want our oil. They must want control over our country."

Even if the Taliban didn't directly spread this misinformation, they effectively highlighted civilian casualties caused by the international community, which had a significant impact on support for the Taliban. Research shows that civilian casualties caused by the international community, or the Afghan government had far more of an effect on support for the Taliban than casualties caused by the Taliban themselves.

The same patterns play out when you look at the backlash against the international community today. It's striking to me that when Russia invades Ukraine or bombs Syria, or when Assad uses chemical weapons against his own people, or China persecutes the Uyghurs, the Rohingya face brutal violence, and so on, these actions don't elicit the same level of popular backlash as we see against some Western countries.

Why do you think that is?

I think it's partly due to double standards, where you can't criticize other countries for actions that you're taking yourself. When I was working in Afghanistan and researching transitional justice, one of the biggest mistakes was promoting human rights, stabilisation, and democracy, while simultaneously making deals with warlords.

If you talk to ordinary Afghans, as I did for years, you'll find that the people in power were often the warlords who destroyed Kabul, Harat, and who were responsible for mass violations, including rape. These were the same actions the Taliban was accused of, and they were almost seen as the worst perpetrators, yet the warlords were in power.

The reality is that the Taliban's rise to power in the 1990s, its resurgence, and its current governance can largely be attributed to the perceived illegitimacy of the Afghan government. From the outset in 2001, the credibility of international intervention was deeply compromised. It is untenable to lecture other nations on governance and democracy while expecting the international system to always align with one's interests. The global balance of power is clearly shifting. In a multipolar world, there is an inevitable reassessment of the role and influence of traditional international actors.

The "war on terror" has proven to be catastrophic. While some may highlight the coalition against Daesh as a success, it is more of an addendum than a continuation of the broader "war on terror" launched post-2001. We are witnessing a period of reckoning as global power centres diversify. Nations now have more choices regarding their alliances, and we are seeing an increasing pushback against traditional power structures.

Between 2009 and 2015, you worked in Afghanistan and Pakistan. Can you tell me a bit about your work and the challenges you faced?

From 2009 to the end of 2011, I was part of a long-term research project with the Afghanistan Research and Evaluation Unit. We studied the legacies of conflict in Afghanistan, working in rural and urban provinces like Kabul, Ghazni, and Bamyan. The focus was on people's perceptions of justice, peace, and reconciliation, and on developing options for transitional justice and Afghan peace and reintegration.

From 2012 to 2015, I joined the EU as a political advisor on the peace process. I worked at the policy level and was involved in the Afghan elections of 2014, among other areas.

What was that like?

The period from 2012 to 2015 marked a critical phase of transition in Afghanistan. By 2014, the plan was to implement both political and military transitions, though the latter ultimately did not materialize as intended. It was a tumultuous and pivotal time, marked by escalating violence and the growing strength of the Taliban. The catastrophic 2014 elections underscored the fragility of the political system. Rampant corruption rendered it impossible to identify a clear winner, and fears of a popular uprising led to the creation of a power-sharing agreement between the two leading candidates.

The unity government was a product of necessity rather than consensus. While Ghani claimed victory, Dr. Abdullah's supporters issued a stark warning: without a cooperative government, they would take to the streets, potentially sparking widespread violence. The international community's primary objective was to prevent such a scenario. I recall traveling with the ambassador to Pakistan to discuss the possibility of a unity government. The Pakistanis, however, dismissed the idea outright, pointing to Afghanistan's history of failed unity governments. Despite their scepticism, it was seen as the only viable solution at the time.

In hindsight, this decision was likely the final step on Afghanistan's path to the collapse of its government in 2021. It was a deeply unsettling and disheartening period to witness. The last time I returned to Afghanistan was in 2019, and I have not been back since the Taliban's takeover.

While you were in Afghanistan, you worked on a project titled "Women in Transition: Securing Gains and Moving Forward." Can you tell me a little about that?

That project was led by someone else, though I contributed to it. For me, it exemplified the profound challenges of engagement in Afghanistan. I vividly recall a senior gender specialist, a consultant on the project, struggling to reconcile the stark dissonance between Afghanistan's commitments on paper and the realities on the ground. Afghanistan was a signatory to numerous international frameworks on women's rights, gender equality, and children's rights, yet the implementation of these principles was alarmingly distant from the written commitments.

This experience underscored the widespread misconception about the utility and relevance of policies, frameworks, and guidelines in such a complex context. While we often delivered formal démarches to the Afghan government on behalf of the EU, addressing a range of issues, the response was usually polite but superficial – a smile, a nod, and a "Yes, thank you." The crux of the matter was always implementation. The consultant, despite her expertise, seemed unable to grasp just how deeply the gap between policy and practice was rooted in the local context. It was a striking reminder of the limitations of external frameworks when disconnected from on-the-ground realities.

You also co-authored a book called "Countering Violent Extremism: Making Gender Matter." What's the connection between countering extremism and gender?

When we returned to the UK and began at Royal United Services Institute (RUSI) in early 2015, I embarked on a project with my co-author, Elizabeth Pearson. Together, we conducted research across the UK, France, Germany, the Netherlands, and Canada, focusing on gender, violent extremism, and countering violent extremism (CVE). The aim was to explore the experiences of both men and women with violent extremism, draw comparisons, and analyse the mechanisms of CVE through a gendered lens.

Our research delved deeply into local communities that had either been directly impacted by violent extremist actions – whether Islamist or far-right – or had been targeted by CVE interventions. Collecting evidence on far-right extremism was notably more challenging, but we were able to develop a nuanced understanding of the gendered differences in radicalization processes. Specifically, we highlighted previously unrecognized vulnerabilities and modalities driving radicalization among men and women who joined Daesh.

For instance, in Muslim-heritage families, we noted that women, with less access to public spaces, were less likely to be targeted through street-level recruitment. Instead, their greater exposure to online spaces rendered them more vulnerable to digital radicalization. This observation contributed to the now widely acknowledged understanding that women are particularly effective at radicalizing other women online, creating unique vulnerabilities in that sphere – something we were among the first to identify.

From a CVE perspective, we also uncovered critical gaps in preventative strategies. In countries like the Netherlands and France, as well as possibly Germany, a significant number of female converts were radicalizing to join Daesh. However, many CVE initiatives at the time were narrowly focused on Muslim-heritage communities, overlooking the radicalization of converts who were often outside those targeted areas.

Our findings shed light on these dynamics and spurred further research. Ultimately, Katherine Brown joined Elizabeth and me in compiling our insights into a book, which was published in 2020. It remains a key contribution to understanding the intersection of gender and violent extremism.

In countries like Afghanistan, where women have limited access to public spaces, are they more vulnerable online?

Yes, we discovered that this vulnerability had not been fully recognized or addressed in counter-radicalization policies. While online recruitment has received significant attention, policymakers and practitioners often overlooked the gendered dynamics at play, specifically, that women are more susceptible to recruitment in the digital sphere than men, and that the narratives used to target them differ significantly.

Extensive research has highlighted how recruitment strategies are tailored to different groups. For men, narratives often emphasize taking up arms, protecting one's family, and demonstrating loyalty and honour.

In contrast, women are frequently targeted with concepts like becoming a "jihadi bride" or fulfilling idealized roles within the creation of an Islamic state. These narratives focus on family, motherhood, and the cultural significance of women in constructing the envisioned society.

Another layer of complexity involves discrimination against women, such as restrictions on wearing the hijab in professional settings in some countries, which can further alienate individuals and make them more receptive to radicalization narratives. In the Afghan context, online radicalization among both women and men is currently a pronounced challenge.

Notably, ISIS-K (Islamic State Khorasan Province, ISKP) has exploited the Taliban's severe gender discrimination. While the Taliban restrict women to their homes and curtail their access to education, ISKP has sought to position itself as a more progressive alternative. Their propaganda asserts that "true Islam" supports the education of women, contrasting this with the Taliban's ignorance and oppression. This portrayal allows ISKP to craft a gendered narrative that appeals to women by presenting itself as a protector of their rights under Islamic principles.

Understanding these gendered dynamics is crucial for developing effective counter-narratives. By addressing the specific vulnerabilities and tailored messaging that resonate with women, practitioners can create more nuanced and impactful strategies to counter ISKP's influence.

What are the dangers of social media, technology, and misinformation for extremism and conflict?

The online space mirrors societal dynamics, serving as an amplifier rather than a direct cause. While I'm hesitant to view social media as inherently causative, it undeniably reflects and intensifies concerning societal trends. That said, I challenge this view by acknowledging how social media platforms amplify and disseminate extremism, exacerbating harmful behaviors.

A major concern is the role of algorithms. Social media companies use them to maximize user engagement, often pushing individuals further down harmful pathways. This isn't limited to extremism or terrorism – it applies to a broad spectrum of online harms. It's increasingly evident that such algorithmic practices are causing tangible harm. Legislative efforts, such as the UK's Online Harms Bill and the EU's initiatives, signal growing recognition of this issue, including attempts to limit the power of harmful algorithms.

There has been a noticeable shift in how tech companies view their responsibilities. In the past, they largely overlooked their role in mitigating harm. Now, there's greater awareness, and companies are taking more proactive steps. While their concerns about the overwhelming scale of harmful content are valid, the continued promotion of harmful material through algorithms remains deeply troubling.

At the same time, we are perpetually lagging behind emerging technologies like generative AI. There's a persistent gap between what we understand and what's possible. Often, we don't recognize the full extent of potential risks until they manifest. If there's a lesson to be learned from the development of the internet and social media, it's the importance of proactively addressing the challenges posed by technologies like generative AI before they become unmanageable.

You've worked extensively in Afghanistan and Pakistan, but you've also worked in other countries. Were Afghanistan and Pakistan the most challenging compared to other contexts?

I didn't live in the other countries I worked in, so my experiences there were quite different. But from a conflict and peacebuilding perspective, every context brings its own complexities. We're dealing with so many unresolved conflicts globally, each reflecting unique challenges.

Afghanistan was particularly difficult because it was often treated as a secondary conflict compared to Iraq. Gaining attention, energy, and focus for Afghanistan was an ongoing struggle. It was also deeply frustrating to see missed opportunities in the early years, moments when peace might have been achieved but they weren't pursued. The international community was preoccupied with Iraq and obsessed with eliminating Al-Qaeda without considering peace with the Taliban. For instance, they turned down chances to negotiate with figures like Baradar, the Taliban's deputy. You can't help but feel that much of this was unnecessary – so many moments when intervention could have taken a different path.

Iraq was entirely different, yet equally frustrating. Despite the global coalition's success in dismantling Daesh's caliphate, the underlying issues remain. Sectarian divisions persist, and the unresolved situation in displacement camps creates conditions ripe for an IS 2.0 resurgence.

In Lebanon, my experience began in 2018. Initially, it felt less intense – a kind of reprieve. We could travel across the country, even to places like Tripoli, which were previously unstable. But within a year, Lebanon's government collapsed, the port explosion devastated Beirut, and the financial crisis worsened. Now, with the resurgence of Hezbollah, the challenges are mounting once again.

Each of these contexts is exhausting to work in, both emotionally and mentally. There's a sense of futility that can creep in – especially when you look back and question what has truly been achieved. Some people dedicate decades to this work and keep going, which is remarkable. But you can't help wondering sometimes if the expectations we set for these interventions do more harm than good. In some cases, doing nothing might even be better than interventionism that fails to deliver lasting solutions.

It sounds like international interventionism is being reassessed. Is this a turning point?

We've reached a point where many countries are increasingly reluctant to intervene in conflicts. This is evident in Africa, particularly in their voting patterns at the UN, where there's hesitation to align with Western positions. A similar trend can be seen regarding Ukraine. These nations are prioritizing their own emerging challenges and are wary of alienating Russia or China, with whom they have important relationships and dependencies. As a result, Western-led UN peacebuilding entities must rethink their approach, moving away from outdated, colonial-style frameworks. This reluctance reflects a broader pushback against traditional interventionist strategies.

I spent six years in Afghanistan, traveling back and forth for nearly a decade. But when I reflect on those years, I'm left wondering – what do we have to show for it? The expectations we created often did more harm than good. In some cases, doing nothing might have been the better option. While there's undoubtedly a generation of Afghans who benefitted from international involvement, many of them are now no longer in Afghanistan or are unable to use the opportunities they once had.

Frankly, conducting research in Afghanistan felt far easier than serving as a policy advisor for the EU. The complexities and frustrations of policymaking made it an incredibly challenging role.

I imagine this work takes a personal toll?

Absolutely. It's draining, particularly when dealing with colleagues on short six-month rotations. They'd often arrive thinking they had the answers, without understanding the context. But the more you learn about a situation, the more you realize how little you actually understand. The more I understand about the way the world operates, the way the different conflicts unfold, the less I understand.

Emily Winterbotham is the Director of Terrorism and Conflict Studies at RUSI, specializing in terrorism, counterterrorism, and preventing violent extremism, with a focus on international interventions in fragile states. Her research group spans London, Brussels, and Nairobi, offering research, advisory services, and training in counterterrorism and conflict. With 15 years of experience in international policy-making, Emily has worked extensively in conflict zones, particularly Afghanistan. She was seconded by the UK Government in 2017 to help establish the Commonwealth Secretariat's new CVE Unit. Between 2009 and 2015, she served as Political Adviser for the European Union Special Representative in Afghanistan. Additionally, Emily is a Deployable Civilian Expert for the UK Government's Stabilisation Unit. She has co-authored two books, *Countering Violent Extremism: Making Gender Matter* (2020) and *Conflict, Violent Extremism and Development: New Challenges, New Responses* (2018). Emily's expertise includes Asia, the Pacific, Afghanistan, and countering terrorism and violent extremism.

HEELA YOON

First, tell me a bit about what you currently do.

I am from the Eastern part of Afghanistan by the border with Pakistan. I hold a bachelor's degree in Finance, International Relations, and Diplomacy, and then I earned my master's in Finance as a Chevening Scholar. That's how I came to the UK. Currently, my nine-to-five job is with Action for Stammering Children as Communication and Engagement Officer.

When I was acting as Cora Weiss Peace Fellow with the Global Network of Women Peacebuilders (GNWP), I had the opportunity to work in the Philippines, Myanmar, and Afghanistan. This experience allowed me to engage in peace agreement implementation efforts in the Philippines and focus on UNSCR 1325 and 2250, which revolve around peacebuilding and leadership empowerment. My role centred on building the capacities of young leaders and peacemakers in various countries.

I later worked with organizations like Oxfam, Amnesty International, and the International Rescue Committee. Much of my professional background involves humanitarian agencies and human rights organizations. In 2019, I founded my own NGO, the Afghan Youth Ambassadors for Peace Organization (AYAPO). The organization focuses on local peacebuilding efforts in Afghanistan's eastern provinces and offers training to young leaders on national action plans related to peace and security. Our programs emphasize leadership development, gender equality, and professional networking.

Since the Taliban takeover, due to restrictions on internal advocacy, our efforts have shifted toward humanitarian work. Many of our aid workers are women, and we've also launched underground therapy workshops to support women during this difficult time. AYAPO has been active for five years, and in recognition of my advocacy, I have been acknowledged as a young leader by the United Nations and serve as a UK Youth Leader for the Global Partnership for Education.

My activism and lobbying efforts – particularly around education and peacebuilding – extend far beyond my nine-to-five job. They focus on advocating with government entities and raising awareness for critical global issues.

What led you to create AYAPO at only 19?

There were many reasons behind starting this organization. One of the most significant motivations was the strong advocacy for peace among young people in Afghanistan. Even before founding this organization, I was inspired by my mother, who was an advocate herself. She worked with United Nations Assistance Mission in Afghanistan (UNAMA) and served as a member of Parliament. Through her work, I was exposed to the world of advocacy. Whenever I traveled with her to the Eastern provinces, her focus was often on vocational training for young women who were otherwise excluded from opportunities.

My mother was a pioneer in conflict resolution, engaging with tribal leaders and legislators alike. I saw her as one of the first women to break those barriers. She showed me the power of local ownership in peacebuilding. Watching her navigate these challenging environments made it clear to me how impactful local efforts could be.

When I started the organization, I didn't have a deep understanding of UN resolutions or the formalities surrounding peacebuilding. Back then, "peace" was a much simpler concept to me. It meant ensuring that girls could access education or protecting them from early and forced child marriage. It meant two communities agreeing on common goals. The term "peacebuilding" itself held a more practical, grassroots meaning for us – it wasn't just about the absence of war but addressing the many smaller challenges that communities faced.

Our first project focused on preventing violent extremism, and it was an ambitious start. At just 19 years old, I found myself working in the Eastern provinces, which were heavily affected by the presence of the Taliban and ISIS. That experience provided invaluable lessons and exposure, shaping much of the work we've done since.

There were many personal and societal motivations behind starting the organization. In Afghanistan, young people often emerge as leaders within their communities, engaging in activism and humanitarian efforts. Given how reliant Afghanistan had been on humanitarian aid for decades, many young people, like myself, saw this as a pathway to create meaningful change.

My early exposure to advocacy through my family played a pivotal role, but there were deeper personal reasons as well. My family's experience as refugees in Pakistan before 9/11 left a lasting impression. We endured immense discrimination, and when we returned to Afghanistan, we saw the devastation that had been inflicted on our home. That deeply personal connection to my country's struggles became a driving force behind my commitment to peacebuilding and advocacy.

What were the challenges of creating an NGO at such a young age?

There were so many challenges, but there were lessons learned as well. One of the first challenges was understanding the complexity when it comes to peacebuilding. When we started working on our first project, we went to eastern provinces. The project was funded by a UN-led youth organization. We got the funding and did a focus group discussion among young leaders who came from very local areas with no understanding of English. Most of our training sessions were conducted in local languages.

Initially, we assumed that because the UN and other organizations had been present in Afghanistan for nearly two decades, people would have some awareness of peacebuilding concepts like UNSCR or the role of UN agencies. However, as we started the work, it became clear that most participants had no idea what peacebuilding entailed. They were unfamiliar with these organizations, and there were minimal resources available for training. Diving into concepts like the UNSCR National Action Plan taught us a critical lesson: understanding the political grievances of all sides involved is essential for effective peacebuilding.

When we started engaging young people, we made sure to include both men and women in the conversations. I recall one participant from Nangarhar who shared his experience of watching many young people in his community get recruited by extremist organizations. He and his own organization were actively trying to understand and address the push-and-pull factors of such recruitment. What struck me most was his personal story, one of his brothers was in the military, and the other was with the Taliban. When asked how he managed this difficult situation, he explained that political grievances run deep within Afghan communities due to years of conflict and war. Accountability was absent on all sides, atrocities were committed by the Taliban, the US, and the Afghan government alike.

Afghanistan's reliance on humanitarian aid created another issue: a lack of local voices being heard. Many UN experts came with peacekeeping templates they had successfully implemented in countries like the Philippines and Myanmar, but those approaches didn't account for Afghanistan's unique cultural and political sensitivities. We learned that a one-size-fits-all strategy was bound to fail here. Local ownership and cultural understanding were paramount.

As a young woman working in peacebuilding, I faced additional challenges. Being 19 and advocating for peacebuilding in a male-dominated field meant I wasn't taken seriously. There was double discrimination, both because of my age and my gender.

Another major obstacle was the lack of political will and hope among young people. Many of the participants we engaged in peacebuilding workshops were sceptical of the entire process. After seeing 20 years of failed initiatives, it was understandable for them to question whether our efforts would make any difference. One of our biggest challenges was breaking through that scepticism and rebuilding hope among Afghanistan's youth.

Financial constraints were another hurdle. As a small local NGO in Afghanistan, we had very limited access to flexible funding from larger organizations. Most major UN and international agencies prioritized national-level NGOs, leaving grassroots organizations like ours struggling for support. Yet, local efforts are critical to sustainable peacebuilding. We've always advocated for a bottom-up approach, emphasizing the importance of involving grassroots leaders in decision-making processes rather than relying on high-profile conferences held in hotels or international forums. Why not bring those directly affected by conflict to the table, instead of cycling through the same political leaders over and over?

Running the organization long-term also posed significant challenges. Being a 19-year-old managing an NGO came with a heavy mental and emotional toll. Working in conflict zones can be incredibly triggering, and on top of that, I was juggling my studies, and a nine-to-five job just to make ends meet.

When Afghanistan collapsed, we were left questioning how to move forward. There were no clear answers. But amidst these difficulties, we learned to adapt. We refined our strategies, understanding that peacebuilding is a marathon, not a sprint. Social causes like this require decades of consistent effort to yield meaningful change.

How do you navigate that scepticism you mentioned?

One way I handled it is to give it space and time. I recognized that addressing scepticism isn't something that can be "fixed" in four or five workshops. Instead, I focused on understanding the root causes of their doubt, navigating opportunities to dig deeper into why these attitudes existed. During one workshop, we conducted a behavioural analysis and asked participants what they believed were the root causes of their scepticism.

The reasons they provided were both numerous and deeply rooted. High unemployment rates, lack of education, limited networking opportunities, insufficient academic support, and a glaring absence of government or organizational backing were at the forefront. They had also witnessed the failures of countless NGOs in the past, including initiatives by UNAMA and UN peacekeeping efforts. These examples cemented their belief that we were just another NGO running workshops for publicity rather than meaningful change.

Interestingly, I shared their scepticism. When I founded the organization at 19, I had to be realistic about the impact we could have. Over the past five years, I've learned that people's attitudes and views are shaped by valid reasons. Instead of dismissing their concerns, we explored them and created a platform where they could voice their scepticism and articulate their problems. One recurring complaint from young people was that they felt unheard. Many of them asked, "What's the point of speaking up if no one is listening?"

To address this, we worked to connect them with key stakeholders – tribal and religious leaders, UN representatives, government officials, and even INGOs based in places like New York. We made sure their voices were heard and their grievances acknowledged. Building this bridge between local young leaders and the international community became a central role for us, and it continues to be one of our core missions.

Whenever there is a conference, we prioritize bringing members from local communities to participate, regardless of whether they speak English. One of the principles we emphasize is that a language barrier should never exclude someone from contributing to important discussions.

Another critical area we focused on was mental health support. In Afghanistan, most young people live in survival mode, and this is especially true for young women. Their fears often revolve around forced early marriages or the constant threat of violence, like bomb blasts. With such overwhelming priorities, it's unrealistic to expect them to engage in peacebuilding efforts without first addressing their immediate mental health needs.

We introduced mental health and mindfulness practices to help them cope. A significant challenge in peacebuilding is the subconscious bias that individuals develop toward one side of a conflict, which often leads to dehumanizing the other side entirely. This lack of empathy creates a barrier to negotiation and reconciliation.

For instance, we encountered a situation where individuals from two opposing tribes were participating in our program. They refused to engage with one another, showcasing the deep-seated personal conflicts between them. Additionally, many men refused to sit with women, dismissing their opinions entirely. Rather than forcing immediate cooperation, we worked to understand the roots of these biases and encouraged dialogue.

One major realization I had was that while identifying the root causes of social issues is relatively straightforward, changing behaviours takes decades. It's a slow and challenging process, but it's necessary for sustainable change.

Another key takeaway for me has been the importance of international organizations, like the UN, stepping out of their headquarters and engaging with people on the ground. Too often, significant resources are poured into conferences and high-profile events, which remain inaccessible to the real activists – the grassroots leaders tirelessly working in their communities. Activism, even today, remains a privilege for a select few, while those making the biggest impact often go unnoticed and unsupported.

What do you think young people and, in particular, young women can bring to peace processes?

There is already substantial research supporting the critical role women, particularly young women, play in peace processes. When women and young women are involved in peace processes, there's a 30% chance of the peace agreement or implementation process being more successful. This is because women and young women experience war very differently and bring unique perspectives to the table. For instance, they are disproportionately affected by gender-based violence, sexual violence, early and forced child marriage, and the challenges of being internally displaced. These are issues that women are more likely to highlight and prioritize during peacebuilding discussions.

I have seen so many examples of this at the local level as well, where young women play the role of mediator. They often propose solutions that reflect these lived experiences, offering a perspective that is both inclusive and comprehensive.

While war affects both men and women, peace processes have historically been dominated by men. I've witnessed countless instances, especially in UN meetings, where male delegates from conflict zones adopt rigid, non-collaborative attitudes, refusing to engage on certain issues. In contrast, young women tend to approach these discussions with greater collaboration, emotional intelligence, and a willingness to listen.

At the local level, young women frequently assume the role of mediators, striving to prevent conflict and bring opposing parties together. Their ability to foster dialogue and understanding is invaluable. There is ample research to back this up. For example, in the Philippines, a woman served as the signatory for a successful peace agreement, showcasing the tangible benefits of women's involvement in peacebuilding.

At this stage, we should no longer be questioning why women should be included in peace processes. It's 2024, and the argument for women's inclusion should be firmly established. Instead, the focus must shift to providing women with the resources, financial support, and safe spaces they need to participate meaningfully.

Safety, in particular, is a pressing concern for women working in peacebuilding. Many face cyberbullying, online attacks, and threats to their character, which further complicate their efforts. This is not unique to Afghanistan but is a pattern across many conflict zones. Ensuring the physical and emotional safety of women involved in peacebuilding is not just important, it is essential to the success of their work.

What is the contact with community leaders and religious and tribal leaders like?

To truly understand peacebuilding in Afghanistan, you need to acknowledge that it is a very tribal country. Peacebuilding efforts cannot succeed if they are limited to just men and women; every stakeholder must be included. This includes religious leaders, tribal leaders, academics, UN representatives, government and former government employees, and women. It's really important to involve every stakeholder if you want sustainable peace. Relying on a few movements or select groups might yield temporary results, but such efforts are unlikely to achieve long-term impact if they fail to address the broader societal fabric.

Recognizing the significance of tribal and religious leaders in Afghanistan, we focused on engaging them as part of our programs. Their influence within Afghanistan's context cannot be overstated and educating them on peacebuilding principles is a critical step. For us, we focused on analysing the influence of every stakeholder and how that's going to impact the peacebuilding programmes we did. However, one of the greatest challenges we faced was connecting with religious leaders. For a woman-led organization, establishing this dialogue was particularly complex.

In Afghanistan, addressing and engaging local leaders requires a careful and strategic approach. Much depends on how you are perceived – your public profile, your social media presence, and how local leaders view your organization. This is a critical consideration for any peacebuilder working at the local level. You cannot adopt a stance that appears anti-religious, anti-community, or overtly aligned with Western feminism or democratic ideals without alienating key players. While everyone may want a democratic country in theory, it is vital to assess whether the society is ready and how to navigate these discussions with cultural sensitivity.

Operating on the local level requires an in-depth understanding of the context. You don't need to agree with every perspective held by tribal or religious leaders, especially when it comes to their views on women or peacebuilding. However, it is imperative to approach these conversations strategically and with a proactive mindset. Our method involved first connecting with young leaders on the ground and then using these relationships to establish contact with tribal leaders. Through these tribal leaders, we were able to reach religious leaders. This step-by-step approach enabled us to build trust and relationships gradually.

A central part of our approach was giving stakeholders, particularly religious leaders, as much space as we can, and we train our young people, especially young women who moderate the sessions, to remain calm and non-defensive. It was essential to understand the perspective of these leaders and to create an environment where they felt invited and valued. This relational approach allowed us to build rapport over time and influence them subtly and strategically. Culturally sensitive and conflict-sensitive strategies were paramount to making progress in this space.

Of course, there were significant challenges along the way. I think the first perception of most of these stakeholders was negative. One time, we did a consultation in one of the academic institutions, and the next day, most of our members received threats. We were accused of promoting Western propaganda, and our banner was burned in a public display of defiance. That was a very strong lesson learned.

Through your organization you have trained over 100 young women and girls to be first responders. Can you tell me about that?

A lot of the training we conducted included both men and women. Back then, there were no restrictions on having training that both genders could participate in, which allowed us to create spaces for shared learning and collaboration. These trainings emphasized the intersection of peace-building and humanitarian aid, demonstrating how both can work in tandem to address crises effectively.

We provided a lot of training on how to be the first responder to humanitarian crisis. This included preparing them to respond to disasters, such as those resulting from climate change, and teaching them how to assess and address the specific needs of women in these contexts. For example, we provided training on delivering dignity care, conducting needs-based surveys, and fostering effective communication with women in camps or disaster zones.

We also worked to connect to humanitarian organizations on the ground, especially the United Nations Development Programme (UNDP) and the International Rescue Committee (IRC), although sometimes that was difficult. We did a lot of testing and trainings to figure out what went well and what didn't.

One of the challenges we faced involved ensuring the safety of women who were traveling to humanitarian crisis areas. In many cases, these locations posed significant risks to their security. Operating with limited funding and resources, we often had to arrange for a male escort to accompany them, particularly in the eastern zones where we work.

Our organization primarily operates in the eastern provinces of Afghanistan, with occasional work in Kabul, we don't work all over the country. That's why we understand the cultural dynamics there, and this has been important when designing training programs for women ensuring they are contextually appropriate and practical. Many of these programs focused on capacity-building, enabling participants to provide direct support on the ground after completing their training.

Additionally, we organized an online exchange program between humanitarian responders from the Philippines and Afghanistan. This initiative facilitated the sharing of experiences and best practices, enriching the learning process for all participants and fostering a sense of global solidarity among responders.

Did you have any feedback from the women who went to the camps and worked as first responders?

A lot of the women felt more comfortable engaging with the female responders when it came to humanitarian aid, as it provided a sense of safety and understanding. But it had a mental toll on the first responders seeing those environments where women don't have access to basic dignity care. One critical gap we identified in humanitarian emergency and response programs was the lack of mental health support for both responders and affected women.

While emergency kits were provided as part of the response, the deeper effects of displacement on women often went unaddressed. Some of them were pregnant, and there was no support in terms of providing pregnancy tool kits. Often when they were given these things, women didn't even understand how to use them. We did a lot of training on how to use these dignity kits.

Another issue was that most of the women needed contraceptive pills during displacement, but there are enough barriers to accessing those products in better times, let alone in times of displacement. In Afghan pharmacies, if you're a lone woman requesting a bunch of contraceptive

HEELA YOON

pills, you're going to face a backlash. Many of our responders, who were young women themselves, felt uncomfortable going to buy these products due to societal stigma. But they needed prescriptions.

We also noticed that some organizations providing first aid and humanitarian support lacked a gender-sensitive lens in their programming. When I asked why these programs weren't being updated, there were often no clear answers or efforts to address these gaps.

As a local NGO, our hope was to learn from the larger organizations on how to deal with these projects, but it was the other way around. It was disheartening to see significant funding being allocated to humanitarian aid while basic necessities for women on the ground remained unmet.

Regarding the mental health support, what are the more prevalent issues, and what kind of help is needed?

The mental health project is called "Peace Goes to School" and it started after the takeover of the Taliban. Right now, tragically a lot of women are committing suicide in Afghanistan because of the restriction on schools and freedom of movement. We realized we couldn't do internal advocacy when it came to gender equality or human rights because there were a lot of security risks, so we shifted our programming. What's one thing a lot of women need? Access to education and opportunities and mental health services. While many organizations are addressing education through underground schools, scholarships, and online learning platforms, mental health support remains largely neglected. The healthcare system is not functioning at all, and the topic of mental health and therapy is taboo. There are very few female therapists or psychiatrists available, and even if they existed, resources are insufficient to meet the overwhelming demand. The government is unable to fund these essential services, leaving countless women, especially young women, suffering from anxiety, depression, and PTSD. We're not experts when it comes to handling these things; we're just a local NGO.

Through "Peace Goes to School," we're using art as a form of therapy and expression. We've managed to secure some local funding through donations, though it's often minimal. For instance, with just £100, we've been able to organize three day workshops for 20 to 30 women. These sessions are held in the homes of our members in Kabul, as securing a public venue poses significant risks. We create a safe and welcoming environment where women can gather, learn, and find support. We give them space, provide them books on mental health, and coach them on how to practise mindfulness, how to do journaling, how to use different resources to have mental health support on the ground.

We conducted a focus group to ask women what they needed most and what activities brought them happiness. A lot of them said they valued art therapy or art sessions because it relaxed them. But no matter the activity, providing them that space to get together and talk and connect has been incredibly important in and of itself. These interactions often foster a sense of community and mutual understanding.

One of the projects we have is the Afghan Changemakers Project where we share their stories on different platforms. This project has been going for over a year, and we hope to expand its reach this year because there's a lot of demand right now.

How do you work around the restrictions to women's education which have been in place?

It varies in every province as local Taliban leaders in one province may be less strict than in others. Our priority is always to ensure no one is put at risk. Most of our activities are conducted either online or discreetly to avoid exposure.

We have a membership and focal points on the ground who introduce us to women in the community. These points have connections to different members of the community, and they're our trusted sources.

Despite a lot of restrictions, we try to find locations that are close to the women's houses and make sure we don't showcase a lot of it on our social media. Additionally, we always seek permission from everyone involved to ensure their safety.

With new restrictions emerging daily, we remain flexible and adjust to the evolving situation. There's no standard template for how we operate; instead, we rely on strategies that have proven effective in the past.

Can you tell me about the work you did with the UN in Myanmar, Bangladesh and the Philippines?

Most of my work with the UN was on advocacy and activism. While working with GNWP in Myanmar, Bangladesh, and the Philippines, our primary donors included UN Women and other UN agencies. Since our office was based at the UN Headquarters, much of our engagement involved working with the UN Security Council on issues related to UN Peace and Security, as well as interacting with various UN mission members and representatives.

In these countries, one of my main responsibilities was to learn as much as possible while also sharing my perspective as a young person. This gave me valuable insight into how peacebuilding initiatives were carried out in places like Myanmar, Colombia, the Philippines, and Bangladesh. We worked on projects such as community peacebuilding dialogues with Rohingya refugees. Much of my focus was on understanding how the UN implements its resolutions, identifying gaps, and sharing my experiences in addressing those challenges.

Every two years, the UN Envoy Office selects 17 young Sustainable Development Goals (SDG) leaders, and I was honoured to be recognized as one of them. This recognition has opened many doors, allowing me to engage with a wide range of organizations. Through the UN, I've had opportunities to speak on different issues, receive training, and deepen my knowledge of resolutions like UN 1325 and 2250.

Currently, the role feels somewhat varied, as it involves a mix of activities. The UN Envoy connects us with local offices in different countries, facilitating lobbying efforts and consultations. I contribute by sharing my expertise, learning about local challenges, and occasionally providing assistance through our ground members. Overall, it's a mix of advocacy, raising awareness through conferences, and identifying ways to address gaps in implementation.

Of all the places you worked with the UN, was there one that was particularly challenging?

My own country, Afghanistan, presented significant challenges. Before the Taliban takeover, we were closely monitoring the UN peace processes. One of the main issues was the overwhelming number of stakeholders involved, leaving no space for young people to meaningfully influence the process. During this time, I had the opportunity to meet senior leaders, including signatories of peace agreements in the Philippines and Colombia, as well as individuals who worked with UNAMA and the UN Committee on Disarmament. It was a lot to absorb, and I struggled to understand the role of young people and where I fit within the larger framework.

Each country presented its own challenges and lessons learned, but Afghanistan remained a focus for me. At that young age, I believed the UN had a substantial mission and wielded considerable influence. Unfortunately, I came to realize that this wasn't the case. One of the biggest challenges was understanding why the UN, despite its reputation, doesn't have strong mediation power. Many perceive the UN as a powerful global organization, but working within the UN system reveals its limitations. Much of its influence depends on the US government and the five permanent members of the Security Council. These technicalities often explain why the UN struggles to make an impact in certain countries, including Afghanistan.

It was especially difficult to shift young people's perceptions about the UN and encourage them to focus on grassroots efforts instead of relying on external organizations. My message was that we could create change within the country itself, but altering this mindset was a significant challenge. Convincing people who had never left their village or country to trust in local action, while bringing in knowledge I'd gained from exposure to UN peace missions, was incredibly difficult. Changing attitudes and fostering self-reliance in such a complex context proved to be one of the hardest parts of my work in Afghanistan.

What should young people be doing to promote peace?

Always approach peacebuilding with a proactive mindset rather than a reactive one. Currently, I work in social media, and I've come to understand the powerful role both social media and AI play in shaping perceptions of peace and conflict. This is an area that remains largely untapped. Social media significantly influences how people perceive war and peace, especially in conflict zones. Unfortunately, platforms like WhatsApp and Facebook have also been used for recruitment purposes, with little to no monitoring in place.

Young people, in particular, are easily influenced by what they see online, and their perceptions of peacebuilding and war are evolving rapidly. I've noticed this even in myself – sometimes I react angrily to certain situations – but I've learned the importance of staying proactive, exercising patience, and critically discerning between fake news and real news.

One alarming trend is the cyberbullying faced by those with differing views on peacebuilding. This can seriously impact the work of local leaders who lack a social media presence but rely on it as a critical source of information. Social media has become the primary tool for young people to access news, so it's vital to strike a balance by analysing information carefully, distinguishing between real and fake content, and responding thoughtfully rather than reactively.

It's equally important to seize every available opportunity to develop your skills, even if it's through online platforms. Peacebuilding is far from an easy task. I've learned something new every day, and I encourage others to make the most of these opportunities while staying focused. Many young people say they work in both human rights and peacebuilding, but peacebuilding is such a broad field. It's better to choose one specific area to focus on initially before branching out.

The concept of human rights is also becoming more complex, with shifting narratives around who is "right" and "wrong." We see these dynamics in situations like Palestine and Israel.

Above all, it's crucial to give young people the space and mentorship they need. I didn't have a mentor and had to navigate everything on my own. Organizations like UNAMA and others involved in peacebuilding should prioritize mentorship programs to guide young people and train them effectively in this field.

Is there anything you want to add?

If you're working in peacebuilding or tackling significant issues, it's essential to give yourself the space to truly understand the complexities. One thing I've noticed among women peacebuilders and activists is that we often take on too much. Growing up in a conflict zone can instil an "impact personality" and a saviour complex, where we feel compelled to solve every problem. However, it's vital for women peacebuilders to establish boundaries between work and personal life. This is something I'm navigating every day.

In peacebuilding, I frequently receive messages from Afghanistan, young women asking for help, telling me their families have no food, or that their brother has been kidnapped by the Taliban. It's heartbreaking, but one of the hardest lessons I've learned is that we can't fix everything. People often have unrealistic expectations of peacebuilders because they don't fully understand what the role entails. It took me a long time to come to terms with this.

Another critical challenge is the lack of genuine support for peacebuilders working within large organizations. While titles may carry prestige, they often don't come with the resources or backing needed to create meaningful change. It's crucial to recognize the toll this work can take on mental health and to prioritize addressing it.

In addition, part of restoring balance in peacebuilding work involves focusing on equity and inclusion in global narratives. All lives should be valued equally, but conflicts in Africa or indigenous communities often receive far less attention than those in Ukraine or the Middle East. This disparity has been a core focus of my work for the past two decades and will likely remain central to my efforts throughout the rest of my career.

Heela Yoon is the founder of the Afghan Youth Ambassadors for Peace Organization (AYAPO), which works on promoting women's rights and peacebuilding in Afghanistan. Through AYAPO, she has trained nearly 100 young girls in gender equality, leadership, and crisis response, and has facilitated peace dialogues with local leaders to support girls' education. Heela focuses on implementing UN Resolutions 1325 and 2250 related to women and youth in peace processes. With over five years of experience in humanitarian and human rights work, Heela has collaborated with organizations like the Global Network of Women Peacebuilders and the Afghan Ministry of Foreign Affairs. She has worked on peacebuilding initiatives in Myanmar, Bangladesh, and the Philippines. In 2020, she was the civil society briefer at the UN Commission on the Status of Women and was recognized by the Kroc Institute for Peace and Justice. Heela currently works with Amnesty International and Oxfam.

AFTERWORD

Jonathan Cohen

Conflict resolution is facing turbulent times. Today's brutal wars in the Middle East, Ukraine, Sudan and beyond normalise perceptions that war is inevitable and also inexorable. There is a danger that we become immune to levels of atrocity that should be unacceptable, and inured to the idea that armed violence cannot be prevented or ended.

The tenacity of these wars, and the evolving 'drivers' that fuel them such as the climate crisis, suggest that the need for peace mediation is greater than ever. Yet, support for peace mediation is shrinking – governments have been increasing defence expenditure, but cutting development, humanitarian aid and peacebuilding budgets.[1]

The interviews in this collection demonstrate that peacebuilding is a long-term endeavour requiring patience, persistence and proficiency. Relationships between people caught up in conflict, and people trying to stop it, have to be nurtured, ideas explored and preparedness for peace cultivated so that moments of opportunity can be shaped and seized.

In a time of shifting geopolitics in which long-standing global partnerships have been thrown into question, conflict resolution becomes ever more difficult. Today's apparent disruptor-in-chief, President Trump, is a paradoxical figure when it comes to conflict resolution. His transactional approach to diplomacy (which is far from new in peacemaking) is often crude and bullying. But he is also explicit that he wants parties to conflict to talk rather than to fight. As I write, the decades long India-Pakistan conflict over Kashmir is flaring again. Trump's response, while simplistic and devoid of contextual nuance, is that the parties should talk – not a bad starting point. In the case of Russia's war in Ukraine he advocates for a ceasefire and a peace agreement to stop the killing. The challenge is that the peace that Trump appears to be pushing is more akin to

---

1 First USAID closes, then UK cuts aid: what a Western retreat from foreign aid could mean, Expert Comment 3 March 2025, https://www.chathamhouse.org/2025/03/first-usaid-closes-then-uk-cuts-aid-what-western-retreat-foreign-aid-could-mean

capitulation for Ukraine than peace with justice – with mineral rights accruing to the US government and US companies without any security guarantees for Ukraine. This is unlikely to provide a pathway to durable peace, and it upends many practices that peacebuilders and peacemakers have developed over years of hard experience. It risks setting dangerous precedents for future stability in Europe and globally.

As international norms and rules are undermined, there is a risk that sovereignty may increasingly become reserved for those with sufficient power to defend it. Trump's recent attacks on the international order such as his proposed 'takeover' of Greenland, Gaza and Canada, raise fundamental questions of sovereignty, identity and governance. This highlights the importance of self-determination as a challenging but key issue in conflict resolution – more than half the world's conflicts are driven by aspirations for greater self-determination[2] – and this could be an opportunity to open up discourse and overcome reticence of states that fear any discussion of self-determination, let alone action to resolve it.

The focus of the media and politicians on high-level bargaining and transactional deals to end conflicts should not disguise the reality that more attention needs to be paid to what can be done to transform conflict at other levels and in other spaces. Supporting local mediation processes and courageous people – often women – striving to resolve conflicts in their own societies, can enable more inclusive and transformative processes than 'top table' negotiations, and can become essential building blocks in the face of increasingly fragmented conflicts. This is all the more acute in the 25th anniversary year of the pathbreaking UN Security Council Resolution 1325 on Women Peace and Security (WPS), promoting women's participation in peacebuilding and yet we are now seeing the rollback of the significant gains made by this agenda.

There is no question the peace architecture of multilateral institutions like the UN and regional bodies have long been under duress and failing to gain traction. Peace mediation itself needs to evolve and demonstrate its contemporary relevance and effectiveness, amid rapid changes in how wars are fought and in the face of destabilised international security. Resolving armed conflict is neither easy nor guaranteed to deliver. The case has to be made for governments to sustain commitment and for

---

2 Mediating self-determination conflicts, report by Conciliation Resources and the Sasakawa Peace Foundation, 2023, https://www.c-r.org/learning-hub/mediating-self-determination-conflicts

civic actors to work in new partnerships to devise bold new solutions to address these pressing challenges. This requires creativity and innovative thinking – weaving together approaches that one leading thinker frames as 'multimediation'.[3]

However, in times of stress, we should not forget that peace is possible. Generational conflicts like those in Northern Ireland, the Philippines and Colombia have been transformed through painstaking and persistent work, prioritising politics over violence, that led to peace agreements. The interviews in this collection are a powerful testimony to what can be done in the face of adversity by putting those affected by violent conflict at the 'heart' of resolving conflict.

Jonathan Cohen is Executive Director of Conciliation Resources, a post he took up in 2016. Over the past 28 years at Conciliation Resources, initially as Caucasus Director and then as Director of Programmes, Jonathan has supported dialogue and peace-building initiatives in contexts including the South Caucasus, Kashmir, the Philippines, Colombia, Ethiopia, and Papua New Guinea.

Previously he served as Deputy Director of the Foundation on Inter-Ethnic Relations in The Hague working with the OSCE High Commissioner on National Minorities. Jonathan is an Associate of the Institute for the Public Understanding of War and Conflict at the Imperial War Museum, a member of the Advisory Board of the School of Slavonic and East European Studies at the University of London and a Board Member of the Peace Dividend Initiative. From 2018-2024 Jonathan was Chair of the European Peacebuilding Liaison Office (EPLO), a network of 55 peacebuilding organisations.

---

3 'Multimediation': Adapting in response to fragmentation by Christine Bell in *Still time to talk: adaptation and innovation in peace mediation,* Accord 30 edited by Teresa Whitfield, Conciliation Resources, 2023 https://www.c-r.org/accord/still-time-to-talk

More from Supernova

The Arab-Israeli Cookbook - recipes
by Robin Soans & Claudia Roden
ISBN 9780951587751

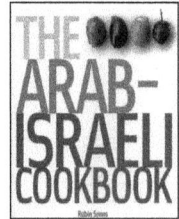

The Original Suffrage Cookbook
eds. L O Kleber & Cheryl Robson
ISBN 9781912430130

*Unlocking Women's Art: Pioneers, Visionaries
& Radicals of Paint* by P L Henderson
ISBN 9781913641368

Edward de Bono: Love Laterally
by Sarah Tucker
ISBN 9781913641481

Not A Number: Patrick McGoohan – A Life
by Rupert Booth
ISBN 9780956632920

www.supernovabooks.co.uk

www.ingramcontent.com/pod-product-compliance
Lightning Source LLC
Chambersburg PA
CBHW040142270326
41928CB00023B/3305